THIS LOVELY LIFE

THIS LOVELY LIFE

*A Memoir of Premature
Motherhood*

Vicki Forman

A Mariner Original / Mariner Books
Houghton Mifflin Harcourt
Boston   New York
2009

For information about permission to reproduce selections
from this book, write to Permissions, Houghton Mifflin Harcourt
Publishing Company, 215 Park Avenue South, New York, New York 10003.

www.hmhbooks.com

Library of Congress Cataloging-in-Publication Data
Forman, Vicki.
A memoir of premature motherhood / Vicki Forman.
p. cm.—(This lovely life)
ISBN 978-0-547-23275-1
1. Premature infants—Care. 2. Premature infants—Development.
3. Forman, Vicki. 4. Mothers—United States—Biography.
I. Title.
RJ250.3.F67 2009
618.92'011—dc22   2008053285

Book design by Melissa Lotfy

Printed in the United States of America

DOC 10 9 8 7 6 5 4 3 2 1

Portions of *This Lovely Life* first appeared in the *Santa Monica Review*
and *Love You to Pieces: Creative Writers on Raising a Child with Special Needs*,
ed. Suzanne Kamata (Boston: Beacon Press, 2008).

IN THIS BOOK, THE AUTHOR HAS GIVEN ALL DOCTORS, NURSES,
AND OTHER PROFESSIONALS FICTITIOUS NAMES.

TERRIBLE BEAUTY

A Foreword to *This Lovely Life*

THIS IS A STORY about children born into circumstances that medicine cannot currently prevent and parents cannot possibly prepare for. It begins with a scene of almost unendurable horror. When the worst (one assumes) has passed, the reader awaits the various authorial balms, tonal coolants, and narrative stand-downs demanded by such a trauma-splashed opening. But the reader quickly staggers into another, even more intimate horror, and then another, and then another. A tiny, cherished hope that things will eventually improve for the author, Vicki Forman, and her increasingly devastated family somehow endures. Such a hope is repeatedly incinerated in reality's unforgiving atmosphere. By the end, the long-delayed first steps of a five-year-old child will seem the fist-pumping stuff of a more traditional triumph narrative. And yet *This Lovely Life* is not at all depressing. Rather, when I finished this book, I felt an electric, wide-awake sadness, as though I had lost a close friend and made a new one on the same day.

In judging this contest I had the pleasure of reading several excellent books, among them a pair of skillful and funny essay collections, a spooky and affecting memoir about life in a convent, and an impressive travel narrative of a decades-old journey through a Middle East that scarcely seems recognizable today. All of these books struck me as both eminently publishable and promisingly vendible. That American publishing (an industry I normally defend, having spent the majority of my twenties in various editorial capacities) has not yet embraced the talented authors of these books can only be an oversight—one, I hope, that will soon be rectified. But of all the books I read, only *This Lovely Life* moved me to read aloud sections to friends and sent me back to its beginning once it had ended. It was also the only book capable of usefully complicating what I thought I believed about the sanctity of life and the altogether different sanctity of death. *This Lovely Life* forced me to think about not only my responsibility to my fellow human beings but also what can reasonably be asked of a society's members when they are dealing with stunted lives that, for the rest of the community, are only abstractions.

Within her memoir's first few pages, Ms. Forman makes a painful, understandable, and yet still shocking decision about the lives of her imperfectly born children. This decision, for various reasons, is not allowed to stand. Because one parent is not granted autonomy, a tragedy involving a single family soon becomes an ever-widening gyre, pulling into it dozens of doctors, nurses, relatives, strangers, and other parents and children. Some of these people are helpful, but many are useless. Some are thoughtless, while others are lovely.

Throughout the book, readers will encounter a number of new words and phrases, among them *adverse neurodevelopmental outcome, extubate,* and *periventricular hemorrhage.* Forman, the daughter of a doctor, manages to use these terms clearly and convey fairly and concisely the importance of the medical decisions she is forced to make. She does not claim that she was always correct; she sometimes expresses anger at certain doctors, and she occasionally behaves in ways that some read-ers may find appalling. But just as this is not a depressing book, it also is not an angry book. It is a book filled with love and wonder—enriched by the kind of grief that those of us who are not parents cannot imagine and that those of us who are will not want to.

Forman, it seems to me, is a nearly ideal writer: tough-mindedly aware of her flaws, deeply intelligent, terrifyingly honest, skeptical of many people, and forgiving of most. Above all else, she is humble before her art—and before her ghosts. That she was able to turn such painful material into a super-lative piece of writing is impressive, but that she has done so without a trace of cant or zealotry is virtually miraculous. *This Lovely Life* is less a book one reads than a book one experiences, and no one who gives him- or herself to this writer's terrible, beautiful story will ever be the same again.

Tom Bissell

Part One

1

I LEARNED ABOUT GRIEF during this time. I learned that no matter the true temperature, grief made the air crisp and cold; that it caused me to drive slowly, carefully; there was very little I could eat. I learned that I didn't notice things until they flew out at me and that most stories and books and news articles were unreadable, being accounts not of the events themselves, but of me. Of what I had lost and would never have again, of what I had once allowed myself to want, the things I used to love. Of small consolations no longer available. I learned that my heart could stop and start a dozen times a day and that my throat felt so sore and tight I often had to swallow air simply in order to breathe. The world receded; everything took place in slow motion and was viewed as if down the wrong end of a very long telescope. So much was unfamiliar that if I was asked my name, I had to think for long moments. "Grief is a visceral process of disengagement," a friend said. In my grief, old versions of disembodiment became a cruel joke. You thought that was bad, not being able to walk into a roomful of strangers without disassociating or turning remote and distant? That was nothing. Try this. Try heart-stopping, immobilizing grief.

The stages of grief were slippery, I found, the boundaries melded, the order mixed up, confused. I backed up through denial, depression, blame, and acceptance. I did my bargaining and got angry all at once. I discovered, somehow, in my grief, that routine would be my only salvation—the routine of familiar places, the same aisles in the supermarket, programmed drives and walks. The same food, food I knew I could tolerate. The less I had to think about, the fewer decisions, the more I might actually find a way to put one foot in front of the other.

I backed my car into a vintage Porsche and crushed in its driver's-side door. I rented a car while mine was in the shop being repaired. As I was parking the rental car in the hospital lot, I heard the crunch of metal going bad. I had somehow smashed the hood under the fender of the high-profile SUV parked next to me. When I got my own car from the shop, I once again backed into a classic car, this time a Mustang. Grief had made me not safe.

In the midst of this grief I somehow betrayed even myself. I put my makeup on. I took care of my living children; I went to the hospital. I did not go back to work. The doctor who wrote the prescriptions for the pills that held me together told me that if I'd had a regular job he would have put me on disability, and it was true: I wasn't functioning.

The day I gave birth was hot, a Sunday. The heat had been rising since Friday, the same day my pains began. My husband, Cliff, had picked this day to visit a friend in from out of town. At the last minute I had to tell him no. "You can't go, I'm not feeling well." Only then did I mention the cramps, the dull pains in my belly. When, at one in the afternoon, I started to bleed, there was no way to deny it was time to get help.

Even as I put my hand to the phone and called the doctor I reassured my husband I felt certain everything was fine, that I was simply having trouble from some early complications, those that had cleared up in the past few weeks. I was barely six months along. I could not possibly be in labor.

The OB on call ordered me to check in to Labor and Delivery. "Things can happen fast with twins," he said. I walked into L & D at three in the afternoon and was hooked up to a monitor that revealed I was having contractions every two minutes.

When I finally connected the news on the monitor with the pain in my belly—or when the monitor made the connection for me—I was stunned, silenced. *Okay,* I thought, *I'm having preterm labor.* No need to panic; there was a lot they could do. In my mind, I was still going home in time for dinner. I waited for the doctor to examine me. The nurse had a glance and said, "Oh my, you are bleeding." The doctor's glove came out red. Another nurse had a flashlight beamed on me below. "Oh God," she moaned, and her expression—a quick glance, a cringe, a look away—told me everything I needed to know.

"Is your husband here?" the doctor asked. "Who's here with you?"

My husband appeared from around the corner—he had simply gone to park the car; our three-year-old daughter was with him still, this was not meant to be a long visit by any means. I was six to seven centimeters dilated, the doctor announced, much too far gone to stop the labor. I was six months pregnant; my twins were no larger than my hand. I was having my babies today.

One of life's great illusions is the notion that we can want—and get—things on our own terms, no matter what. It's human nature to seek pleasure and avoid suffering, but what happens when suffering finds you? My husband and I had tried for two long years to conceive these twins, had lived through miscar-

riages and fertility treatments to bear them. When I learned
they were coming so early and so fragile, I had only one wish:
to let them go.

I begged and pleaded with the army of doctors and nurses
who came around in the hours between three and seven. I told
them I knew about morbidity and mortality; I knew these babies could not possibly survive or be normal if they did. "Let
them go," I said. "I know what their lives will be like. I want
you to let them go."

The OB pulled my husband aside. "Tell your wife to calm
down," he said. "These babies will be born with signs of life. The
laws of the State of California dictate that they be resuscitated."

At twenty-three weeks' gestation, my twins were at the very
edge of viability. I could terminate a pregnancy up to twenty-
four weeks in this country. If that were the case, how could babies this early be born alive? *This is a miscarriage,* I thought.
What I did not know was that in the years before my twins were
born, as extreme measures became available for use on very
premature infants, every hospital had developed a different set
of standards for resuscitation. A hospital in Portland, Oregon,
had recently drawn up guidelines that advised withholding intensive care for babies born prior to twenty-five weeks. Before
that gestational age, the risks of negative outcomes were too
high. At this hospital, where I'd arrived unarmed and unpre-
pared, no such plan of care existed. A young, dark-haired doctor appeared at my bedside and introduced herself as Dr. Tam,
the neonatologist. I pleaded my case to her.

"Let them go," I said. "It's too soon. I want you to let them go."

"I agree the risks of morbidity and mortality are high," Dr.
Tam said. "Even so, what you're asking, I cannot do."

The same hospital in Portland that had adopted guidelines
for plans of care in cases like this had discovered that decisions

about extremely premature infants and their resuscitation varied even within its own neonatology unit from day to day, shift
to shift. If Dr. Tam had not been on duty that Sunday afternoon, or Dr. March, the OB, would the outcome have been any
different for me or for my twins? I will never know.

"I don't want them to suffer," I said. "They're too small.
Please—"

Dr. Tam put her hand on my arm, shook her head, and said,
"I'm sorry."

They took away one set of measures then and replaced it
with another. The anticontraction medication and catheters
and all else were removed. An anesthesiologist arrived to administer an epidural. Cliff held my hand, and I kept saying,
"Why is this happening? Why is this happening?" It was after six already. I had been in this small room since three in the
afternoon. They were letting me labor. I was going to deliver
these babies. They would be born with signs of life and they
would be resuscitated.

In the delivery room, my husband had on scrubs and a shower
cap. He sat at the head of the operating table and kept his eyes
fixed on mine, trying to stay calm for me. Several nurses and
Dr. March were there. I turned my gaze away from Cliff's, determined to keep my eyes closed throughout the delivery. I was
convinced the twins would not survive and I wanted no memories of their birth. The last image I saw was of myself: I looked
up into the mirrored light that hung from the surgery ceiling.
The light showed me all—my body on the table, my husband
sitting next to me, Dr. March at the foot of the gurney. His
glasses reflected what he did below. I closed my eyes then; I let
it all unfold.

At seven forty-five, Dr. March broke my water. Our son,

Evan, slipped out a moment later. It was an easy birth. I did not watch but heard his frail, angry cry. I forced myself to look, and my frightened glance showed me his flattened body, surprisingly large head, and fragile limbs, shaking now in unison with his cries. Five hundred and forty grams was his weight. Later, I would learn just how small this was: one pound, three ounces. Not two weeks earlier a national magazine had featured a baby this small on its cover, a baby attached to tubes and lines, kept alive with a respirator and all else. SMALL MIRACLES, the headline read. At the time, I'd shivered at the sight. There was no connection between this image, this baby the size of a human palm, and the babies growing inside me. I had my own tiny version now, a boy from whom most would turn away and think, *That's not a baby; there's nothing here that resembles a baby.*

Ellie lay in a breech position, with her head under my sternum and her feet pointing down. In order to deliver her, Dr. March would have to invert her inside me. Her birth certificate states that Ellie was born twenty-three minutes after Evan. For a full twenty minutes, then, this went on, the excruciating task of Dr. March struggling to extract my daughter from inside my womb. Finally, when it was all done, I heard, "I can't get a heartbeat—" A nurse? The doctor? The team surged forward, and soon a ruddy form was presented to me. "Your daughter," another doctor announced, pushing Ellie's forehead toward me. "Give her a kiss."

My daughter? My daughter was a blooming toddler at home with friends. This was my daughter? Nothing resembled the human. I saw tendons and muscles. Only the palest sheen of skin hid her blatant shape. Her color shocked the most: rusty, raw, more skinned animal than human being.

In the aftermath of the delivery, the room fell quiet. The

team, and the babies, vanished. Only my husband, a doctor, and a nurse remained. Like the scene of an accident in the last moments of cleanup, all was silent, businesslike. The technicians had removed their machines, the nurses had disrobed from their gowns. An ennui descended, and as a nurse wheeled me out of the delivery room and into recovery I looked at the clock. Eight thirty. Not even six hours from start to finish. The sun would be down, our daughter in bed.

At times, in the hours and days that followed, my mind tricked me; sometimes, if I let myself, I could nearly forget what had happened. The babies would die, this would all be a memory. In the recovery room, Cliff and I watched the clock and waited for someone, anyone, to come and report this as true. Instead, my brother arrived and we saw the clock turn from nine to nine fifteen to nine thirty to nine forty-five. And still no one came. At ten o'clock, a nurse placed a white plastic bag labeled PATIENT BELONGINGS beside me on the gurney, put an ice pack underneath me for the pain, and moved me again, this time to a room in the maternity ward. In other rooms, newborns cried, flowers and balloons arrived. At eleven that night, when it became clear that no one was coming to tell us anything about the twins, I sent my husband and brother home. The clock crept toward midnight and still I forced myself to stay awake, both waiting and willing. I somehow knew that if I fell asleep it would all be true: the labor, the delivery, my ruddy baby girl, Evan's fragile cry. I shut my eyes to the memories and made myself stay awake and began a ritual then, in my vigilance, that would accompany me during the next days and weeks and even years, one where I rewound the clock to the moments prior to my walking through the hospital's sliding glass doors that afternoon, as if by staying awake and rewinding the clock I could also change it all, have the story turn out differently. The moment I felt those dull pains, earlier that morning. I call the hospital before noon, I don't wait until I am bleeding. Or earlier. Saturday night. We'd been out to dinner and I'd almost been unable to climb the steps to the restaurant. Why didn't I turn to my husband then and say, *I think I need to go to the hospital*? Why didn't I recognize my pain as signs of labor? Or Thursday, at the park; I sat on a bench after pushing my daughter on the swings and asked another mother, "Did you have contractions early on in your second pregnancy?" I felt tired, sluggish. Stop the clock there, make myself pay attention to that moment. And back even further, to the doctor's appointment I'd canceled two weeks earlier. A client had called an impromptu meeting. If I rewound to the place where I kept that appointment . . . And so it went, from that night on until years later. I watched the clock turn and knew I could not make it go back, could not stop time at any of the moments where it might have made a difference, where I could have changed this outcome.

In the middle of the night, with the hallways dark outside but my light still on, my mind still praying for an exit, a knock came at the door. An older woman, dressed in blue scrubs and wearing a heavy pewter cross pinned to her chest, came in. "Mrs. Forman?" she asked, her voice accented and soft. "I am Dr. Kress, one of the neonatologists here."

If ever there was a vision, this was it. Dr. Kress with her cross and her voice, here to tell me, finally, about my children. All at once, I recognized her voice. This Dr. Kress was the same one who had given me Ellie to kiss. "Your daughter," she'd said. "Give her a kiss." Now, Dr. Kress took a seat, her back to the wall. "Your babies are very sick," she said. She paused. "It is unusual for babies like this to survive more than a day, no matter what we do to keep them alive. Their lungs are too fragile, their systems too immature."

"So they're going to die?"

"Yes," she said. "I think they will."

I told Dr. Kress I wanted a do-not-resuscitate order placed in their charts. "If they're going to die, we need to let them go," I said. "No more heroic measures."

"I understand," she said. "Of course."

She left then, the news between us. The babies were going to die. It was just a matter of time; they were too fragile to survive. Dr. Kress assured me that the do-not-resuscitate order would be put in place so that if the twins did lose ground in the middle of the night, they would be allowed to die. After she left I turned off the lights, finally, and tried to sleep.

At six that morning the hospital's noises woke me. I'd slept maybe four hours, no dreams, just darkness. With the morning's light I knew the truth: nothing had changed. My babies were still alive, they had been born too soon, they were extremely premature, and we were now in the extended process of waiting for them to die. The phone by my bedside began to ring—friends calling to find out what had happened, my parents, my sister and brother. My friend Lee's confusion mirrored my own: "You asked them not to save these babies and they didn't listen to you?" she said. "Whose children are these? I don't understand."

"I want to bury them in Hawaii," I told my brother-in-law when he called. "Next to your parents."

"I know you don't want to hear this," my sister said. "But you can always get pregnant again."

"I'll just pray that whatever is supposed to happen is what happens," my friend Maria said.

I was still on the phone trying to offer explanations though none seemed at hand when I looked up to see three doctors standing at the door to my hospital room: Dr. March, the OB who'd delivered the twins; my regular OB, Dr. Yamada, who had been on maternity leave with her own twins; and, finally, Dr. Bath, who had overseen my pregnancy and had been unreachable during the delivery the day before. Dr. March, with his clipped gray hair and sartorial manner, was the senior of the three. He took the one available chair while the others stood in the doorway. Dr. Yamada, the youngest, and the only woman, seemed the most disturbed. This was her first day back from maternity leave and I was her first visit.

Dr. March cleared his throat. "I think given everything that happened we can all agree things could not have gone any differently," he said. "My sense of it is that due to your previous miscarriages you were simply unable to hold on to these babies."

"Sometimes the uterus can only handle so much volume," Dr. Bath offered.

Dr. Yamada remained silent.

"What's going to happen to these babies?" I asked.

"I'm guessing the girl will probably make it and the boy won't," Dr. Bath said.

"Dr. Kress told me last night she thought they would both die," I said.

"The boy is saturating at eighty percent oxygen," Dr. Yamada said. "The girl is only on seventy." I must have looked confused. Dr. Yamada went on. "The higher the percentage, the sicker the baby," she explained.

"So the boy will die," I said. "Because his numbers are higher?"

"Only forty percent of twenty-four-weekers survive," Dr.

Bath said. "The odds are pretty good that at least one of these babies is going to die."

Everything I knew to be true about childbirth—the pain followed by the joy—had been turned upside down. When my older daughter, Josie, had been born three years earlier, I had learned of the giddy euphoria that came from giving birth, how that joy helped pass the sleepless nights and conditioned the anxieties and fears of being a parent. With Evan and Ellie's birth, I had been shown a different coin, one where the pain of childbirth could be followed by more pain, where sometimes the truth of childbirth was not the birth of something one had expected (a healthy child) but instead the birth of something very different (a sick child, a child with the potential for life-long complications, a child who might die). Only years later would I understand how these births were more similar than I'd thought; that past the fear, the results were the same: a child to nurture and love.

I told the doctors I didn't understand. "I knew these babies would suffer if they were resuscitated, and now they're doing everything they can to keep them alive, even if we all agree they aren't meant to survive? None of this makes any sense."

"The answers aren't that simple," Dr. March said. "You have to realize—this is going to take a great deal of surrender on your part."

After the doctors left, I forced myself out of bed. I still wore my hospital gown, felt sick and sore and had barely slept. Even so, I pushed aside the breakfast tray, put on the yellow hospital socks I'd been given the night before, and went to see my twins.

In my first glimpse of my son, he lay in an open bed directly across from the front door of Special Nursery A. The bandages and cotton dressings that surrounded him glowed larger than his body. Bilirubin lights hovered over his incubator. Gauze pads protected his eyes from that same light. I soaked it all in—the tubes, the lines, the IVs. His tiny chest vibrated from the high-frequency ventilator that rumbled beside him. His skin was dark, translucent, muscles and tendons visible beneath. There was an IV line stuck into his small forehead, and no fewer than a dozen syringes filled his bed, connected with medical tubing to various parts of his body, dispensing fluids in shades of red, yellow, white. Overhead, three monitors displayed his stats in spikes and graphs: wavy green, jittering blue, loping red.

Here it was, then, physical proof. My babies had been born. They were hooked up to machines, getting blood transfusions, being kept alive. There was no rewinding the clock, no going back. Around me the unit bustled with nurses and doctors. Alarms sounded, machines vibrated and hummed. I asked about Ellie. "Shouldn't she be next to him? Shouldn't they be together?"

"We try to keep twins on opposite sides of the room," the nurse who tended Evan explained, "so as not to confuse their care. Each baby has its own nurse. We're here twenty-four hours a day to answer your questions. Please, just call."

When I was ready to cross the room to see Ellie, the nurse who escorted me to her bed gave me details, facts, and figures about Evan's status. Evan was saturating well, he was receiving 80 percent oxygen, he had had insulin and phenobarbital and some Ativan to keep him calm. His head ultrasound had been normal. He had received two blood transfusions already. If my husband and I wanted to donate blood, he could receive ours, assuming our types matched.

"Do the babies have names?" she asked. "We want to make signs, to call them something other than Twin A and Twin B."

"We . . . we hadn't decided," I said. I answered the nurse and tried to incorporate. I was a mother. I had had my babies. They were in this hospital now, no longer inside me. I could pump my milk and they would store it. Visiting hours were unlimited. The nurses and doctors would answer any and all questions. Support groups met, chaplains visited. I had to wear a gown, scrub in the hall outside each time before I entered and scrub inside between babies. No jewelry, no cell phones. I don't know why it took so long, but when I got to Ellie, my stomach finally heaved. Here was the same bruised and ruddy thing I'd seen at birth, twitching and shivering now. My baby, my daughter. Her legs were long, desperately thin. Her body trembled. Her eyes, like Evan's, were still fused shut. Thin slits of eyelids, a soft downy coat of black hair. A person, and yet not. Nothing could protect her, nothing could change what had occurred. I began to cry. The nurse offered me a chair. I refused, stumbled my way back into the hall, got lost, then finally found my room. On the way past the nurses' station a young woman handed me forms to fill out for birth certificates. "Congratulations!" she trilled. I asked her for a Coke and a cup of ice and crawled back to bed.

It was eleven in the morning. I had the birth certificates; I had seen the babies. I called Cliff and asked him to come pick me up. "I want to go home," I said. Even Dr. Bath, after I asked when I could leave the hospital, had said, "It's not hard to deliver one-pound babies. You can go home whenever you want." Inside the Patient Belongings bag that had followed me from recovery to the maternity ward, I found the same denim maternity shirt and black stretch shorts I'd worn into the hospital not twenty-four hours earlier. By the time I had dressed and downed half a Coke, my husband had arrived. I saw from his tired eyes that he hadn't slept much more than I.

Cliff and I had met in our late twenties, in New York. I'd been married and divorced just out of college, and wasn't looking to get serious. "I don't think I want to have anything to do with you" were probably my first words to him. "I don't think you have much choice," he'd said, and proceeded to convince me.

Shortly after we began dating, I was accepted into a graduate program three thousand miles away, in Southern California. "I'm coming with you," he'd announced. "I don't believe in long-distance relationships." A day before we were scheduled to drive across country, I totaled the car I'd bought for the adventure. Cliff was there, in the front passenger seat, and as soon as we collided with the other car, he instantly reached for me to make sure I was okay. I'd never met a man more able to handle the tough stuff—a girlfriend moving across country, a horrible car wreck—all without turning away or blaming someone else. I loved him for this, and because he was gentle, kind, forgiving. "The thing we need to remember," he'd once said to me during a fight early on in our marriage, "is that we're both good people, and we love each other." The morning after the twins were born, I couldn't imagine going through what was to come with anyone else.

"I'm so sorry," I said. "I can't believe this is happening."

"Don't apologize. This is not your fault."

I showed him the birth certificates. "They want us to fill them out." Name, date of birth, sex. In Evan's case, we'd already agreed on his name: Evan, after Bruce Springsteen's son, and the middle name, David, in honor of my grandfather. In the case of our girl, Twin B, we hadn't yet settled on a name. As I filled in the forms, I put down *Eleanor*, the name Cliff had preferred, instead of *Alexandra*, the name I had wanted. For a middle name, I wrote, *Anne*.

"Anne?" he said. So far out of the proper course of events, that my own husband didn't understand the middle name I'd chosen for our child.

"My mother's middle name," I said. "I thought it went well with Eleanor."

And so it was. Now the nurses could tape a sign at the foot of each baby's crib, call them something other than Twin A and Twin B.

Before we left, Cliff wanted to see the twins. I took him back down the hall to the NICU. In one short hour I'd become a pro; on this, only my second, visit, I knew how to find the NICU, that we had to put on gowns and scrub, and how to operate the foot pedal that dispensed water into the big, laundry-style sinks. Knew that there were two different kinds of soap: an iodine-based variety that stained one's hands and left them raw and red, and a less caustic but still industrial-strength brand that was labeled with the hospital's own name: HAMPTON. It would take visits to three other hospitals and countless doctors' offices before I realized that the soap was not made *for* the hospital, it simply and coincidentally had the same name. It was also the case that whenever I went to scrub, I'd be reminded that a father at my daughter's preschool worked for the company that made the soap. These details, however inconsequential they might seem to someone else, would somehow hold me together. "Hey, Tom," I'd tell that dad many times in the months that followed, "I used your soap the other day."

I showed my husband the yellow gowns and the eponymous hospital soap and the individually wrapped scrub brushes. I pointed out the instructions—"Remove your jewelry, wash for five minutes, use the red plastic stick packaged with the scrub brush to clean under your fingernails"—and watched him follow the rules. He worked slowly, methodically, moving through each step. He soaped his hands, his palms, then his long fingers. After that, he used the plastic stick to clean under his fingernails. My husband liked to follow the rules, and even though later on I would wash my hands for fewer than the requisite three minutes, Cliff always took precisely that long. Above the sink I found a box of safety pins for attaching jewelry to the gowns. Our wedding rings hung from these pins as we entered the unit.

This time, the second time, it wasn't me who collapsed on viewing the twins, but Cliff. He started to cry as soon as we got to Evan's bed—tight, wet tears. "I thought you'd seen them already," I said. "You came to visit last night."

"I stood outside," he said. "They were too busy. I didn't want to get in the way."

I would come to see this often: the new father standing outside the theater of the NICU, looking through the windows, trying to understand, take it all in. To step through the door and be center stage with the noise and the machines and the nurses and doctors required a great deal of strength, one mothers were sometimes better able to muster than dads. Even a man as strong as my husband couldn't be blamed for collapsing. He and I held on to each other by Evan's bed, and I felt him crying softly in my arms. "The chaplain came by," a nurse said. "She wanted to know if you'd like to do a blessing for them."

"What kind of blessing?" I asked. "We're not churchgoers . . ."

"It's nondenominational," the nurse explained. "Sometimes parents like to do naming ceremonies for babies—"

Her words hung in the air. In my mind, I finished the sentence: *For babies who aren't going to survive.*

I asked about the do-not-resuscitate order I'd requested the day before. The nurse checked the chart and shook her head. "It's not here," she said. "Let me find it for you."

After twenty minutes, the nurse still had not found the form, and she called Dr. Tam, trying to figure out how to proceed. Cliff and I took turns at Evan's and Ellie's bedsides. My shock at the sight of these ruddy, fragile beings, taken from me much too soon, had not worn off. I could not imagine the thinking that presumed they ought to be kept alive in this way, with drugs and ventilators, this most complicated set of interventions.

"Mrs. Forman?" a nurse said. "Dr. Tam wants to speak with you."

The nurse led Cliff and me into an empty nursery across from the NICU. Dr. Tam stood there, along with another woman. "I'm Sally," she said. "The social worker." The room seemed to serve as both an office for the nurses and doctors and a backup unit for patients. There was a computer on the desk and several empty Isolettes lined up along the wall.

I took in Sally's clipboard of notes and Dr. Tam's strained expression. "What's going on?"

"We need to discuss the DNR," Dr. Tam said.

"What's there to discuss?" Cliff asked.

"These situations are complicated," Dr. Tam said. "What you're asking for isn't easy."

"What we're asking for isn't easy?" I repeated. I thought of my children: red, dusky, small. Syringes stuck into their bodies, ventilator tubes snaked through their tiny mouths. I started to cry. "What makes you think it's easy to ask? If it were up to me, I'd go over there and pull every last tube out of them. I don't understand what you're doing. I told you last night I don't want any of this to be happening."

Cliff pulled me into his arms. I was sobbing now.

"Please," the social worker said.

"If you are unhappy with our decisions you can look into transferring these babies somewhere else," Dr. Tam said. "I can recommend another hospital."

"I don't want these babies anywhere else," I said. "I want you to institute a DNR. These are our children, not yours. What gives you the right—?"

"You're aware of the consequences?"

"We are," Cliff said.

Later, I would read the following distinction made for preemies of this gestational age: that there was a difference between living, existing, and surviving. To the doctors, survival was all that mattered. To the parent, living was what you wanted for your child; pure existence would never do. To us, the existence the doctors had arranged for these babies, hooked up to machines, kept alive with an army of drugs and interventions, wasn't any kind of survival, not in the least.

"We want the DNR," I said.

From this conversation, the social worker stated the following in Evan's chart, under the heading Psychosocial Interventions:

Dr. Tam met with parents on 7/31 in the presence of Sally, the MSW, to clarify things regarding the "DNR" status they have been requesting. They have discussed this "DNR" together and both parents strongly feel that a "DNR" order be placed in the chart and that they are aware of the consequences/ramifications. They do not want their babies to suffer. The mother stated that if she's allowed, she will discontinue life support. I told her that this is not an option at all at this point in time unless a major catastrophic event such as a major bleed in the brain, grade IV IVH, occurs. Prognosis for neurodevelopmental outcome is too early to be determined at this time. Extreme prematurity alone puts a baby at increased risk of neurodevelopmental problems but these are extremely premature babies who are doing reasonably well. Dr. Tam expressed to parents that she respects their wishes of a "DNR" order and it will be placed in the babies' charts. Another meeting is scheduled today at 1300 hours.

Years later, I would reach a point where I could love Evan apart from (or because of) his disabilities, for the person he was. At the time of his birth, I did not want this life, this kind of birth. I have learned in the years since the twins were born that my honesty about not wanting them to survive provokes a strong response. A young man who read my first attempts to understand this decision wrote me that he believed in the laws that preserved Evan's and Ellie's chances at life, and disagreed with my determination to let them go. My father calls my insistence heroic but what I know, and what I'd like to tell that young man and my father, is a simple truth: looking at Evan and Ellie, seeing them so small, giving birth so early. I was terrified.

Like many privileged members of the middle class, I grew up in a family where normal was nothing short of perfect. As a child, my younger brother read the encyclopedia for pleasure and had so many facts and trivia memorized that when he went on *Jeopardy!* at the age of twenty-two, he was fully primed for success. This same brother graduated summa cum laude from Princeton and went on to Harvard Law School. My older brother and younger sister are each their own version of perfection: talented, successful, good-looking. My mother has a PhD and a law degree, did all this while raising these four astonishing children. My dad is known throughout the country for his psychiatric work with disabled children and their families. Children brought into this middle-class life are supposed to follow in the footsteps of their parents; they are meant to be born full-term, thriving, lovely.

Even the very word *preemie* was too cute for what had happened to us. *Preemie*—with its long vowel sounds and diminutive flavor—didn't capture the reality of these babies. *Preemie* meant a few weeks early, a baby with large eyes and tiny, precious hands. Preemie babies were micro versions of newborn babies, those whose miniature clothes spoke of being half baby, half doll. When Evan finally was ready for a preemie gown at two months of age, even then it was massive and oversize. There was no word to describe babies the size of one's palm, those whose breathing apparatuses outsized their heads.

Once the twins were born and I had become their mother, this reluctance to accept them as they were and my fear of their futures swiftly found an equally powerful counterpoint in the fact that they were, indeed, my children. I couldn't hold or nurse or feed them, but I could change their diapers, question the doctors and nurses about their health. By the time my parents arrived, three days after the twins' birth, and my father tried to tell me all the neurological implications of such young brains—mental retardation, cerebral palsy, learning and developmental disabilities—I couldn't listen.

In many respects, the scientific, problem-solving orientation of the medical team facilitated this acceptance. I have heard neonatologists describe babies born this early as a series of problems to solve, and we soon learned the extent to which Evan and Ellie were bodies to preserve, a collection of levels (sugar, oxygen, blood pressure, respiration) to manage. There was a wall of fame in the NICU where photos of graduates went on display for all to see and admire. The afternoon we met with Dr. Tam and Sally, a nurse case manager stopped me on my way out and pointed to the picture of a former twenty-four-weeker. "That's Amanda," she said. "She's four years old now and doing great. I know this is frightening, I know they're tiny and you're scared, but this will work out. It will."

Friends, too, had me thinking in this direction. Within

hours of the twins' birth, I began to hear story after story of twenty-three- and twenty-four-weekers who had survived without complications. Some vision problems, some delays; they were small, of course, but they came home and they grew and learned. One ex-preemie even learned his colors by the age of eighteen months. So yes, this was a scary world, and yes, Evan and Ellie were very sick. Still, it might just work out.

I now see this initial phase of acceptance as primarily a form of protection. Once Evan developed lifelong disabilities, I learned true acceptance: loving your child apart from his limitations or how others see him. Loving him if he can't talk and doesn't know his colors. If he can't even see his colors. In the days after the twins' birth, I protected my babies and myself. If they were to live, I had to watch over them. Watching over them meant not paying attention to every fear (and potential reality) but clinging to the hope that they would be okay. It would be years before I put aside those hopes.

But all these preconceptions—and misconceptions—about how my life and my babies could or should turn out were yet to come. At one o'clock in the afternoon, a day after the twins were born, Cliff, my brother, and I sat in a conference room down the hall from the NICU with the head neonatologist, Dr. Lamb; a new social worker, Betty; and Dr. Tam. The team took up their place at one end of the table while Cliff, my brother, and I sat at the other, ready to hear, finally, what the doctors had to say about our twins and their prognoses.

It was hard not to like Dr. Lamb, a soft-spoken man in his late fifties. Behind thick glasses, his eyes were soft, compassionate. I would come to learn that Dr. Lamb's knowledge of medicine was impeccable, his instincts and his attention to detail equally remarkable. I once saw him personally cover an air-conditioning vent so that the baby who lay underneath it could more effectively regulate his body temperature. I did not know about this attention to detail during this first meeting. What I heard was his expertise and authority as he discussed our twins.

His first concern was about the DNR. "Perhaps you could explain to me why you are requesting this?" he asked.

"We want the twins to be DNR," I said. "I was against resuscitation at birth and I'm not in favor of prolonging life support. These babies were born too early. They're too fragile, the risks of morbidity and mortality are too high."

Dr. Lamb paused. "It's not typical for us to include this type of order in a chart."

"Why not?" Cliff asked.

"There are various things that can happen when a baby is intubated and on a respirator," Dr. Lamb explained. "He could pull the tube out and have to be reintubated. He could have a pneumothorax, which is when the lung develops a hole in it due to high-frequency ventilation. In themselves, neither of these situations is life threatening. But if there is a DNR in the chart, I would not be able to intervene, and the babies, who otherwise might survive, would die." He stopped for a moment and let this news sink in.

I nodded and held on to Cliff's hand. "Go on," I said.

"The same is true for withholding nutritional support or antibiotics. All these measures do indeed keep a baby alive who might otherwise not survive. But they are all part of a typical plan of care for babies like yours and it is our policy at this hospital to provide care for twenty-three-week babies and not withhold it unless there is a catastrophic event."

"So no DNR," I said.

"I would prefer not to," Dr. Lamb said. "For all the reasons I have just stated."

I understood then more of how the wheels were turning, and how they'd been turning since the night my twins were born. There had been no catastrophic event. The babies, as the social worker had reported in her Psychosocial Interventions, were doing reasonably well. Dr. Lamb wanted to be able to treat them without restriction.

I looked to Cliff for an answer. His expression was as lost as my own. We had thought we knew what to do, and that was push for the DNR. Now we were being told that this would somehow be a mistake and hinder care. That the care was going to come either way. Did we want to interfere with the doctors and their ability to do their jobs? Would we accept that responsibility?

Both my husband's parents had died while we were still in our early thirties. Our first married years had taken place with these deaths—after long illnesses—prominent in our lives. Three years earlier, when Cliff's father was in the hospital and dying, his chart had included a DNR. We did not want him to suffer, and his quality of life, at the end of his life, was nil. In that case, it made sense to let him die in peace. In this case, with the issues Dr. Lamb had raised, the situation was more complicated.

"If we insist on the DNR, the twins could die when they might otherwise survive?" Cliff said.

"Precisely."

Cliff and I held each other's hands tighter.

"So no DNR?" Dr. Lamb said.

"No DNR," Cliff replied, looking at me.

Dr. Lamb had a pad of paper in front of him and made a note of what we had just decided. "I need to tell you a few things about the complications your babies might face." He went on to describe a series of conditions that each had its own abbreviation or acronym: RDS, IVH, PDA, NEC, CLD, ROP;

there could also be hearing deficits and adverse neurodevelopmental outcomes. There was no crystal ball, he explained. The twins would be in the hospital for a long time. Evan and Ellie might become blind due to the high levels of oxygen from the mechanical ventilation—oxygen that kept them alive but was toxic to their fragile, undeveloped retinas. They might have lifelong lung conditions that would leave them dependent on respirators. They could fall prey in the hospital to infections in their intestines and bowels that would cause the organs to stop functioning. Kidney function, liver function, blood pressure, sugar levels—all depended on the army of drugs the medical team now administered.

"We try to manage these conditions," Dr. Lamb said. "We do our best. But you need to know the possible complications we are facing here. And, again, if there is a catastrophic event, such as a bleed in the brain, we can discuss removing life support. Dr. Tam has already reported to me that your daughter appears to have what we call a grade two bleed. There are some signs this afternoon that her condition is worsening."

"What signs?" I asked.

"Her oxygen needs are higher," Dr. Tam said. "There seems to be some pulmonary bleeding, which we discovered when we suctioned her ventilation tube. If the bleed worsens, we will consult with an outside neurologist to determine quality-of-life issues. If we find that future quality of life is nil, we encourage parents to remove the child from life support."

Later, I would learn that the head-to-toe we received that afternoon offered rare opportunities to get the facts; news about the patients was conveyed most often bedside or in the hallway outside the unit. A half-hour in the conference room with the doctors and the parents was a unique event. Later, I would also learn that our twins' arrival had tapped major resources in the NICU during those first twenty-four hours, and that the struggle to keep the twins going was far more challenging than the doctors had let on in that first meeting. While we were told quite a bit—no doubt far more than we could handle at the time—we actually weren't told even half of it: about Ellie's metabolic acidosis that portended severe cerebral palsy; about the discussion in the NICU the night before regarding the decision not to perform a C-section. That the twitching I'd seen earlier in Ellie was probably seizure activity. And what none of us knew: that Evan's retinas were so immature and unformed, he would always be blind. That Ellie's bleed had worsened already, and her quality of life would be deemed nil.

I try to picture the scene from their end of the table. My husband and I are terrified and grief-stricken and very much alone. We have two sick babies who ten or even five years earlier would not have survived. To the neonatologists, these babies are a series of problems—very complicated ones, to be sure—to solve. As the meeting ended, I had only one question, a silly question, given all I had heard. "When will they come home?" I asked. And Dr. Lamb, of course, did not have an answer. There was no crystal ball.

Dr. Lamb finished by explaining the immediate care he and the team would provide, asked us to sign consent forms for various procedures, shook our hands, and urged us to come to him with any questions we might have. Then he and Dr. Tam left.

"Most parents describe this as a roller coaster," Betty, the social worker, said as we got up. "I think you just found out how true that can be."

In the days that followed we moved haltingly. Evan's eyes stayed fused shut; my parents bought plane tickets with grievance fares. "To see them before they die," my mother said.

"You think they're going to die?" I asked. "The doctors seem to think they'll survive."

"I don't see how," she said. "I can't imagine them living for more than a week."

I didn't know how to explain to my mother what I now witnessed on a daily basis, how every medical effort and intervention was being employed to keep them alive. Nurses administered drugs and transfusions; IV drips and ventilators performed their own tasks mechanically, diligently. It all seemed nearly unconscious, except that I also knew Dr. Lamb and Dr. Tam and the others all managed and orchestrated these efforts. Where my mother could not conceive how they might survive, I watched this business and could not imagine how my twins would ever be able to die, even if this were what was meant to be.

I wore a T-shirt for days that read *Zombie*. A snapshot from these moments shows me staring downward at nothing, eyes glazed. I don't know why someone thought I'd want a picture from this time, but there it is, my sideways glance, the dark circles under my eyes, my hair unbrushed. Friends called; messages stacked up. Pages and pages in our phone log recorded the dozens of calls we received these first few days. "What's going on?" the world wanted to know. "What's going to happen?" I had no reply.

I collected my breast milk and stored it in the two-ounce bottles supplied by the NICU and labeled each with the date and time, and the drugs I now took: *July 31, 7 p.m., Seconal*, a bottle read when I found it six months later, buried deep in my refrigerator. And I remembered, *Yes, I asked for sleeping pills. The doctor wrote a prescription for ten tablets, as if in ten nights I would be done with my grief.* And this: *August 1, 10 a.m., Seconal/ Celexa.* If I labeled the bottles with these signs of my grief, I never once considered this as evidence of my clearly declining mental health; I simply thought that when the time came to give the twins this milk, if the time ever came, some doctor would need to know that I had taken medication, what kind, and when. Already I had gleaned that doctors liked to know those things.

Late in the afternoon of the twins' second day of life, a social worker from the hospital called us in to meet with a pediatric neurologist to discuss Ellie's prognosis. As Dr. Tam had warned it might, Eleanor's bleed had moved deeper into her brain. A grade III bleed meant the brain had been compromised enough to present significant challenges to future learning and development. A grade IV predicted the vegetative state Dr. Tam had spoken of during that first meeting. Our daughter would be nonambulatory and nonverbal, with zero intelligence. We would not be able to care for her ourselves; rather, she would live out her life in a subacute-care facility. An institution, in other words. The hospital had called in an outside pediatric neurologist, Dr. Masters, to confirm these findings. In a small room off the social worker's office, Dr. Masters presented us with his impartial view. According to him, the bleed wasn't as serious as we'd been told. "I see children in my office all the time who have had grade three and four bleeds," Dr. Masters stated. "Some of them are just fine."

Fine was a word we would come to hear a lot in our time in the NICU. But the doctors' versions of *fine* and mine were not the same. I pressed Dr. Masters.

"With all due respect, what percentage of these children are fine? What are their medical needs? Prognosis? We've been told Ellie will be vegetative. Are you saying that isn't true?"

"It is, and it isn't," he replied. "In these cases, the truth isn't so easy." I thought of Dr. March's prediction the day before about my future encounters with surrender. *The answers aren't that simple.*

"You people need to get your facts straight," Cliff said. "This isn't what we were told."

"I would not recommend at this point removing life support," Dr. Masters concluded.

"This is a life here, a spirit," I said. "There is a family involved. We have a three-year-old at home and another twenty-three-weeker fighting for his life. Are you going to raise this child?" I twisted the tissue I felt I'd been holding for days now. "Are *you* going to wait for her to be just fine?"

Not forty-eight hours earlier I had been the expectant mother of twins; today I raised ethical and moral questions with a doctor who seemed unwilling to confront the reality of his recommendations, or who, apparently, had never had his judgments questioned by distraught parents. Dr. Masters had spoken to us for all of fifteen minutes, but once he delivered his opinion, he stood up, convinced that he had finished the job.

Cliff and I were not done. My husband corralled the social worker and demanded to speak to the neonatologist on duty. Fifteen minutes later, yet another man arrived. He sat down and introduced himself as Dr. Vine, one of the neonatologists on staff at Hampton. This was the first time I'd met Dr. Vine and I was immediately suspicious of the gold chain around his neck and the cross hanging from it. Would he be another one at this hospital to invoke a higher authority, this time God rather than the State?

"We just met with Dr. Masters," Cliff said. "He's not recommending that we terminate life support."

"I see." Dr. Vine crossed his legs.

"He said children with grade four bleeds sometimes do just fine. Yesterday, Dr. Tam informed us that she'd be vegetative. Which is it?"

Dr. Vine entered into a cagey explanation not unlike what Dr. Masters had just told us, citing the gamut of outcomes but agreeing that Ellie's prognosis was poor. "I understand your concerns," he said. "And in principle I agree with your decision to deny life support in this situation. Unfortunately, I will have to speak to my staff about this. I have a team of doctors and nurses who will need to agree with this decision before we can move forward." Dr. Vine would consult with his staff that evening and get back to us the next day with their decision. "There is also a bioethics committee associated with the hospital if you have concerns with the decision," he concluded.

And so my incantations began: *Don't do this to me, don't change my life this way.* Coupled with *Who will love them if not me?*

I will never have the answers to the questions surrounding Ellie and her short life. What if we hadn't insisted—would she have survived? What if we had been more ready to raise a profoundly disabled child—would that have made us better people? What if another set of parents had been in the same situation—would they have made the same decision?

A life at its end is a life that has been lived, a life others can look back on with fondness and memories. A life at its beginnings ought to be a life full of potential, not a life whose future is dreaded and feared. Today, when I reflect on our decision, I look for proof that Ellie would not have been anything other than profoundly disabled. But even if that were the case, I now know that these lives are worth living too. A friend writes to me, *The strength and character you display is how everyone pretends they will be if their child is born with disabilities,* and this is all the reassurance I need, beyond the what-ifs and the whys.

The next morning, our third day as Evan's and Ellie's parents, my parents arrived. My father's first words to me, the moment he walked into my apartment, came via a friend of his, a pediatric neurologist: "If this were my daughter and this happened to me," that man has told my father, "the first thing I would do would be to throw up." The second, apparently, would be to demand that both twins be removed from life support. Before he even sat down, my father entered into a long description of how preemies like this fared, ending with "The neonatologists have their walls of fame and their stories of miracles but they don't see these kids, they don't follow them. Call Willits," he said, writing the neurologist's name in our phone log. "He'll tell you." When I looked at the log later, I saw my dad had left every bit of information I would need: the man's home and work numbers, his pager. I almost expected to see his golf tee times as well, and I had absolute confidence in my dad that if this information were relevant, it would have been there too. When my father said, "Call Willits," he meant it.

In the kitchen, my mother took me aside. "I know what Dad means," she said. "But I don't necessarily agree. I think it's impossible once you have a child, no matter what is wrong with it, to walk away."

Although my parents lived in Philadelphia, three thousand miles away, we had a close relationship, one in which we could be honest, kind, and forthright no matter the circumstances. My mother had made clear her unhappiness with my first, early marriage, as well as her relief when it ended, even as she visited me during my worst moments at that time, to help me through the wreckage. For as long as I can remember, my father has celebrated each proud accomplishment of mine—straight-A report cards, admission to an Ivy League school, published writing. With the pride has come a balanced fatherly worry—over the dead-end jobs I worked after college, my uncertain future as a writer. Together, my parents each kept his or her own individual counsel about my decisions—they didn't always agree, but they always respected each other—finding a way, all the while, to understand those decisions, weigh in, express their concern.

When Cliff and I told my parents about our conversations the night before with Drs. Masters and Vine about Ellie's prognosis and the team decision, my father became visibly distraught. "Their decision?" he said. "How is this their decision? Are these their children? This is just incomprehensible to me."

My whole life my family had been deeply involved in the medical. We believed in medicine just as we believed that medicine was not meant to let us down. My father had been a child psychiatrist for going on forty years; we had spent our lives around doctors and hospitals, lived with the MD after my dad's name and the names of all kinds of other clinicians who provided us with answers when we were sick, when my grandfather was dying. On a weekly basis, some relative would call our house to discuss a medical condition with my dad. So what were we to do now that the medical had hoisted us on its own petard, and now that, when we wanted humanity as much as science, we were woefully adrift? When I told my father that the neonatologist and the neurologist had said that some children with grade IV bleeds did "just fine," my dad nearly exploded. "They're lying to you," he said. "I've seen these kids. They don't end up just fine. Who do you think my patients have been all these years?"

My memories of my father's patients were of children who came around on Saturdays, kids in trouble at school or those with behavioral problems. Children of divorce. Those were the kids who needed a psychiatrist. That morning, listening to my father, I understood. He spoke of his other patients, children in the hospital where he worked, those with seizure disorders and brain injuries, the ones so far gone with mental illness or disability their parents could not raise them. Those in institutions where my father visited to monitor their meds and check on their progress. I'd never thought about these kids, never realized that when he was finding beds for them in hospitals, he was dealing with much more than the children of divorce or kids with mild learning disabilities. And for the first time I could see in my dad's face what he meant when he told me about his friend and throwing up. He was trying to tell me how worried he was, how much he knew about what lay ahead. He wasn't just a doctor who knew about my twins' potential outcomes; he was my father.

"You're talking about very immature neurological systems," he said. "These are tiny brains, completely undeveloped. Ninety percent of kids born this early end up with some kind of disability. Someone needs to be telling you. The majority of these kids do not turn out just fine."

I tried to listen and hear him out. The day before, I had stood outside the NICU and cried and threatened to rip out every tube and line attached to my twins. But something had changed in the past twenty-four hours, something I wished I could explain to my father—how I had come to lose my resolve, that I could no longer fight but saw this instead for what it was: a train wreck no one could stop. Where the day before I had argued and cried and demanded the do-not-resuscitate order, today I held my breath and waited for the decisions to come down from on high. While I was only three days into this ordeal, I had already begun to accept these compromised babies as mine. My milk had to come in. I had to figure out moment to moment what the information meant that I was being given about Evan and Ellie and their care. I needed to decide if I would pump my milk or not, if there was a purpose to that act of motherhood. Everything was happening in the now, and there was no standing back. I wished I could find the words to describe how this whole mess felt oddly fated, that I was somehow meant to be Evan and Ellie's mother, that there was a reason why these babies were born at the worst possible moment—not before twenty-three weeks, when they certainly would have died, nor after twenty-five weeks, when their prognoses would have been so much better. Call it fate or destiny—whether or not my father thought this was crazy, which I could see he did—I didn't seem to be able, nor were the doctors making it possible for me, to do this any differently.

At eleven that morning, the phone rang. I was alone in Josie's room and answered it to hear Betty, the social worker, on the line. "The team has agreed," she said. "We all feel the best course of action is to remove your daughter from life support."

I hung up then and before I could tell Cliff or my parents I flattened myself onto Josie's bed and cried. From something, it appeared, I had been released.

At 12:20 p.m. on August 3, they gave us our daughter to hold in our arms until she died. We sat in an empty nursery across the hall from where Evan lay, still alive. A nurse was there with us, Anne, and Betty, the social worker. They had wrapped Ellie in a blue quilt, one that became ours after she died. For the rest of my life, I would be this girl's mother, the mother of a dead child, a child who had lived for four days and who died when we removed her from life support. Before I was that mother, I was a writer whose favorite book included the death of a child. Richard Ford's novel *The Sportswriter* begins with a father and mother visiting the gravesite of their son. This death has brought about their divorce, and yet once a year on his birthday they find each other again to honor their son. I don't remember how the son died or even how old he was, but I do remember feeling the power of this death throughout the book, and how, to my younger self, my nonmother self, this death felt so real and significant. Before the twins were born, I had even begun writing a novel in which the main character visits a cemetery early on in the story. This cemetery holds the bodies of many young children. It is a place my own daughter could now rest.

The afternoon I arrived to hold my daughter in my arms until she died, these points of reference meant nothing; the death in Ford's book was distant and abstract, the cemetery meaningless. My emotions weren't clean and ordered. I was relieved and scared and guilty all at once. I wanted to be present for Ellie and for Cliff but I also wanted this to end. I had never been around a death before, never seen one happen before my eyes. That this death would also be my daughter's made me all the more unsure of what was to come. I was a parent and I was meant to know what to do and how to behave, but mostly I remember feeling lost. Years later, when asked at Ellie's gravesite, "Who are you here to visit?" I would be able to respond, "My daughter." On this afternoon, in this place, I didn't know the most basic skill, and that was how to be the mother of a baby about to die.

I took her first. Compared to Evan's, Ellie's medical record was brief: fourteen pages. What stood out in this short history was one small detail: *Infant was extubated on 8/3 at 1220 hours. She received morphine 0.7 mg IV × 1 prior to extubation, for comfort.* And so the baby I held in my arms was slowly dying already with a small dose of sedative to help her make the transition from life to death. I brought her small body toward me. She was so light there was nearly nothing to hold on to. I was greedy for her and wanted to keep her, but there was Cliff and it was his turn.

I watched my husband hold his daughter and remembered the first pictures of Josie, how happy he was, a smile I had never seen before, the smile of pure love. This time, the opposite time, it was a sadness and longing I had never seen before. I knew only my fear until I looked at my husband and saw what this death would do to him. He held Ellie and stroked her forehead, those dark eyebrows, her hair, her tiny hands. All at once, I wanted to take her from him and make her live, make this all change and go away.

Anne, a nurse, had volunteered to be with us for the next few hours. She also let us know she would leave if we preferred. "I don't have to stay," she said. "You can call me in when you think she is gone." None of us knew what to do or say. Should we be alone? Should there be company? Over the next several minutes we shuffled our way through logistics. Cliff handed Ellie back to me, the nurse checked her heartbeat, Betty took a note or two. Later, I would see other parents in this room in situations similar to ours. I would hear heaving sobs of grief, see priests leave, watch nurses take away white-wrapped bundles I would recognize as babies that were no more. On this day, with us, there were only hushed words and silence.

Dear Daughter, I would write much later, *the last day: we held you, touched you, gave you our warmth. They placed a stethoscope on your sternum and the nurse said, Not yet.*

For that is how I would forever remember it. That we passed our daughter back and forth and even gave her to Anne at one point so that we could hold each other, and that this went on for a very long time. I don't know what I expected: a movie ending perhaps, a final cry and then stillness. What happened instead was this: my daughter's body grew cold and then colder, her skin turned dark and then even darker, and when I felt nothing from her at all, no warmth or movement or breath or heartbeat, I cried and asked the nurse to check again and pulled back the quilt so she could reach Ellie's chest and she put the stethoscope on my tiny baby and shook her head and said, "No," meaning, *No, not yet,* and that this went on, over and over, a dozen times perhaps, over the course of the next two hours. That my daughter's heart slowed and slowed until it felt like it would never stop. How the nurse found its beat again and again, over the minutes and then hours. And how what felt like the last time kept coming because I knew she was already gone even as the nurse said she was not.

And then Anne looked up at us and said not yes, not no.

We held her longer then, our lost child, because once they took her from us we knew we would not see her again, just as we knew we would not know what to do with ourselves when we left, where we were supposed to go or how to find our way. And then it was too much even for us. We handed back our daughter, we took the quilt, we let her go, we left.

The last two details to my daughter's brief life:

TIME OF DEATH: 14:34 p.m.

CAUSE: periventricular hemorrhage grade IV; extreme prematurity (23 weeks).

Before she signed off on these details so that they might appear on Ellie's death certificate, Dr. Tam made the sign of the cross on my daughter's forehead. I did not stop her, though I thought, through my grief, *Did anyone ask you to do that?* And *What right do you have to send her to your God, or to think she is not already there?*

At home, Josie raced to embrace me while my mother hung back, wanting to know, I think, not wanting to ask. I hugged my mother and said only this: "It took so long, I never realized it would take so long." We had been gone almost three hours. I was not hungry but it was nearly four in the afternoon and so I agreed we should eat. We went out to lunch in the next town over, and afterward we drove through the streets, looking at houses. There was a place I knew of for sale in this same neighborhood, one with high home values and good schools; I had even called the realtor about the house on Friday, the weekend before the twins were born. One of the first messages on our answering machine the following Monday had been from the realtor, offering us times to see the house, telling us the price. That Friday, we'd been the potential parents of three children in need of good public schools. Today, all we had was Josie, and there was no need like that. Even so, I humored my parents, who wanted nothing more than to find something completely ordinary to take my mind off what had just happened. "This is a nice neighborhood," my parents agreed, admiring the well-kept ranch houses with views of the mountains to the north. "You really should consider buying a house here, no matter what happens." It all seemed incredible. Our daughter had just died and we were eating lunch and looking at houses. For the rest of my life I would remember this disembodied feeling, that when a person died, it was surreal and almost unfair that life went on, that dogs were out on walks with their owners, that people took strolls on sidewalks, that food could be cooked and eaten. This was the caprice of the physical world: that a person could have a body and live and walk and eat at one moment, and in the next moment none of those things existed or were necessary because that body was gone. And this would be the pain of losing Ellie, that each day we still lived in this world, even though she did not.

I had asked my parents to take charge of the funeral arrange-ments. Cliff and I discussed the details and decided on a cremation. My mother and father made an appointment at the funeral home sometime the same week Ellie died. They picked out an urn to hold the ashes, met with the funeral director. Years later, my mother would ask me how Cliff and I had been so sure about cremation. "Because we didn't know where she would go," I told her. "We weren't in a position to make a decision about burying a body."

Two days after Ellie died—a Friday—Cliff and I arrived at the funeral home to sit with Ellie's ashes before they were sealed within the urn. In place of her body, this time we held the smallest gray box, the kind I might buy at a craft store for less than a dollar. Inside were our daughter's ashes, half an inch deep, three inches wide. Cliff and I sat in a room with this box and held it together, even though there was not enough space for both sets of our hands. Me: I dreamed of a girl on a playground, her feet trailing in the dirt. Him? To this day I don't know. This was not something we discussed, how our hopes and dreams might play themselves out differently. We knew they did, we could see it in each other's eyes. Why put those dreams into words? They were gone.

We lit incense and we cried. We took turns holding the box. As with her body, we were greedy and bereft all at once. We didn't want to let go, we didn't want to hold on. There was no other way to be in that space except to go back and forth, to stay in the moment until the moment became oppressive. I have read that human nature has us fear the engulfment of grief, but that the human body spares us from this out of compassion for the nervous system and all else. In the moments like the one where we held Ellie, I knew how true this could be. I came right up against a pain I thought might suffocate me, so dense and hard was its weight, only to find that just when I could not take another breath, the weight lifted and I was back in a living body again, no longer in the stasis between the no-where I had gone to and the somewhere of this new life I knew to be mine. And so we cried and traded the box back and forth and then, when we didn't know what else to do, we gave the box back and went home, just as we had given her body back and gone home two days before.

2

I N THE FIRST DAYS and weeks after Evan was born, after
Ellie died and we took her ashes home, we heard the phrase
a lot: "We're waiting for him to declare." To the doctors the
phrase meant the obvious: "Will his blood sugars level out now
that we're giving him glucose?" "Will his blood pressure increase with the dopamine?" "Will his white blood cell count
lower with the antibiotics?" "Will his blood gases improve with
the change in the vent settings?"

To us, the words had another meaning: Does he want to
live? Is he willing to stay? What kind of life is he looking for?
Why was he in such a rush to be here? When Evan opened his
right eye for the first time, I saw this as a declaration: *Okay,
I'm willing to look around.* But the left eye stayed fused shut for
many days, almost in a squint, and the declaration became less
Yeah, I want to see this world than *Hey, I'm not so sure about this.*
When I thought back to his very delivery, those first kittenish
cries certainly seemed more like a question mark than a definitive *Hello, world, I'm ready for my close-up!*

Several years after Evan and Ellie were born, a good friend's
husband died suddenly, tragically. I compared my situation to
hers only to be told, "Yes, you both had terrible losses, but at
least you had something to do after your daughter died. You
could take care of your son. In this case, our friend's case, she

is alone." It was true that I had something to do, and that this something involved taking care of Evan. But the caretaking was unlike any other I'd done in my life. It didn't involve anything concrete or performative—other than changing my son's diaper and questioning the doctors on their every move—so much as it involved witnessing this process of waiting to declare. Being there to see first one eyelid open and then the other, to watch the slow drip of drugs and fluids into his body, to measure his weight each night. To look at the flashing lights and monitors. Evan didn't do anything in the months we waited for him to de- clare—he simply lay there and went, as I told a friend, from looking like an animal at first, then a very old man, and then, finally, a very small baby. At first he looked like no one; then, with his hooked nose, my father; and after that, with his high forehead and wrinkle lines, my brother Bill. Eventually, when his eyes opened and his full-lipped mouth was no longer taped up to a breathing tube, he finally looked like himself: a boy with a round face and dark skin, eyes more Asian than Josie's, a double chin. A little bit of Josie, a little bit of Cliff. Not much of me, except that same high forehead my brother boasts, the one my husband calls the Forman forehead. But to even say *at first* and *then* and *then* is to make it seem as though these pro- gressions took place in a way that was visible. In reality, this all happened so slowly it was not unlike watching the drip of those same drugs that had kept him alive. Eventually, there was something solid as evidence of all that had been happen- ing. Eventually, he turned into Evan, a boy who had declared himself.

In this time and for months afterward, I could read only one book, a Buddhist book. *When Things Fall Apart*, it was called, and it spoke of essential Buddhist concepts: suffering, compassion, loving-kindness. Listening to the beeps and wheezes of Evan's ventilator, I read about fear and came to understand how this one-pound baby needed me in a way I had never conceived before. I read about compassion and saw that over my reluctance to have my son live and my fear of what his life might be, his needs began to triumph. I read about suffering and came to understand that if I didn't sit there, learn how to change his three-inch-square diaper, wait for the moment he opened his eyes for the first time, and question the doctors about their every move, then who would? *I* was suffering? *I* had not gotten what I wanted? What about Evan and this early, fragile life?

Faith and spirituality were all around me in the NICU; every parent seemed to have his or her version of my Buddhist book. For some it was the Bible and prayer. For others it was the invocations placed over their tiny babies' incubators: *Protect Baby F.,* and *We are looking out for you.* I heard a lot about God in those days and wanted my own kind of faith to keep me going, but God had never done it for me. Instead, I considered myself to be an atheistic-religious mongrel. My father was Jewish, my mother Episcopalian. I grew up going to synagogue on Jewish High Holy Days and, occasionally, church on Easter or Christmas. We celebrated Hanukkah in my house and I have memories of my dad fasting on Yom Kippur. But my parents' mixed-religion marriage hadn't gone over too well with the Jewish side of the family, and, growing up, I had always thought of religion as both hypocritical and a potential source of conflict. My Jewish grandmother wouldn't come to the house if we had a Christmas tree and she had even gone so far as to wear black to my parents' wedding.

My religious upbringing was further splintered by the Quaker private school I attended from the time I was nine years old until I went to college. Quaker Meeting, in which the congregation sat in silence and members stood up to speak as "the spirit moved them," became my only habitual religious experience, said experience being, essentially, one of contemplative meditation and patience. Over the years, as my friends discovered meditation, I always laughed and told them, "I had forty minutes of Quaker Meeting once a week from the time I was nine. I know all about meditation." In my adult years, this early practice with silent meditation had taken me to New Age spirituality in the form of yoga, relaxation techniques, Zen Buddhism, and the I Ching. Nothing had ever consistently given me a clarity or faith I could call religion, however, and while I appreciated the perspective meditation and these other languages and answers could give, I certainly never felt the need for an explanation of any kind of higher order or purpose. Fate was fate, destiny destiny. That was all I needed to know.

Until the twins. When faced with a future of uncertainty (Evan) and a past of loss (Ellie), I wanted to believe in the power of prayer and saw the allure of potential answers. I went to the hospital chapel often, adding Evan's name to the prayer list. At home, I lit candles and incense. On bad days, I got on my knees on the altar at the chapel or in front of my candles at home and prayed—not to God, but simply for compassion in the midst of my grief. For release and help. Mostly what I experienced in those moments was pure invocation: *Help me, take this away, make it better.* These thoughts were of a desperate nature and not addressed to anyone in particular, just to a higher power if one existed. Today I read of a study that has determined scientifically that prayer does not help patients who undergo medical procedures or those who are hospitalized, and yet I think anyone, scientist or doctor, would be hard-pressed to find family members not willing to consider prayer in these circumstances.

It was impossible, looking at Evan, waiting for him to declare, not to wish for answers, or want a higher purpose to this life and the lessons I was learning. This is where my Buddhist book came in and why it was all I could read during that time. The Buddhists, I learned, explained the material world as a continuous cycle of life and death, birth and rebirth, and, along with it all, impermanence and suffering. Buddhists call this cycle samsara and describe life as a process of trying to avoid and conquer its dimensions while getting caught on it all the while. We think we can escape samsara when our needs are met; we think when desire is fulfilled, the suffering won't return. We think we are immune from the cycle of life and death and that we can hold impermanence at bay. There was solace for me in these concepts because if I needed anything it was a sense that this situation was not permanent, and that, in the shifting tides that comprised Evan's life in the NICU, I might find something different the next day or the next.

While I remember every event from Evan's hospitalization, I remember very little of Josie's third year. On the days she was home from preschool, I went about my living daughter's routine dutifully and with little attention. We incorporated visits to the hospital to deliver my milk into trips to the park down the street from our house. I pumped my milk six or eight times a day, every three hours, for a baby that still received all his nutrients from TPN, or total parenteral nutrition, a pouch of yellowish fluid that hung from a metal stand and dripped into an IV poked into Evan's head, the head being the easiest place to start an IV on a preemie his size. I have very few memories of this time as Josie's mother. Photographs remind me: Josie in a green-and-white-checked jumper, standing in front of our apartment building. Her smile is still all baby teeth but her hair has grown long, curly locks that reach her small shoulders. Sparkly red shoes on her feet, those we bought on a rare shopping trip to the local mall. She called them ruby slippers and demanded a pair so that she could look like Dorothy. For a year, until she outgrew them, they became a ritualistic part of her attire. I remember walking in our neighborhood, up Orange Grove Boulevard, the route of the annual Rose Parade, to Wrigley Mansion, to hear those same ruby slippers clatter and echo on the steps. I remember yoga poses in the fall by the water fountain there. My daughter liked to see me do sun salutations, and hold my hands in front of my heart at the end of the series of poses and recite the Sanskrit prayer *Namasté*.

I began a story about a woman who has lost a child and in it there was this scene:

> Clara plays with Elyse's daughter, a game they call Hello, Luna. Together, they walk to the park and search the blue sky for last night's moon. When they find the crusty remnant, cold and silver in the morning sky, they stop and cry, "Hello, Luna." The girl then strikes her version of a yoga pose: hands in front of her heart, thumbs touching her chest. She grins and says to her, "Mama-stay."

I thought I was writing in the third person, never saw that this Elyse was me.

My last memory of Josie at age three comes from a picture taken at Disneyland in mid-July, a week or two before I went into labor. My daughter is a wispy-haired pixie in her green-and-white-checked jumper. I was twenty-two weeks pregnant. Even on that trip, I didn't feel well. Later I would hear from a friend, in passing, some modern-day folklore: if you're pregnant and want to go into labor, head to Disneyland on a hot day.

My next memory of Josie was of her fourth birthday the following May. By then Evan was home, blind, having seizures.

To maintain and manage, I turned my attention to the details
and language of the world we'd entered. The night the twins
were born the doctors handed Cliff a booklet that offered a
guide to the neonatal intensive care unit, with phone numbers
and definitions and advice and suggestions. *Be sure to get support,* I read. *Don't be surprised if friends and family can't figure out
what to say or do* came another adage, which explained why I
kept having the same conversations over and over: "When is
he coming home? I know about another preemie that was born
at twenty-four weeks; he's great! He's a little small for his age
but otherwise he's just fine!" And more advice too: *If you don't
understand a procedure, be sure to ask your child's doctor.* Books
and suggested reading: *After the Death of a Child: Living with
Loss Through the Years; Empty Cradle, Broken Heart: Surviving
the Death of Your Baby.* Handouts with titles like "What Every
Parent Needs to Know: Taking Care of Yourself," and "Riding
the Roller Coaster, Dealing with Setbacks," and "How Your
Marriage Adjusts," with such tips as *Decide on decision-making*
and *When in doubt,* CLARIFY. There were numbers for social
workers and the chaplain, directions to the cafeteria and the
chapel. I became a student of these handouts and kept this
manual, my anchor to the world my son had entered, by my
bedside for months. At night, I read passages aloud to my husband, who would endure about ten minutes before asking me
to stop. "How can you stand reading that stuff?" he'd ask. "It
doesn't help one bit." Cliff coped in his own way, by wearing a
set of worry beads the chaplain had given us, reading his own
Buddhist books, and, in his visits to the NICU, sitting by our
son's side quietly, not badgering the doctors and nurses with

questions from the handouts. In the early days and weeks of Evan's hospitalization, we established this pattern: me needing to know more, Cliff wanting to focus on fewer details, the bigger picture. What mattered to Cliff was Evan, his survival and eventual homecoming. What counted to me were details, comprehension, understanding cause and effect. The image I encountered again and again—how fathers stood outside the theater of the NICU while mothers took their places center stage—would continue to play itself out, in the hospital and beyond. No matter how strong they might be, fathers, like Cliff, often felt helpless in the midst of these details, unable to fix things, and so they stood back, looking for the bigger picture. Mothers, like myself, felt equally unable to fix things, and yet our helplessness somehow fed our compulsion to know and understand it all.

My whole life I'd been fascinated with the details of how things worked and were made and functioned. During the same Quaker Meeting that taught me meditation at an early age, I often spent the forty minutes of silence taking apart my watch and putting it back together again. My grandfather was an inventor who built a cello from scratch, knew how to melt gold, and, apparently, came up with the compound that was Silly Putty before it was officially invented. He died before I was born but I felt inside me some endless capacity for investigation I believed I inherited from him. I rarely have to read instructions; my sense of direction is tremendous; and I can fix things, or determine what needs to be fixed, on items as varied as sewing machines, lawn mowers, and computers. At a gathering, I am always the person handed the video camera and asked to make it work.

Until the twins' birth and Ellie's death, I had never encountered a situation I could not either fix or abandon. The book they gave us, and the NICU itself, told me we'd entered a different world. The woman who could operate every machine and had a solution to every problem faced some big obstacles in the form of advanced medical technology hooked up to one very tiny baby. In the first days and weeks of Evan's hospitalization I asked a lot of questions; if I didn't understand the answers, I asked more questions. I made it clear to the staff that I was smart and educated. Once, when I looked at Evan's chart, a nurse told me that since the chart was not mine, I didn't have the right to inspect it. I fought that nurse just as I later fought what actually got written in the chart.

Despite my questions and probing, despite my fix-it fingers, I quickly became aware that in the NICU, control and solutions were not in the offing. There were the sticky rules, like who could read a chart. There was the trial and error of determining what was wrong and finding the right solution, that alchemical mixture of treatments and drugs. There were the common ups and downs of the preemies themselves. Finally, and most important, there was the essential not-knowing even the doctors acknowledged—that lack of a crystal ball. My fix-it self wondered why it took something as arcane and magical as a crystal ball to know what was going to happen to my son. Surely the doctors did know that this was a painfully complicated picture and that no matter what they did, Evan would suffer, as would his family. And yet few of them mentioned the lasting complications Evan might face, or the lifelong disabilities. In their defense, the doctors were also right in telling me they couldn't predict Evan's course; the cruel joke in the world of preemies is that two babies born on the same day at the same birth weight can have two absolutely different outcomes. Even now I know of a little girl the same birth weight as Evan who can walk and talk and see. The boy who was Evan's roommate for so long, who looked to be doing so much worse more days than not—his eyesight was in danger, but then all the risks receded. And another boy born even later term and at a bigger birth weight than Evan—he is deaf and oxygen dependent. None of that explains what happened to my son.

According to statistics provided by the Centers for Disease Control, in the entire United States in the year 2000 there were only 4,241 live births from twin deliveries in the weight range of Evan and Ellie, five hundred to one thousand grams. Even more relevant is the statistic of babies born weighing less than five hundred grams, those termed "very-low-birth-weight infants." There were only 1,148 twin deliveries (and live births) in this weight range in the entire United States in the year 2000. If one were to (arbitrarily) divide this by the number of states, the statistic gets even slimmer: only 22.96 women in all of California in the year 2000 gave birth to twins the size of Evan and Ellie.

Since the 1990s, progress in neonatology has resulted in more babies surviving from younger and younger gestational ages. Advances in fertility treatments have also increased the number of multiple—and premature—births. Multiple births are six times more likely to end in prematurity than singletons. And while only 3 percent of all births in the United States in 2000 were multiple births, they made up 30 percent of the cases of infant mortality. My own doctor had told me that if I reached twenty-four weeks in my pregnancy, the babies would have a 40 percent chance of survival; the doctor never revealed the actual odds of having a child this early. During the fertility treatments that gave us the twins, the doctors had described multiple births as a risk of fertility treatments. Those risks never included clear, factual statements about prematurity. Put together, the increase in multiple births and the increase in techniques aimed to save these very tiny babies have resulted in statistical realities like Evan and Ellie. In the year 2000, myself and twenty-one other women went through this experience. Slim odds indeed, and yet also a reality. Perhaps this was why I had never been prepared by any of my doctors to become this kind of statistic. As the doctors often told us later with Evan, "The statistics don't matter until they happen to you."

Unexplained preterm labor is most often attributed to some kind of infection. Neither I nor the doctors ever addressed what kind of infection might have occurred, where it had originated, or whether it could have been prevented. I never pressed for an explanation, never posited my own theory for the premature labor and delivery. I was simply convinced that by missing the signs and symptoms of preterm labor, I was to blame. I was an unfortunate statistic; there seemed to be no point in searching for an answer. *Stupid*, I told myself. *So stupid.* At twenty weeks my OB had warned me that the following four weeks were important and told me to arrange my appointments for every two weeks from then on. I'd canceled my twenty-two-week appointment because of a work-related meeting and rescheduled it for twenty-four weeks. I went into labor the day before that new appointment. I read of other women pregnant with multiples who saw high-risk specialists, were primed for the signs of preterm labor, and put on bed rest at twenty-four weeks, no matter what. This was not me. Despite my education and background, I'd opted out of a high-risk specialist and settled instead for my regular obstetrician and his practice. I'd been pregnant before, had had no complications the first time around, was still under forty, and knew what to look out for—or so I thought. Rather than making a career of the pregnancy, I tried to keep things as simple as possible.

And yet in the days before I gave birth there were small signs things were wrong, signs I ignored: contractions on Thursday at the park. Not feeling right Friday. Tiredness and pain on Saturday. When I read afterward about the signs of preterm labor, I saw that there were often these inconclusive feelings, the sense that what were otherwise typical pregnancy symptoms were more intense or somehow different. In my case, and in many other cases, the signs weren't distinctive enough to call the doctor. At eighteen weeks, I'd had what I knew were contractions, those that worried me enough to phone the doctor's office. "Drink water, rest on your side, call us if they keep up," the nurse said. The contractions subsided but still I mentioned them at my twenty-week appointment. The doctor examined me and pronounced me okay.

So how was it that the woman who knew to recognize those signs and to discuss them as they arose didn't know enough to recognize spotting that Saturday morning as the start of labor? Or the intense, sharp pains that same evening as another version of contractions? Looking back, I wanted to rail at myself for my denial. *Stupid, so stupid.* That Saturday-night dinner with friends, I put up my feet and had half a glass of red wine and told myself to relax. Nothing was wrong. Then Sunday, more cramps, more strange feelings. I wasn't getting better, only worse. "You don't think you're in labor, do you?" my father asked me over the phone. "No, I don't," I told him, "but if my whole pregnancy is like this, it's going to be a long one." I remember the conversation so clearly, that and his advice to me: "Take care of yourself." The next time we spoke, the twins had been born.

Even at the hospital the Sunday afternoon the twins were born, when I started telling Cliff and the doctor about the other signs I'd noticed, I felt so dumb for having kept them to myself. *Stupid. Just so very stupid.*

I also read afterward that many women who experience preterm labor blame themselves for the outcome and for ignoring the signs. The morning after the twins were born, I told my mother how guilty I felt. "Oh, Vicki," she said, "I was so worried you would blame yourself. You know this isn't your fault, don't you?" Of course I did. I brought my husband along to a therapist appointment a month after the twins were born to hear him say out loud that he didn't blame me. Even so, I knew different.

As women and mothers, we think of ourselves as omnipotent, not impotent. Our instincts and nurturing help us know from the first moments our children are born how to distinguish cries, recognize real distress, tell the difference between a cry of hunger versus that of a soiled diaper. When Josie was an infant I'd awaken an instant before her, ready to nurse. When we were getting her to sleep through the night I always sensed before Cliff whether the cries were easing up or increasing. Later, when Evan started having seizures, this same ability to tune in told me something was wrong even if no one else could see the signs. Cliff and I once had a conversation about maternal feelings of omnipotence and he insisted that they were both real and misguided. Of course a mother couldn't stop an accident from happening. I disagreed. In the stories I read later of children dying and bereaved parents, there was always the sense of foreboding, of having made a mistake by allowing the night out, the boat trip on the lake, the ski weekend. A mother's refrain is not unlike *Madeline*'s Miss Clavel's: "Something is not right." In the same way that a mother clings to details, she also believes that if she simply pays attention long and hard enough, she can prevent anything from happening.

Today I read that fetal cells migrate to the mother's brain and live there for up to twenty-seven years. This is why we blame ourselves as mothers, because the cells are there: to tell us there is risk and danger, to help us prevent tragedy. Because I hadn't listened to the cells, or myself, I had altered my family and our lives forever.

Early on in Evan's hospitalization, there was a young couple who looked upon their baby, a boy the size of Evan, and asked, "When can we bring him home?" as if the answer would be "Next week"; I heard how confused they were to learn their son would be in the NICU for several months at least, of how they kept coming, day after day, more or less unaware of how serious his situation was. Even Cliff marveled at how little this young couple understood of their lot. "They just don't get it, do they?" he asked after watching them during one of our visits. He turned back to Evan and said, "I guess on a certain level, that makes it easier." Cliff wasn't being cruel; he was simply stating an essential truth: the more we knew, the less we could accept. Together, he and I asked about Evan's weight and his vent settings and his saturations and looked at this couple and wished for the same level of naiveté. When could Evan come home? We heard replies like "Close to your original due date," which meant a four-month hospitalization, and "We don't have a crystal ball," and "When he weighs five pounds and is stable." None of these answers felt relevant to the fourteen-ounce package stretched out before us, all limbs, sealed eyelids, half a dozen syringes sticking out of his body. Friends and family members wanted to know, "When?" and I tried to describe what I saw and compare it to where I knew we needed to be. To come home, Evan had to get off the ventilator, take forty ounces of formula a day by mouth, and weigh five times as much as he did right then. From six hundred grams to the astronomical four thousand grams that had been my older daughter's birth weight. How long could it take? At the moment, our boy's lungs were each the size of a dime, his heart the width of a penny. A favorite baby doll of Josie's was longer than him by two inches and had a head the size of Evan's: the dimensions of an orange. How long would it take for that same head to become a grapefruit? A hundred days? Twenty-four hundred hours?

Every detail became a kind of measurement. A baby across the unit took two ounces of formula at a time. She'd certainly be out the door long before Evan would. Another preemie was already "nippling," or taking a bottle by mouth. PO—from the Latin *per os,* "by mouth"—was pretty important. Breathing on less than 20 percent oxygen from an oxygen supply or, better, on room air alone was another important threshold. Evan was still on 80 or 100 percent oxygen most of the time. The truth of the numbers? I could nearly have another baby in the time it would take to bring Evan home.

On a hot August morning, three weeks after the twins were born, I drove with my brother-in-law Curt deep into the San Gabriel Valley to look at gravesites for my daughter. Cliff was at work, Josie in preschool. Earlier in the day, while I sat by Evan's bedside, Curt, a radiologist, had gone with Dr. Vine to look at Evan's most recent chest x-rays. He and Dr. Vine bonded in radiology over the medical facts and figures of Evan's case—*bronchopulmonary dysplasia* and *infiltrates* and *atelectasis*—while I held fast by Evan's bedside with my Buddhist book and my intentions. "Vicki, I know this is hard and you don't want to do it," Curt said to me when he returned from the radiology lab, "but we really need to look at graves."

Not wanting to do it was an understatement. At the time, I had a guided meditation tape I listened to at least once a day that took me through all the stages of the body and the chakras and their healing lights—"Now imagine your head, and the healing purple light of the crown chakra. Imagine your crown chakra covered in light, healing purple light. . . ." In the same way that I charted the drugs I took on the bottles of breast milk I stored, this guided meditation was another clue to my deteriorating mental state. On the days Josie was at daycare, I listened to the tape three or four times in succession, entranced by the thought that the colors I envisioned might also heal my heart. It was only ten thirty in the morning, but what I wanted more than anything at the moment of Curt's suggestion was to head back home and bathe myself in that healing light.

Ellie had been dead three weeks. Her ashes still rested on the radiator in our bedroom, the remains safe inside a square metal urn my parents had picked out. Along with the urn, we also had a permit to keep her ashes at home. I had no idea that such a permit was required until the funeral-home director asked us when we came to collect the urn if the ashes were to be interred.

"We're keeping her at home for now," I said. "Is that a problem?"

"Of course not," he said. "But you'll need a permit. I've included one in the bag." I looked inside and there it was: an official permit from the Department of Health allowing the "bearer to keep the ashes of Eleanor Anne Kamida at a personal residence." "Don't remove the permit from the bag," the man said. "You'll need it if you decide to inter the ashes at a later date."

Later, I offered this detail to a student after I'd read a story of his in which a cremation urn rested on a mantel in his character's living room. The student looked at me quizzically. "Believe me, you need a permit to keep ashes at home," I told him.

"I know it sounds weird, but it's true. If you put that detail in, your reader will know you have your facts straight." Together, Ellie's ashes and the permit rested inside a green velvet bag, open at the top. Some days I removed the urn and read the inscription: *Eleanor Anne Kamida, Forever in Our Hearts.* Most others I burned incense and lit candles and listened to my guided meditation and tried not to think about the next steps. At first, after the cremation, Cliff and I felt certain that Ellie needed a funeral and a place in the ground. But as we became involved in the daily intensity of Evan's care, we also grew less and less able to let go of Ellie. In my mind, and in Cliff's, it was increasingly true that she didn't need to be anywhere but with us for now.

As the oldest brother in the Kamida family, Curt is often given the job of caretaker. This role had become especially operative since the death of both Cliff's parents, several years before. It wasn't simply the Japanese American heritage of the Kamida family that demanded this respect; it was Curt's own intelligence, strength, and decisiveness, his ability to cut through to what mattered and to make what mattered happen. Before his visit, I had even asked Curt to help us with the task of finding a gravesite, certain he was the right person for the job, all the while knowing I wasn't ready. And so it was that despite my desire to be home with my healing chakras, I found myself driving east in the San Gabriel Valley that morning to look at cemeteries at my brother-in-law's behest.

After the twins were born and I felt certain they would die, I had told Curt I wanted to bury them in Honolulu, where Cliff's parents are interred. There, the gravesite lies in a lush, green valley, surrounded by other cemeteries. The niche for the urns is indoors, but it's open to the outside, and there is a glass pane that gives a view of the urns and those of their family mem-

bers who are with them. In my routine life, this is the graveyard I am closest to, the one I visit most often, even more often
than that of my own grandparents, who are buried somewhere
out in deepest Northeast Philadelphia. We visit Cliff's parents
and grandparents at this cemetery each time we go to Hawaii,
to light incense and place flowers. When I'd suggested this option to Curt, he'd voiced the concern that if we buried Ellie in
Hawaii she would be too far away for us to visit on a regular basis. "You should try to find somewhere in Los Angeles," he said.
"She needs to be close by."

I could see how, from Curt's perspective (and that of my
own family, my brothers and sister and parents), we needed to
move on, and that in burying Ellie we were also better accepting the reality of what had happened. I could also see how Curt,
like so many others who visited us during that time, wanted to
do something and couldn't find a way to the place where Cliff
and I found ourselves on a daily basis—the place where there
was nothing we could do and where we had to learn to live in a
seemingly permanent stasis, that same cycle of birth and death
and impermanence I clung to every day. Even so, the idea of a
child of mine being buried in San Gabriel, or Glendora, or Al-
tadena—all cities near to us—was so striking as to be nearly
implausible. I had grown up in Philadelphia, thousands of
miles away. Cliff's family was in Hawaii. What did any place
in Los Angeles mean to us? How did we know that in ten years
or even five we'd still be living here? Our immediate families
were too scattered to think of putting Ellie near any of them,
and the very idea of having a child to bury seemed even more
inconceivable.

On even the most glorious Southern California day, the valley east of Pasadena isn't the picture of tourist fun: the 210
Freeway, eight lanes wide, looks out on either side at strip malls

and car dealerships, lights flashing in the bright sunlight, advertising deals and low-interest loans. In the winter, the mountains are snowcapped, purple, and immediate. In the summer, they are brown and wrapped in smog.

"This isn't the nicest time of year to visit," I said to Curt as we drove.

"It's not like I'm on vacation," he said.

"Even so."

The farther we drove into the valley, the worse the heat and smog, until we couldn't see the mountains behind the yellow sky. When we reached the first cemetery, an empty landscape of gravestones, flat green lawns, and walls of mausoleums, stark and white in the heat, I thought to myself, *Even the dead deserve better than this.*

I'm not sure what I expected in a graveyard. On that day and in the moments since we'd watched Ellie die, I came to this question in a very real way. I knew I loved the cemetery in Nuuanu, where Cliff's family was buried—the place itself feels haunted by spirits. At my old Quaker high school there are two cemeteries, the "live" graveyard and the "dead" one. The live graveyard, on the south side of the school, still took reservations; on sunny, spring days, we ate lunch in the dead graveyard. Quakers believe in demure markers, no larger than a brick placed flat and sideways, since in death as in life, simplicity is key. In high school, we never thought twice about eating lunch in the dead graveyard; it was just a pretty spot with a cherry tree in the middle and a decent amount of sun and shade, depending on the weather. Some teachers held classes there, and study sessions during exam time, and the place was even a make-out spot during dances. There have been other cemeteries in my life throughout the years, and they have all been some version of peaceful and appealing. None of them were baked in smog, flat, and expressionless. Perhaps this was what I sought: a place for the living.

I wanted to move along, to keep driving and leave that blank spot, but Curt said we should stop and park and get out and look at one of the mausoleums. We walked along the length of the building—a thick stucco wall exposed to bright sun. The niches were large, each the size of a coffin rather than an urn. "Where's the columbarium?" I wondered aloud. Even Curt seemed to be at a loss. We crossed to the other side and saw the smaller squares, those that would hold cremains. We wandered like unwilling shoppers, hoping not to find a salesperson.

"No one should have to do this," Curt said.

"Do what?" I asked.

"Bury a child. No one should have to bury a child." His eyes rested not on me but at the wall of plaques before him.

But I am, I thought, *that is exactly what I'm doing.*

What I knew, and why I didn't say the words aloud, was that grief was not clear-cut, the way Curt and the others wanted it to be. A mother didn't drive around looking at cemeteries and accepting the fact that her daughter had died and that she was waiting for her fourteen-ounce son to declare himself. Instead, she put everything off until the putting off was more unbearable than the thing itself. I didn't want to be on this cemetery-shopping trip. I didn't really want to be home in bed with my meditations either. If anyone had asked what I wanted, my answer would have been this: to be in a place where I wasn't doing any of it. Even Curt did not want to be here. I could tell from his twisted expression and the way his hands stayed jammed in his pockets. I also knew that even if I couldn't do this now, there would come a time when I would have to, when I would be burying my child, the one who had lived for four days and took two hours to die in my arms. I didn't blame

Curt. Everyone thought it was important for us to bury Ellie and to move on. What Curt and the others didn't seem to know was that when we reached the point where we had to do it, it would be us doing it, not anyone else, and that this burial was not only impossible at the moment, it was also an impossible sign of how permanently things had changed.

On the way back to the freeway, we stopped at a nearby gas station for a Dr Pepper. A sign in the window of the mini-mart announced a lottery jackpot of $18 million. "Let's buy a ticket," I said. "Who knows? Maybe we'll win." I certainly didn't feel lucky, but it seemed like something normal to do, something ordinary, and in those days whatever I could do that felt ordinary felt joyously ordinary.

Compared to the first cemetery we toured, the second was a model of what a graveyard should be—shaded, beautiful stone markers, benches on which to sit and rest. It lay in a small town just east of where we lived, one established in the late nineteenth century. Some of the oldest graves belonged to the town's original citizens. I saw graves dating to 1870, ancient by Southern Californian standards, and I felt the presence of these founding fathers comforting and familiar, something more East Coast than West. Old-growth California oaks provided shade and thick roots to climb over as I walked the dirt paths. There were children buried here, with old-fashioned names like Beatrice and Lowell. The cemetery stood on a hillside that looked down on a community center. Below, I saw kids swimming in the town's pool. A playground, a basketball court, a preschool. Up here, the smog wasn't as visible on the mountains, and my eyes traced the fire roads among the brown vegetation. Not the blank expanse we'd seen before, but very much the world of the living.

Curt and I walked around the graveyard in slow, opposite circles. I didn't want to say, and clearly he didn't want to push me in that direction, and yet I knew as I stood on a path under the oak trees that this might be somewhere we could put Ellie, somewhere I would not mind visiting. We left the place, drove in silence. Back home, I called my brother Bill that afternoon to tell him. "I think we may have found the place," I said. He listened as I told him about the children in the pool below, their noise and cries. "It will be good for Ellie," I said. "And for us. She'll have company, someone to listen to. . . ." Before I could finish the thought I was crying, and he was saying he was sorry, and I found myself wondering yet again, *Did the dead really notice, did they care about the living?*

That same evening, the day of cemetery shopping and lottery tickets, Dr. Vine called us to tell us that Evan had taken a turn for the worse. "I'm not saying anything dire is about to happen," he said. "But you wanted to know if his condition deteriorated, and I think it has. You might think about coming back tonight after shift change." I hung up the phone and told Cliff. We both knew that in the world of waiting to declare, this was not a good sign. It was still early, not even seven. Since shift change—when the day nurses handed over their cases to the incoming night crew and discussed any issues that had come up during the day, or might come up that night—started at seven and didn't end until eight, we headed out for an early dinner at a local Chinese restaurant. I didn't feel like eating but Josie was hungry, and there was no point in sitting in the house, waiting to return to the hospital.

Over dinner, Curt mentioned in passing all the phone calls he'd seen us receive in the past few days. That same evening, after Dr. Vine had called, the phone had rung half a dozen more times. I ignored the phone each time, the way I let it ring and ring in the days and weeks following the twins' birth. "You know, you have a lot of friends," Curt said. "A lot of people who want to know how you're doing."

"So try being a bit nicer to them?" I said. "Is that what you mean? That we should pick up the phone and talk to them?"

I knew I was being insensitive, I knew I had disappeared into another round of grief over the news about Evan, the trip we would have to make that night to the hospital, the possibility that we might be looking for not one gravesite but two, and the knowledge that there was absolutely nothing I could do to change a thing. In my grief and panic, I also resented the fact that Curt still lived in a place where if you were good and honest and right, if you were polite and answered the phone and called people back, if you did all that, everything would turn out okay. Our time in that place had ended.

The look of shame and anger my husband gave me told me what I already knew: I had gone too far. My apology came out mangled and angry and wasn't an apology at all. "I'm sorry, but you try getting a million phone calls every day about your critically ill son and then we'll see how nice you manage to be."

For the rest of the dinner, Josie played the joker, as she would do so often over the next few years. Curt turned his attention to her, and I picked at my string beans, not willing to meet Cliff's eye, fearing his anger. I felt awful, of course, because I hadn't wanted to hurt Curt's feelings and I knew he was simply trying to do what he considered to be the right thing. Back home, Josie, Curt, and I sat in the courtyard of our apartment building in the fading light, waiting for hospital shift change to end and visiting hours to start again. In my mind, I tried to find ways to describe for Curt how I felt, ways I might apologize and tell him I wasn't as mad as I seemed, or that I was, and to explain why. As I pondered a dozen openings, a stray black Labrador wandered into the courtyard. In the same way that my grief would take me by surprise as the years went on, so too my anxiety. The dog, in the safety of my territory, on the prowl, sent me into a panic. "Go away!" I shouted. "Leave us alone!"

Curt moved between me and the Labrador. "It's just a stray," he said.

"I'm afraid of dogs," I told him, holding on to Josie. "A German shepherd jumped me when I was little. Can you get rid of him, please?"

Curt calmly took the dog and walked him out of the courtyard. When he came back, I said, "I'm sorry. I don't know what came over me."

"It's okay," he said.

"I'm sorry about what I said before too. At the restaurant. I just can't do this the way you want me to."

"There's no one way," he said. "I thought I was doing the right thing. We're all just trying to cope, aren't we? No one really has the right words, Vicki. No one knows what to say."

I reminded him of something he'd said when the twins were born, the reluctance he'd expressed about removing Ellie from life support. "You told Cliff you hoped we could live with the consequences, as if maybe we were doing the wrong thing. I need you to understand. There's no living with any of these consequences."

"When we were in the radiology lab this morning, Dr. Vine said babies like Evan have only a forty percent chance of surviving their first few days," Curt said. "He's amazed he's made it this far."

"Do you think Evan is going to die?" I asked. "Is that why we're going back tonight?"

"Doctors usually don't call unless it's serious," he said. "But honestly, I don't have an answer to that question."

We left Curt with Josie on the couch, reading books. On our

way out the door, I turned to Cliff and said, "I'm scared. I'm not sure I want to go."

"Stay here. I'll go by myself."

"I don't want you to be there alone."

"I don't mind."

"No. I should go. What if something happens? I'll wish I had said goodbye."

I went to the hospital that night with the absolute certainty that this was the night my son would die. Doctors didn't call unless it was serious. We would have to bury two children. Perhaps this was why we hadn't found a spot for Ellie yet; we were waiting for Evan to join her. As soon as we arrived, I saw the tense bodies around Evan's bed—Dr. Vine and the respiratory tech and two nurses—and I saw Evan himself, his numbers dipping wildly, and I knew how serious the situation was. I hadn't seen faces that worried ever, even the morning after the twins were born. Later, Dr. Vine himself would tell me, "I had the whole team here to keep an eye on your son. I had no idea if he would make it or not, but I wanted everyone to know we had done everything we could. The situation was that dire."

The night Dr. Vine called us to the hospital, the monitors above Evan's bed told the story the doctors and nurses didn't have to: an erratic heart rate (green); low blood pressure (red); and, finally, a separate machine, the pulse oximeter, which measured the level of oxygen saturation in Evan's blood. The pulse ox told us, via a sensor on his toe, if Evan was saturating well; that is, getting enough oxygen in his bloodstream. This was also the machine that sounded an alarm every time the saturations went below a certain number, usually 85. This was the machine I followed intensely in those first few weeks, as if by counting the numbers, I might also watch Evan survive. That night, Cliff and I sat by Evan's bedside and watched his saturations veer wildly, from 85 to 90, then down to 70 and below.

A normal pulse ox reading registered around 99 percent; what did it mean that his oxygen saturation rarely climbed above 80? What happened to his brain when his levels dipped as low as 65 and stayed there? I was too afraid to ask. Instead, we sat by his bedside and watched all his numbers careen wildly and I gripped Cliff's hand in a panic like none I'd had since the day Evan and Ellie were born. In the process of waiting to declare, this was a very bad night. I touched my son's inch-long foot and saw the numbers go down even farther and I knew I couldn't stay. "I can't take this," I said to Cliff, and I fled the room.

Outside the unit, I paced back and forth, didn't know if I should take off my yellow gown or not, couldn't decide if I could go back inside. My panic existed on the level of pure instinct, fight or flight. Cliff came out a few minutes later. He held the meditation beads he'd taken to wearing since the twins were born—my husband's own version of his Buddhist book—and his eyes were dry.

"I'm sorry," I said. "I just couldn't sit there any longer."

"It's okay," he said, pulling me into his arms. "I'm not doing much better."

"But you could take it. I couldn't."

Where I wanted to flail and yell and lose my temper with everyone, my husband was staid and firm and in control. I don't know how he did it. He once said, apropos of being Japanese, "My culture just accepts people who are sick and maimed. We take care of people when they get old and we take in people with disabilities." When he said this, I remembered a photograph taken after Hiroshima in which a woman holds her naked and profoundly disabled child in her arms after a bath. The mother's expression is one of sadness, certainly, but not anger. Instead, it's sorrow and love, and the viewer knows this woman will bathe her daughter every day for the rest of her life. Even before I became Evan and Ellie's mother, I had known I could not easily make that same sacrifice. Here was Cliff telling me he was ready and that he could. He told me that night and the nights that were to come, when we knew Evan's lot was going to be much rougher than the doctors would tell us. My husband was the first one to say out loud, many months later, "He can't see anything, can he?" and follow it with "That's okay."

We went to bed late that night, expecting a call telling us to come back. And yet, the morning light came without one. I called to check on Evan that morning to hear, "He's doing better. He made it through the night."

When the lottery numbers came out on Saturday, Josie and I checked our tickets. I had lost, but Curt had won twenty dollars. I called Curt to tell him I'd put his ticket in the mail. "Keep it," he said. "Buy yourself some Dr Pepper."

3

People seem to often fall into a few categories after a preemie birth: the Rocks, the Wanna-Be-Theres, and the Gingerbread Men. It is helpful to know this.

The Rocks attempt to do anything and everything to offer encouragement, support, understanding, and love. The Wanna-Be-Theres are often neighbors, casual close friends, and coworkers with whom you work closely, but they can also be close family member or friends. They want to help, but often don't know how. Wanna-Be-Theres are not Rocks. They do not offer the right type of compassion to you and often see the baby only in terms of how it makes them feel.

This leads us to the Gingerbread Men. Just like the story, they run, run as fast as they can from you when they hear of your baby's birth. They will not call or contact you. They might ask, always secondhand, about your baby. But go no further.

—*Preemie Parent Page*

I COULD ALMOST HEAR a social worker's voice as I read the words. *It is helpful to know this . . .* And yet, no matter how saccharine the words, the truth of them would come back to me again and again. In the months Evan lay in his hospital bed, we learned that there were indeed friends who were gingerbread men, friends we had thought of until then as loyal, devoted, and present, who found a way to distance themselves and disappear. In the same pages that warned of these gingerbread men, there came a prediction: *you will be angry, you will not know how to process this anger.* No advice as to what to do—"What do you do with all your rage?" a neighbor would ask much later. *You mean my rage at you, for starters? For bringing a toy into my house my son can't see or hold? For daring homilies about his future? Let's start there, because my rage is boundless. . . .*

What did I do with my rage? I swallowed it. Sometimes, as with Curt, I snapped and said what I really felt, that I didn't want to be nice or understanding. I had a very sick child and a dead child. I tried to understand the perspective of those who didn't know, to appreciate their attempts, no matter how incomplete, but it wasn't easy. While Evan grew and I learned how to be his mother—or began to learn, very slowly, what it would be like to have a child like him—I also learned how hard it was not to be angry, disappointed, and alone.

August 22

Today a friend said, "Well, I don't know why you were chosen for this but I'm in awe of how you're handling it." Sometimes I do wonder why I was picked to do this and a hundred other mothers weren't. In my more egotistical moments, I think it was to show others how lucky they are, to give an example of strength and grace. In my moments of self-criticism, I think I must have been meant to learn something about myself, my arrogance, my conceptions about what is normal, right, fair. The truth is that this was something over which I had no control and the question is not why but what. What am I going to do with this? What am I going to make of it?

I've been given an opportunity: to look at fear, forgive myself, learn how to love (myself, others, my son, no matter how imperfect he may be). To practice detachment and patience. To love my daughter no matter how large I perceive her demands to be, even though I have a son whom I feel needs me more. It's what I do in the face of this experience that matters. Do I find ways to go on, or do I stop?

August 25

I don't know how my son will be, having lost his twin. I do believe that from six months of feeling each other move, he knows the loss of that person next to him, just as I feel the loss of those children inside me. Some nights I think of him lying in his hospital layette, all hooked up and being cared for by others, and I feel desperate that I cannot hold him, lonely that he cannot be with us. My friend M. says not to focus on his vulnerabilities but his strengths, and that is what I do. I envision his high school graduation, how Cliff and I will drive away and I'll think, *This was the boy I begged them not to resuscitate, this is the baby my father worried over, trying to prepare me for his deficiencies.* Someday he will visit his sister's grave and wonder about her and how she would have turned out, wonder why it was that he got to stay and she had to leave. I will love him fiercely and teach him what a gift it was for him to remain.

August 30

I do fine until I compare Evan to the others, the babies that arrive and depart, those not on a ventilator or oxygen, the nearly full-term babies. "Monsters," I call them. "Monster babies." My walk to the neonatal unit takes me

past the nursery, where a fresh crop of newborns appears
daily. Even harder is my glimpse down Labor and Delivery. Mothers-to-be stand waiting for their turn at birth. I
remember seeing a pregnant woman the day after I gave
birth to the twins and feeling so confused: Why me, why
not her? How long will it take for that confusion to go
away?

Thirty-two-week twins arrived in the nursery the
other day—I heard the nurses discussing the mother's
labor, how the doctor had planned to deliver them soon.
Thirty-two weeks! A whole eight weeks longer than I
was able to keep Evan and Ellie. Had I made it to thirty-
two weeks, I would still have two babies now, babies that
would be going home soon. I felt the tears well up and
I knew, once again, that if I can learn to accept my tiny,
skeletal child, the loss of his sister, and the uncertain future, then I can learn to accept anything. To accept all
this, everything else needs to fall away: the pregnant
women, the full-term babies, the preemies older than
mine. In any comparison, I come up short, as does my
son. It does him (and me) no good to dwell on this, to re-
sent being so much at the bottom rung, to wish another
super-preemie would show up so that I could feel better.
Nothing I can do will make Evan bigger and better, able
to hold his own against the monster babies. We're alone
in this.

September 2

Saw Rachel today, the chaplain who helped us with the
naming ceremony we held for Evan and Ellie that first
day after they were born, before I filled out their birth
certificates. I remember how she took the time to make

blessing certificates for us, and find the tiniest dharma beads, those that might actually have fit around the twins' small wrists. I keep them in a dish that contains other important objects, the one that also holds the candles I light all the time now. I mentioned my rituals to Rachel and I said, "Don't have children. You'll only have heartbreak."

"Yes," she said. "It's true that when your heart opens it can also break."

September 4

My strangenesses are transparent now, my defenses don't exist. Anne's been watching Evan for the past few days, the same nurse who was there for us when Ellie died. I had the chance to tell her how much it meant to me that she was there for us with Ellie. She said that some nurses have a problem being with the parents when a child dies but that she was able to do it because she knew that everything God does has a purpose. She got down on her knees that morning, she said, and begged God to give her the strength to do and say the right thing.

And you did, I told her. Everything you did was right.

To hold a small being until its life blows out, to feel a human body turn cold—this is something Anne, Cliff, and I did together. I never knew Anne until then, and yet there she was, instrumental in a moment none of us will forget. I try to make sense of what this means and I can only think that I am simultaneously being challenged and given grace: when I must speak I do, and when I speak I find the grace to say what is necessary. For others, I am leaning how not to speak. It's not up to me to describe what we've been through and so I am learning to be silent in a way I've never been silent before. And yet when it comes to someone like Anne, I need her to know how important her actions were, how right and necessary, and how grateful I am.

Later—in this same spirit, I told Dr. Tam, whom I'd begged not to resuscitate my babies, that I was grateful to her too, that I was glad to have Evan.

September 9

Today I read about the tonglen meditation—deliberately bringing all the rough stuff of the world into your body so that you can relieve others of their suffering. How by bringing that suffering into yourself, you know the full depth of pain, and learn too that you can survive. *Okay*, I thought. I can do that; sometimes it nearly feels like I'm doing that already. But why? I don't like these spiritual tests, I'm not enjoying them. Just like having a child like Evan, this is not what I signed on for.

I get angry at anyone and everyone who doesn't have to deal with what I'm dealing with, then I feel guilty about all that anger, then I try to replace the anger with gratitude and loving-kindness because there's absolutely no point in getting angry. Rage doesn't affect my situation, or improve it. What do I do with all my rage? I displace it, repress it, swallow it. I beg for it to be lifted from me. Then I go back and I count all the reasons to be angry all over again.

I've learned something about myself, something awful and raw: I don't want to forgive, not myself or others.

September 13

Nearly seven weeks. Slowly, life returns to normal, and so the challenge becomes how to stay grounded and focused as I'm pulled back into the world of distractions. When the twins were born, Cliff said to me, "We'll survive this, we'll feel joy again." I didn't believe him, but now I see. He knew. Life goes on, ineffably, inextricably. Work may be coming in, I'm getting dressed and having lunches. The days are not as leaden. Evan's had some great weeks now, gaining weight, a bigger bundle filling up the Isolette, a presence I can sense, increasingly, as I witness that growth. Lurking out there are germs that could be serious but that have not, so far, materialized into anything real. And why do I worry about them? Because part of me needs to accept that he still has a long way to go, that as strong as he is, these great weeks he's had may not last. Is that pessimism? Fear, certainly. The potent fear of the first few weeks after his birth has retreated, and I'm left with lingering fear instead: about his eyes, possible infection, bringing him home and living through developmental milestones. These fears are all deeper challenges to living in the moment.

I saw my son's back today. I came in and the nurse had him lying on his stomach, and there it was, the back of his body, a naked expanse of baby skin without lines or probes, just smooth and soft, visible to his mother for the first time more than six weeks after he was born. Such a normal thing, my son lying peacefully on his stomach, as though his big struggle to get here is over. No more fighting for his life; now he can lie there and grow.

October 4

Took Josie into the unit yesterday, as I've been doing for weeks now—just the hallway, not the room itself—only to be told that it's not okay, not kosher. Visiting days for siblings are Sundays and Wednesdays, no exception.

I got upset. We weren't going to visit, just stand at the end of the hallway long enough to restock his milk. "Are you saying she can't be in the hallway either?" I asked. That was exactly what they were saying, even though we'd been there before, over and over. "It must have been at night, or some other time," a nurse demurred. "Oh, you look so disappointed," another one said. "Go in, I'll watch your daughter. I can see it in your face, you're so disappointed."

I've lost a child. I've been doing this for sixty-five days. My son still weighs only a thousand grams. I have a three-and-a-half-year-old at home, and the closest I can come to bringing my family together is to have her here, six feet away from where he lies, behind glass. *Disappointed* was not the word for it.

We left. I took Josie to the park; I was in tears. I could see in my daughter's eyes how scared she was—sad mommy was back. They always say, "Don't cry in front of your kids, they're too little, they'll fall apart." I had no choice; the grief was back full force. Today when I talked to the woman who runs the parent-support group about what happened, I broke down again. There's only so long a person can go on without breaking down, only so many rules and barriers and loss of control one can handle. To have Lou Ann, a nurse I truly dislike, telling me I cannot put my daughter in proximity to her brother and to hear another one say how disappointed I look because of it—it was just too much.

So, if I am to come with Josie to drop off breast milk or pick up bottles, I must use the back door near the freezer. They will move Evan to a bed by the window so that Josie can see him from the hallway. And me, what of me? There is nothing they can do to make me feel better, nothing at all.

(And Lou Ann was upset! This I heard secondhand. How Lou Ann went to her boss to talk about how bad she felt, how upset I was and how that upset her. Too bad for Lou Ann.)

They say it's your baby, but until you go home it's not your baby.

October 11

Dr. Brown examined Evan on Tuesday and said that he has "tortuous" cells in his right eye, the beginnings of retinopathy of prematurity—ROP. The blood vessels in his eyes are growing abnormally due to the high levels of oxygen he received in the weeks after he was born. Cliff and I have put off thinking about this; we have paid attention to his breathing and his growing, we haven't wanted to think about his eyes.

I looked at the drawings Dr. Brown did of Evan's eyes to see if I could understand more, but the sketches look like spider webs, inscrutable. And of course I'm getting my information from Dr. Tam, whom I would not praise for her communication skills. When explaining a condition, she rapidly goes back to the very beginning of the issue, all set to draw a diagram. She's rarely able to digest the information and present the salient facts.

This is my cross to bear, of course; I, who used to crave all the information in the world, collected it with relish, am now in a position to say, *Please, no, enough.*

Because he's my son, because I'm his mother.

And Evan, there is Evan. Always the unsuspecting recipient, from the moment of his birth. He lies in his

Isolette, that same plastic home to him these past two and a half months. Who else could do this, live a life shaped by drugs, machines, surgeries? I cannot begin to imagine the spirit inside this boy, the patience and will, the endurance. Not doing, just accepting.

When I first arrived this morning, I asked the respiratory therapist and the nurse my usual round of questions. The respiratory therapist brought out Evan's chart and showed it to me, a big no-no. Parents aren't supposed to see the chart, not without making prior arrangements. He asked if I was in charge of the baby. Oh no, I told him, I'm the mother. He was flustered and apologetic; I had put one over on him. My questions, he said, were just too deep.

I sat then with my hand on Evan's body, felt the small warmth from his skin and listened to his breath. I closed my eyes and slowed down my thoughts, hoping to gain perspective. The NICU was filled with grief, I realized, and it was my job to protect myself and my son from the grief of others, so that we might stay focused on and process our own. I will write a story about this one day—that was another realization. Something long, about my own endurance. I had cascaded into another round of thoughts—about when we'd be coming home; I should call my parents and tell them to cancel their trip, since he wouldn't be home by December 7—when I felt a hand on my shoulder, as if a spirit itself were there to hold me down on this plane where decisions become manifest in their own good time. I looked up to see Rachel, the chaplain.

"I'm staring into the face of an angel," I said, and I started to cry.

I can endure all this and do everything possible to

take care of myself and be present for my son, to stay calm and grounded, to keep perspective (*he will come home, he will*) but that doesn't mean I have to be happy about it or like it or even enjoy the process. Sometimes I wonder if I'm not grateful enough, if I should stop thinking about what isn't happening (or about how terrible this all is, what a drain it is) and start thinking more about how lucky we are. But even here in this very thinking I'm searching for the thing that will bring me my big reward, his coming home, and sooner rather than later. I'm still bargaining. . . .

October 12

A blip—infection, higher vent settings—but Evan is back on track. When I go to the hospital it's not just to be with him, it's to get everyone else on track with him too. To marshal the attention.

October 13

In Chicago to see my sister. Didn't want to come. Evan was so close to getting off the vent; I wanted to be there. Now that I'm gone, he's worse again. Something about bowel loops? I can't get a clear answer over the phone. The escaping I used to do so well, walking, on a plane, a train? Gone from me now. Nothing can bring back the time I lost, or give me the perfect monster newborn. My friend M. says to focus on the golden coins that are my everyday life: Josie, Cliff. Evan and Ellie.

October 18

He sneezed. They took the tube out of his throat, and he breathed on his own, took several deep swallows of air. He wrinkled his face and, like that: a sneeze.

And then I realized: to sneeze you need to breathe.

I laughed, giddy at the sound. "Did you know you need to be able to breathe to sneeze?" I asked them all. "I had no idea."

The nurse had told me when I'd arrived that morning that the vent settings were low enough, they wanted to try to take out the tube. "You're going to extubate him?" I'd asked. "Today?"

Dr. Tam was on duty. She smiled. "I think he's ready." She studied the machine, told the tech to keep her posted, to lower the settings even more and see how he did. "He's mostly breathing on his own already," she said. "I think he can do it."

I told her I had to go home to take a phone call for work, and that I wanted to be there when they took it out. This was a big moment, one I'd been anticipating for eleven weeks. Nearly eighty days since he was born, and the tube had been there this whole time. "Don't do it until I get back," I said. "I want to be there."

I had never seen his mouth, his lips, his nose.

I rushed home, then rushed back, and he was already flying solo. My boy. I went to his incubator and saw, for the first time, my son's whole, unencumbered face. I sat beside his incubator and watched his mouth move—I could finally see his upper lip, watch it tremble in his sleep—and my tears came and came. Such a small thing, breathing on his own, and so huge too. I sat there for hours, cried harder than I could remember crying even after he was born, just cried and cried as I listened to his voice. Baby breaths, baby coughs, baby sneezes. No noisy vent next to him. Gone were the sounds. Just the quiet of a baby breathing.

He woke up at one point and looked around and took more deep breaths, and in one long pause between breaths, even he seemed surprised that he could do it on his own. Incredible.

Later

With every gain comes a loss. The same day we exulted in his breathing on his own and what a miracle that is, we heard the news about Evan and his eyes. He will need surgery. I saw the chart on Wednesday, finally met with Dr. Brown on Friday. We know the issue; we can only hope that this abnormal vessel growth becomes less aggressive. Dr. Brown says that sometimes the abnormal vessel growth regresses and the baby is fine. He also says that these are fragile cells and there's no controlling their development. We have to watch and wait and hope for the best. I've prayed and visualized and tried to get behind the positive outcomes in my thinking. I even crossed the Rubicon of talking to my parents and presenting the news in such a way that they could remain positive as well. I've put up psychic protection and bought an amethyst. I'd do anything for him, but ultimately it's up to Evan.

October 27

More samsara. We're permitted to hold him now, an hour at a time, once a day. If one parent comes to hold him for an hour, the other parent will have to wait until the next day for his or her turn. The theory is that while holding preemies helps them grow and feel loved, holding them too long interferes with their body's ability to regulate breathing and temperature. A little bit of holding is good, in other words, but too much is stressful. Three months since he was born and still we can hold him for only one hour a day.

Cliff and I fight for the right. "You held him yesterday," he says. "Today's my turn." He brags about how it feels to hold his son. "He's so strong," he says, "for being so little. I can't wait for him to come home."

Like Cliff, I make the most of my time. I unwrap my son's blanket and put him skin to skin on my chest, feel the warmth from his small body, the heat. I return him to my lap, take in his small features, and stroke his cheek, his eyelids. He falls asleep in my arms, his hand stuffed up under his chin, and soon he snores. Baby gestures, his own.

I'm in the unit, holding Evan, when the new chaplain comes by. Where Rachel was intuitive and wonderful, this woman is all that can be wrong with religion. She talks about herself, wants desperately to show how much she understands. She asks nothing and has no interest in listening. "I looked at this deathly ill child and gave myself up to God," she says to me. "Do you know how that feels? Has that feeling ever come to you?"

"Yes it has," I say. "But I only have thirty minutes to hold my son so I'd rather take this time to visit, if you don't mind." Of course, of course.

There was a time when I said, "The day I get to hold him will be my big payoff." And I believed it and meant it. That day has come and gone—like the day he came off the vent, the day he started on breast milk, the day I heard him cry—and I'm putting new goals out there as fast as the old ones are met. I've relished all these mo-

ments, but they haven't made me complete. The day
he starts talking? Walking? Can write his name? Read?
When Josie was born, I enjoyed holding her and loved
her infancy and was in a hurry all the while for the days
she could accomplish the things I thought would make
me happy: hold a toy, crawl, sit up, take steps, say a
word. It's so difficult to love another person and yourself
for who they are and not what they do or who they could
be. To stay in this moment and know it in all its pleasure
and its pain. The world is a beautiful place. How often
do we say this aloud?

November 5

Three pounds, nine ounces. Taking a bottle now, more
cuddle care. I go to the hospital twice a day. I feel like a
mother. I have a son.

Entering the hospital on Halloween, the night I had
in my mind I would give birth: the newborn nursery was
empty, the census in the NICU a low fifteen. It almost
seemed as if babies weren't supposed to be born during
this time (this after a whopping four sets of full-term
twins showed up last week). It was okay; I was going to
hold my son, he'd made it, and everything was going to
be all right. He's here, I've survived. It's okay.

It's a strange sort of nesting then, as if my body were
in touch with the final days of his gestation (one that's
happening outside of me), preparing itself for his arrival (even though we know what he looks like and what
his temperament is), and facing the anxiety of being a
mother again. Holding him with Josie hovering by, I
flinched when I saw her breathing on him. Then Cliff
and Josie left the unit and it was just me and it felt won-

derful. All this leaves a gaping hole where Ellie would have been: the second baby, the other baby, the wandering soul. Evan's homecoming means that I must also process her loss. And that I must accept too that I will have to give her up, find somewhere to put her ashes, allow her spirit to go.

Part Two

4

TWO DAYS LATER—Election night, November 7, 2000—
found me not heading home with my three-pound son
but, rather, driving behind the ambulance transporting him to
the acute-care hospital deep in the city where a team of expert
doctors would try to restore his sight. In reality, I wasn't behind
the ambulance at all. I had taken the shortcut I knew through
the hills, while the nurse and the respiratory tech and the ambulance driver who accompanied Evan didn't know the city
well enough to avoid the freeways. It was five o'clock on a Tuesday night. I drove as well as I could, in my husband's truck, because I knew the parking garage at the hospital couldn't accom-
modate my tall car, or at least I thought so. I was to find out
later, in the months we would be in this new, different hospital, that my car fit just fine, but on this night I was holding fast
to the road in the slow lane in this truck I knew would get me
where I needed to be, hoping the ambulance wouldn't get stuck
in traffic and that they would arrive before me.

Until this night, I had believed my son would escape the lit-
any of ex-preemie problems, that he might be okay. I had held
him and given him a bottle and thought of our homecoming.
Even though it revolved around the hospital, our routine had
become so normal. Tonight, all that would change. I must have
known this as I drove, taking turns in the hills without think-

ing. Grief was back; I was once again unsafe. This must have been why I drove so slowly, as if I hoped to put off my arrival at this new hospital and with it my arrival at the place where Evan was not okay.

Dr. Brown had spoken to us in his office the day before and said, "This baby will need surgery; the only question is when." We had assumed he meant a simple laser procedure, one that was minimally invasive, had a terrific success rate, and could be performed at Evan's bedside. We had assumed that the bleeding in Evan's retinas could be controlled by the laser surgery and that the disease would regress.

In the book on prematurity at my bedside, the one I used for reference each time a new complication arose, the section on retinopathy of prematurity explained the disease in terms of zones of the eye and stages of severity. The retina grew outward from the base of the optic nerve: Zone 1 was closest to the eye and surrounded the area where the optic nerve connected to the base of the eye. Zone 2 was the stage the next farthest out, and zone 3 the outermost region. By the time the retina grew as far as zone 3, it was mature and fully functional. A retina that stopped growing at zone 1 due to bleeding and the fragility of the system remained immature and offered only a thirty-degree range of vision.

The disease was also described in terms of stages. Stage 1 resulted in a full recovery; stage 2 led to some visual impairment (the patient might need glasses, for example); and stage 3 almost always necessitated laser surgery to stop the proliferation of abnormal blood vessels. The surgery destroyed abnormal vessels so that normal, healthy vessels could grow over and beyond them, allowing the retina to finish its progress toward the back of the eye. The agony of this disease was that remission was always possible. The abnormal growth could stop, leaving room for the better vessels to take their place. Laser surgery was often successful enough to rescue the retinas, the vision, the eyes.

In the most serious cases, however, those of stages 4 and 5, more intricate surgery was called for: removing the eye's vitreous humor and with it the more serious scarring that had edged out of the retina deeper into the eye's structure. This procedure, called a vitrectomy, was done to prevent retinal detachment, which could result in blindness.

"If your child becomes blind," read the book's final section, the one I forced myself to go over many times in a terrified dance of approach-avoidance, "love your child, remember to speak to him before you approach him, find out what services are available in your area. There will be a period of grief when you realize your child has not turned out the way you might have wished."

Before the mad race to the new hospital, before our lives had become yet another emergency, Evan had been examined by Dr. Tran, a retinologist called in by Dr. Brown. My husband had left work on his lunch hour to be there. He and I waited in an empty nursery in the NICU for the retinologist to finish his exam; had been waiting, in fact, since noon for the man to examine Evan. It was two thirty before he finally arrived, only to announce that he had left the necessary instruments in his car. "What is wrong with these people?" Cliff asked, rhetorically, I hoped. "Don't they know what torture this is?" Like my very first arrival at Labor and Delivery on the day the twins were born, this visit was meant to be short, informative, and efficient. Simply a confirmation of what Dr. Brown had suspected and told us over the phone the night before.

My husband hadn't read the chapter on blindness; he didn't know the big words, the zones, or the stages. Like so many moments in our journey with Evan, I required and absorbed the information while Cliff was there to hold up and be a witness. And so I was alone again with my vast store of knowledge when the retinologist finally stepped through the door, told us to sit down, sat down himself, and announced, "The baby has the beginnings of a retinal detachment on his right eye and a definite detachment on his left. He needs a vitrectomy and laser surgery and I'm recommending he be transferred immediately to Central Hospital."

"The baby needs a *vitrectomy?*" Without warning, we had skipped straight to chapter's end. "He needs to be transferred to Central?"

Cliff wanted to know what a vitrectomy was; Dr. Tran listened as I explained. He hardly needed to correct me except to add, "Vitrectomies are done more aggressively now. We consider them preventative."

I knew from the book on my nightstand that this was what my mother and I would call painting a rose. Hearing that your child needed a vitrectomy, even and maybe especially a "preventative" vitrectomy, was not good news. Dr. Tran and I both knew we were well beyond a simple laser surgery at my son's bedside. "How could this happen?" I asked. "How could he go from not needing surgery a week ago to detached retinas today?"

Dr. Tran didn't have an answer. "The main thing is to get your son to someone who can help. The doctor I'm recommending at Central is young but she's an excellent surgeon. She's someone I'd want to have operate on my own child."

But this isn't your child, I wanted to say. *He's mine and he's supposed to be coming home, not going to another hospital. For eye surgery. I don't want anyone to have to operate on him, not you or me or your superstar. I want him to be okay and I want him to come home.*

"I'm sorry." The conversation ended.

After Dr. Tran left, everything happened quickly. By four thirty that afternoon, Evan had been loaded, along with his oxygen, formula, and medications, in a transport Isolette and sent on his way to Central Hospital. Nurses and doctors rushed around the unit at Hampton, preparing his discharge, giving instructions, coordinating his care. When would he need to eat again? What was his formula? What papers did the mom need to sign? Betty, the social worker, passed through the hallway and said, "Don't worry, I know what's going on." And then a lingering look, one I understood much later to mean *And yes, I know some things you don't. These situations never turn out well.* All I could think about was that we were meant to be going home—up the road, to our apartment—not heading in an ambulance to another hospital. He'd been taking a bottle, we were weaning him off the oxygen, I'd been holding him, friends of mine had even planned a baby shower for the following week. This was not how it was supposed to go.

Cliff and I agreed that I would stay with Evan while he went to pick up Josie from preschool. "You're still better at this than I am," he said.

The transport ambulance and I left the hospital at the same time. If Evan needed the surgery that night, my brother would take over with Josie, and Cliff would come down to the hospital. And me? I took that long, bargaining drive to our next destination.

Later, much later, I would have long conversations about the words we eventually came to use to describe Evan: *mental retardation, developmentally disabled.* For any parent, the words were loaded with grief and misunderstanding. Much later, on my way home from an appointment with the neurologist after Evan had been diagnosed with a catastrophic seizure disorder, I'd ask my dad over the phone if Evan would now be at risk for mental retardation. "I don't know, Vicki," he'd say. "This disorder often results in some form of mental retardation." At the time, the news of the seizure disorder was even more devastating than Evan's blindness (a word no one had yet used to describe him; at that point he was still simply visually impaired). We had a visually impaired child on oxygen and a feeding tube. Now our child would also face lifelong developmental disabilities.

What did the words really mean? A diagnosis of mental retardation, as Evan did indeed eventually receive, had very different implications for different children. For some, speech was possible; for others, not at all. The medical definition of *mental retardation* itself came subdivided into three categories: mild, moderate, and profound. If Evan at three was described (for the purposes of social services) as "moderately mentally retarded," this would have more to do with his blindness and his lack of speech than his genetic makeup. So too his other diagnoses, other words and phrases: *cerebral palsy, seizure disorder, congenital heart defect.* Later, when I listed these for friends and family, I'd hear, "How do you manage?" The simple answer being, of course, that eventually I found a way to go beyond the words, the diagnoses, the shadows of uncertainty they cast. Eventually, I got to a place where I could see Evan as not just a boy with problems—or words that described those problems—and not just a kid who might not walk or talk, and who obviously couldn't see. Instead, I saw my son. His beautiful smile, his sense of humor, and his delight in the world. That he could laugh his ass off at a joke only he knew or understood. The diagnostic words didn't make a difference; they didn't change what he might do, and they certainly didn't help me feel better.

• • •

I arrived at the hospital before Evan. A receptionist directed me to Admissions. I was the grief-stricken mother of a baby who weighed three pounds and who was somewhere in transit from one hospital to the other for emergency eye surgery. My son could turn out blind. He most assuredly would not be okay. I wanted to communicate with no one, but I was forced to handle the details. Name, date of birth, diagnosis, admitting physician. Consent forms, agreement to arbitrate. Signature, date, relationship to the patient. The office was cold and empty. Only the most serious cases arrived after hours, and a sole clerk worked the night shift to handle the emergencies. She handed me my finished forms at last. I had given her three words, maybe, two of which were "Thank you."

Upstairs, in the unit, Evan had arrived, having slept through the ambulance ride. They had dilated his pupils for the second time that day in preparation for the superstar eye surgeon's exam. I rushed to his bed, held his hand, stroked his back and neck. "I'm sorry," I said. "I'm so sorry."

Compared with Hampton, a comfortable community hospital where the lights were dim and the voices hushed, the unit at Central was bright, cold, noisy. The room smelled strongly of antiseptic. There were no good cases at this hospital, and I had resisted the transfer for this very reason. I had been here for a meeting involving Evan's future social services; the place was crummy and badly in need of a renovation. There was no maternity ward here and hence no easy case; every baby was, like Evan, a challenging patient transferred from another hospital, one that didn't have the ability to solve the problem. It was here that complicated open-heart surgeries were done on infants. Chronically ill and disabled children came here for cancer treatments and regular medical care. Parents, when I saw them, were mirror images of myself: zombies, sleepless, losing weight with each passing day. Later, I would read a description of the NICU as "the one room in the hospital even the surgeons were afraid of," and I would instantly grasp this description as the most honest report of what it was like at Central, as if the unit itself managed to mirror the desperate nature of our children's medical status. The nametags we wore, the ones given to us at the security desk in the lobby, came color-coded for the floors we visited. Our tags, the blue ones, always received looks of dismay in the elevators from doctors, nurses, and even other parents. The blue label meant we were getting off at the third floor and would enter the dismal world of the NICU. Here, the soap was harsher on our skin, so harsh that many of us stopped scrubbing up before entering the unit. The gowns were kept not in clean, folded layers but heaped in piles on metal crash carts. Medical residents prowled the units, and the neonatologists, when they passed through, rarely made eye contact. Instead, all the care was managed by nurse practitioners. It was at Central Hospital that I truly learned to be an advocate for my child, mostly because I had so little faith in its Dickensian netherworld.

Evan's first night at Central, I told every nurse I met that we would do the surgery and head home immediately thereafter. "Home"—that was, back to Hampton, within walking distance of our apartment, where the only wheelchair-bound patients were new mothers being taken, babies in arms, to their cars. As far as I was concerned, Evan didn't belong with the hard cases, the seriously ill kids, the permanently disabled. Just like the hard words involving his disabilities, the hard facts of Evan's new peer group were inconceivable to me. When I told a friend about this sense of Evan's not-belonging—among the kids in wheelchairs, the chronically ill, the kids on respirators—she told me that actually he did belong, because he was there.

A super-preemie lay in an Isolette across from Evan, birth

weight on transfer six hundred or so grams. The parents were young, the mother, like me, thin and hardly postpartum. Along the row of incubators lay Abby, another super-preemie, who was recovering from intestinal surgery. I could see her stoma, the bag taped to her belly to collect her waste. There it was then, the triangle of preemie complications: the early birth, the middle stages of recovery, my own son's arrival for eye surgery. Other preemies, when I met them, would have shunts and feeding tubes and chest tubes; there would be babies in heroin withdrawal, with seizures and congenital heart defects.

I saw Evan through his physical exam, answered the questions about oxygen, diet, medical history. We had started all over again, right back to questions about the delivery and his twin. "What did you do with her?" a nurse asked, curious. "I mean, do you actually have a funeral for a baby that little, do you bury her?"

When I was finally alone with Evan, I sat and rocked him, tried to feed him, then held a syringe of formula and watched the milky liquid slink through the tube into his nose, all this through a veil of tears. Since three that afternoon, I had been in a state of adjustment. Evan's sight was in danger. We were in a new hospital, a frantically busy unit with new nurses and doctors. I watched the clock and waited for the retinologist. At ten to seven, a nurse approached me. "Mrs. Forman? I'm sorry. . . ." I looked at the clock and realized I had committed a cardinal sin: I was bedside during shift change. Even though I had hardly arrived, even though I was clutching my son and in tears about his fate, she had no choice but to ask me to leave.

"Of course, of course," I said, because shift change was sacred, and even the most grief-stricken parent could not possibly sit bedside during shift change. At shift change, confidential patient information was exchanged between the off-going nurses and the incoming crew, so no one but the nurses and doctors was allowed to be in the room at that time—not even parents. I gave up my baby, gathered my purse, and headed for the door. It was a testimony to my mental state that rather than being angry about getting kicked out, I felt grateful that they had actually given me twenty minutes of grace before telling me to go.

Later that year, when I finally returned to teaching, a student asked me to read some letters he'd written in prison, with an eye toward whether or not they were publishable. There were talks of cellies and lifers and drug addicts and every other person had hepatitis C, and amid the anecdotes of prison culture, I had an odd sensation, as if I had been among these people, or at least understood the feeling: shut in, demoralized, dependent on arbitrary rules geared toward controlling interaction and behavior. Reading John's tales of Folsom Prison, I felt exactly that disembodied sense. I'd had it at Central Hospital the night they kicked me out at shift change; I was to feel it every day I stepped off the elevator on the third floor and saw the grimy, giraffe-pattern linoleum leading to the unit. Already beaten down and terrified, already at the mercy of the kindness of others, it took so little to make me feel I had no rights at all. That night, like the specter I was to become, I retreated to the lounge and waited out my sentence—and Evan's.

A bank of phones against one wall, vending machines along the other. Two TV sets hung from the ceiling. A U-shape of necessity, accompanied by three banks of chairs. There had been no such waiting area at Hampton. Here there was the need. Waiting for bedside procedures to end, exams to finish, surgeries to be completed. In the months that followed, we would sometimes come out here simply to relieve the monotony of sitting by the bed. To drink a Coke and eat a bag of chips and call a friend. We'd sit here on Christmas Day and meet friends and family members of the babies we knew inside. I'd say a tearful goodbye here to my first and closest friend whose child had also turned out like mine: imperfect, disabled.

The night of Evan's transfer, the waiting area had none of this meaning for me. All I saw were the phones I dreaded using, the calls I knew I had to make—to my parents, to tell them the news—and the food I had no desire to eat despite the fact that I had skipped lunch and it was long past dinner. The TV announced news of the national election taking place that night. Bush was winning? Gore? Earlier in the day, before the retinologist's exam, I'd made Cliff go to the polls with me. Somewhere my vote was being tallied, while here I waited for a doctor to examine my son's eyes and brace me for his future.

I picked up the phone. My mother answered. I told her what had happened and where we were. "I'm waiting for the retinologist."

"Let me put Dad on, he wants to talk to you."

I started to cry. "Tell him not to ask me a million questions."

"He just wants to hear your voice."

My dad came on the phone. "I can't tell what's happening with the election," I said. "Is it Bush or Gore?"

"It's down to Florida," he said.

From this moment on, my father and I entered a realm in which we could discuss serious matters like Evan's blindness and ordinary matters like sports, current events, movies, and dinners out. It didn't seem odd at that moment, nor does it seem odd now, years into our routine. Even so, I found myself, beyond the small talk, apologizing. "I'm sorry, Dad. I love you."

I could feel him about to ask the questions to which he

craved answers. In Evan's first weeks, my dad had warned me about Evan's eyes and about retrolental fibroplasia, the original term for retinopathy of prematurity, ROP. "Have you asked them about that?" he'd asked, and I'd been short with him and said, "Yes, we've discussed it, but I have to go now." I'd been angry and unwilling to tamper with the good news I had just delivered about his vent settings. Since then, I'd avoided any talk of Evan's eyes with my dad. Now there was no avoiding the topic. We hadn't been in this kind of crisis since Evan and Ellie were born. With Evan's transfer to Central, we had naturally returned to the place where there were a million questions and where there wouldn't be a lot of answers right away. I could hear all the worry in my father's voice and in the questions I wouldn't let him ask and I wanted to find a way to tell him across the miles that I had what it took to take this next step, but I couldn't. I wasn't sure I did.

"I've got to go," I said. A doctor had appeared from around the corner, clearly headed for me. It was hard to believe that this very young, very petite woman—no older than twenty-eight, no taller than five feet—had the spectacular expertise Evan was going to need and a reputation that preceded her, but I was in her hands and had no choice. Nor did it occur to me to question that same expertise, since I was also very aware that we were pretty much at the end of the line, considering how serious Evan's condition had become, and how rapidly that had happened.

Dr. Chang led me into a nearby conference room. As the parent of a sick child, I knew that when the door was shut behind me, the news wouldn't be good. I knew this earlier in the day with the retinologist at Hampton, and I knew it immediately with Dr. Chang.

"Your son has a partial retinal detachment in his left eye," she announced. "The best we can hope for from the vitrectomy is to reclaim some peripheral vision. Probably we are looking at mostly central vision in that eye, if any vision at all." She paused and allowed me to digest the information. "I don't know what Dr. Tran told you."

"He didn't want to predict," I said, remembering then how he had deflected some of our questions, telling us to wait and ask them of Dr. Chang.

"The detachment is serious. It's hard to tell how much retina there really is at all since the scar tissue itself is in the way. I'll know more when I go in to remove it."

I looked at the clock. Seven twenty. Each moment of the day had turned the news more and more serious. More than anything, I wanted to flee this room and this news, but I was Evan's mother and tonight that meant my job was to sit and listen.

"The right eye is also showing signs of traction," she said. "The retina on that side has begun to detach too. I'm going to do laser surgery on that eye to halt the traction and stabilize the retina." She drew a picture of each eye to show me what she had planned. Unlike Dr. Brown's or Dr. Tam's sketches, Dr. Chang's diagrams were precise and made sense. I wondered how many sketches like these she had to draw each day, and how serious Evan's pictures were compared to others. "The best-case scenario," she said, "is that he will have some central vision in his left eye, and central and peripheral vision in the right eye."

"And the worst?"

"No vision whatsoever in his left eye, peripheral vision only in his right eye."

In retrospect, my next questions sounded more than banal. I asked dumb things like "Will his left eye look strange?" and "Can we correct the musculature?" "Will he be able to drive? Write?"

From her responses, I could tell Dr. Chang had been on the other side of dozens of these conversations. "Hopefully," she said, and "We'll see."

For the first time, I understood how serious this was, and just how much we would have to pay for our ignorance. Dr. Chang was not making predictions, nor was she being evasive. She wasn't going to say very much at all, in fact, until she operated on Evan, which she would do the next day.

A year later, to that same student who had his tale of prison to tell, I would say, "You have a moral imperative to write this story."

"It's true," he said. "How many people know what it's like to lose it all? It's as if you've been put into a machine, spun around, and spat out at the other end, and nothing is the same."

"Write the story," I said. "People need to know."

At home, Cliff and I desperately bargained. Peripheral vision in one eye, central and peripheral vision in the other. Not bad. "Sammy Davis Junior was blind in one eye," Cliff pointed out. "So is Sandy Duncan." We'd gone from parents who wanted our child to come home and be normal to parents who could accept a child who was blind in one eye. Before I went to bed, Cliff joked: "Remember when the cat swallowed flea shampoo and went into the closet for three days? And how we couldn't get him to come out and drink or eat? Remember how worried we were?" All by way of saying *Look at what we used to think of as hard times.* My husband likes to claim his place of comic relief, but that night and many nights later I simply loved him for being able to make me laugh in the midst of my grief.

The surgery was scheduled for two o'clock the following afternoon. Cliff would go to work half the day, then join me in the waiting room later. I arrived early and held a very hungry Evan, who had not been fed since six that morning; he was, according to orders, NPO, short for *nil per os*, or "nothing by mouth"—a common order prior to any surgery. In our time at this hospital, Evan would be NPO half a dozen times and it would never get easier to see him furious with hunger. He sucked on his pacifier, held it with his hand up to his mouth. I stroked his forehead and waited, minute by minute, for two o'clock to come. Time crawled to a halt with a hungry child in my arms, a surgery awaiting him. Finally, at one thirty, they called for him from the OR.

Downstairs, I joked with the anesthesiology resident the way I always did when under stress, as if joking could take care of both Evan's sight and the cold twist in my stomach. "Nice shower cap," I said, pointing to his headgear. The resident asked me about Evan's heart murmur, which was suddenly "significant," so significant that the man scratched under his shower cap and invoked the aid of someone in a white coat, whose DR. X embroidered across the breast lent more authority than the young resident's green scrubs. Together, they murmured, then agreed that they could proceed without harming him, and I was aware that beyond my jokes about shower caps and the discussion of Evan's heart, beyond my fears about his eyesight and his future and mine, they meant business.

Upstairs, Cliff and I waited it out. Dr. Chang had warned us that the surgery would be long—three hours inside his eyes to tackle all the problems. By five o'clock, it was time for one of us to head back and pick up Josie. "I'll stay," I told him. "You go."

A little after five fifteen, Dr. Chang arrived, looking tired. She took me back inside the same conference room as the night before, shut the door, and sat down across from me. "The left eye was much worse than I had thought," she said. "Once I was able to remove the scar tissue surrounding the optic nerve, I saw very little retinal development. I'm sorry."

The boy I'd thought could track my face from inside his Isolette had not been looking at me at all. I met Dr. Chang's gaze as she went on. "There was no real opportunity to save much sight. At best, he will only see shapes and colors with that eye. With the right eye, however, I'm more optimistic. The baby responded well to the laser, and I'm hopeful that we've been able to relieve the stress the scar tissue was causing on the retina."

Of all the doctors we would meet during all the years with Evan, Dr. Chang was the most direct and honest, no matter how weary or busy she might be. Over the next few weeks, as Evan's eyesight deteriorated beyond even her control, Dr. Chang always took the time for a phone call or a bedside visit. She called me at eight at night; on a Sunday morning; at home and on my cell phone. She tracked me down in the unit to give me a report on a surgery and to brief me on what was to come. When my father met Dr. Chang for the first time, I asked him, "How old do you think she is?" to which he replied, "About twenty-two," which was a joke, of course. After all my experience with doctors it didn't escape my notice that the most helpful, direct, and honest doctor in my time with Evan was not only a woman, but also one who could be mistaken for a teenager, and that among all the professionals, the only one who had genuine compassion for a tiny baby and his family was a woman who gave parents hard news every day, all day long. Once, after a long conversation full of this same hard news, Dr. Chang actually thanked me. "You're very knowledgeable and understanding," she said. "You make my job that much easier."

And so it was no coincidence that it was with Dr. Chang that I finally came to a place where I could ask the questions I needed to ask, where I finally overcame deep fears about

Evan's future in order to hear the answers to those hard questions—not false promises, not vague or evasive responses, but answers that came directly from someone who had been inside my son's eyes. I asked her about prognosis, about what we should expect next, about our chances of going home any time in the near future.

"What will his recovery be like?" I asked.

"At first, I'll need to examine him every two to three days," she said. "We have to keep a very close watch on these cases, they can turn that fast."

"And more surgery?"

"That's also possible."

"Do you think he'll see well enough to read? I mean, I know that's a stupid question—"

"It's possible. There are also devices like large-print magnifiers that make reading easier. Really, there's a lot that can be done."

"Of course," I said, not at all ready to consider the fact that my son would need a large-print magnifier in order to read.

The fear and surrender I recall from those conversations with Dr. Chang feel as though they happened to another person. What did I fear? I hark back to Evan's birth and to my demands to let Evan and Ellie go and wonder how I would react in that same situation now, being on the other side, knowing what it means to be the mother of a child with profound disabilities, with friends in similar situations and a family that mended itself around those truths. Things changed so much in my time as Evan's mother, I have a hard time remembering why I was so afraid, only that I was. When I came home from the hospital after this first surgery, I asked my brother and sister-in-law if they would be comfortable as the aunt and uncle of a blind child, and they said, "Of course." But I couldn't imagine being the mother of a blind child, a boy who would never know his mother's face or see his mother across a room. What became clear to me eventually, and what wasn't clear to me then, was that my life and that of my family could and would go on.

Very quickly on the heels of my learning more of the truth and less of the fiction, I also realized that I had to report these truths to my parents. It was nearly six before I made the call. This time, I told my dad all in a rush what Dr. Chang had reported. "Oh God," he said. He sounded devastated, as though the words went right to his heart. "There's nothing more she can do?"

"Not right now. Right now, we just wait." On the TV, a reporter discussed a Florida recount. A day later and Gore still hadn't conceded the election. "I'll call you tomorrow."

Finally, I went into the unit to visit Evan. There, lying in the bed, was the truth no doctor or medicine could reveal, and that was this three-pound boy, my son. Underneath heavy cotton gauze, his eyes were red and swollen, the same eyes I'd thought the day before could see me and take in the world. Blood spotted the dressings covering his eyes. "Is he in pain?" I asked.

"The doctor says it doesn't hurt but I can't imagine it's not painful," the nurse tending him replied. "We've got him on fentanyl. If he is in pain, he's not feeling it."

His hand was flung up above his head and I pressed my fingers into his warm palm. I received not even a reflex by way of a response. The pacifier he'd sucked on so furiously hours before lay cast aside in his crib. We were so very far from even a day ago when I sat with him in my lap and fed him from a bottle, my little man. So much had changed.

I spent the weeks following this first surgery with desperate thoughts, piles of fear of what it would be like to have a blind child, as if I were getting ready, even then, for who he would become. I reread my journal from these days and weeks of surgeries and bad news and see page upon page of incantations. Sometime around Evan's transfer, I read or was told that if you asked for something three times in a row, or even ten, that wish stood a better chance of coming true. That the more often you asked, the better your odds. I wrote the sentences during his surgeries, while I waited in the hospital chapel, during phone calls with clients. Looking at these pages now, I see the rows and rows of pleas:

I want his retina to flatten and grow.
I want his retina to flatten and grow.
I want his retina to flatten and grow.

And when this seemed too presumptuous, when I thought perhaps I should put the wish out there without demanding it, I wrote,

Please let him see.
Please let him see.
Please let him see.

People called and I didn't recognize their voices. A realtor reporting to me on my cell phone about a new house on the market and I was in the chapel, crying. Friends telling me their babies had been born. My brother trying to track me down to see how I fared. And, always, my parents: always there, always willing to hear about every last detail, to commiserate and to listen. They refused to cancel the trip they'd planned for December, back when it had seemed Evan would be coming home then, insisting that they wanted to visit anyway and keep me company at the hospital.

In the midst of these calls and details, I returned to that place—the ghostly place from the days and weeks after Evan and Ellie were born, the place where things happened beyond my control and where my job appeared to be to clutch at whatever I could find to keep me afloat. Sometimes it was the blue pills I took in the morning to keep depression at bay; sometimes the little white pill I took at night to help me calm down and sleep. Often it was a bag of French fries and an iced tea in the hospital's basement cafeteria. In the early evening, a glass of wine or two or three, then to bed next to my husband, our daughter sometimes sleeping between us. Nothing had changed; all the happiness, joy, and anticipation of bringing Evan home had been replaced by yet another hospital, worse news, and fear.

November 13

Waiting, waiting, waiting. On Friday Dr. Chang will call to report to us on Evan's eyes.

In the morning, before I left for the hospital, I nearly burned down the house with my candles. I had left a votive lit when I got into the shower and when I came back my page of incantations had fallen into the candle and was in flames. Up in smoke went my wish: for his retinas to flatten and heal and grow. All had turned to ash. The bamboo shade caught fire, smoke swirling upward into the window frame. I doused the fire and now my Buddhist prayer card is singed at the edges and there is melted wax stuck to the plate where the votive once was. If I'd taken just a moment longer in the shower, I wonder if I would have emerged to see the wall itself aflame.

November 17

Time crawls to a halt. The report on Evan's eyes comes back: the retinal detachment has stabilized and the retina is growing. Dr. Chang wants to go back in and perform more laser surgery next week on the right eye. Cliff and I discussed all that was still unsaid about Evan's overall prognosis, and on Wednesday I finally faced my fears and called Dr. Chang with our long list of questions. I tracked her down in the eye clinic, and she sounded annoyed. "You aren't supposed to call me here," she said. Even so I pressed her for answers. Yes, it was true that the traction and scarring on the right eye posed a threat of detachment. The fact that it had stabilized didn't mean it would resolve itself or go away. Evan faced a sixty-forty chance of needing a vitrectomy in that eye. At best, he'd have a thirty-degree range of vision in that one eye. Certainly better than being blind. I think back to the days and weeks after his birth and see how easy that all was compared to this. Those moments passed and were replaced by new ones. This business about the eyes is permanent and real. We don't need a crystal ball this time.

I read again last night in my Buddhist book about facing fear, how miraculous and difficult that is. What is the fear here? That I won't be able to love my child because he's impaired? That I won't want him home or in our family? I suppose this is where faith comes in, and endurance in the face of the unknown. We don't know how this will turn out or what his purpose is. Evan could terrorize the playground with one eye. Cliff says he's the yang to Josie's yin: where she is beautiful and smart and brilliant and totally dependent, he could be vulnerable and strange-looking but utterly his own person. He'll charge into things, hurt himself, recover.

Another hospital, more nurses and doctors, different rules. It's impossible to live normally and yet this has been going on for so long that it's impossible to remember another time. A hundred days. Maybe more.

November 21

My original due date.

In the chapel, while Evan undergoes laser surgery on the right eye, a voice comes to me: *You're going to love him no matter what happens.* And *You are a beautiful soul.* Only to be followed by: *Please let this go well, I want him to see. Please let it go well, I want him to see.* That and *I'm so afraid.*

"Suffering begins to dissolve when we can question the belief or the hope that there's anywhere to hide."

However he comes back is how he is.

November 25

Thanksgiving. Sarah and Kalea host dinner, and offer to baby-sit Josie so Cliff and I can visit Evan in the hospital. We sit in the unit and take turns holding our son. I've dressed him in his first true preemie outfit, green pajamas with a reindeer pattern, in honor of the season. He's intubated again; the surgeries have been too much for him and one of us holds the vent tubing while the other holds our son. He's grown. He fills out those same pajamas. His left eye, the bad eye, seems to have shrunk. "Is his left eye smaller?" I ask Cliff. "I think so," he says. And I remember then what Dr. Chang said, how without blood flow to the retina, his left eye might not grow. The difference is noticeable already. Already he has become the words *visually impaired.*

"What else have you been doing?" someone asks me later when we return to the gathering at our friends' house and take our place at the table, beside the turkey and the trimmings.

Nothing. This is my life. There is nothing else.

December 1

I've gone from pinning my hopes on good news from Dr. Chang to knowing that whatever happens we'll adjust. I feel like two people now: one is moving forward with each bit of news, coping, growing, accepting, and being at peace, and the other is stuck in "Why?" and "How could things have been different?"

Holding Evan helps me stay grounded. No matter what, I am his mother and it is and will be my job to take care of him. I walk into the unit and demand this each time. "Let me hold my son," I say. Forget the rules about holding preemies, about limiting the time. This is what I need, this is what matters and makes the difference, to me and to him.

Cliff says that in Japanese culture there's an acceptance of flawed people. I'm just realizing how much of my life has to do with something that is less perfect being "wrong." He also says that for a long time it will be harder for us than it is for him, and that then it will be harder for him than it is for us. For us, this will end; for him, this will go on and on.

Thanksgiving passed as Evan recovered from his second surgery. The presidential election was still undecided; the hospital tuned in every day to CNN, and I listened to the news on the radio as I drove back and forth to the hospital. One day at the end of November I noticed a shadow across Evan's now smaller left eye. "Is that a cataract?" I asked a nurse. Dr. Chang called me that night and I mentioned the grayish shadow. I had guessed right. The cataract was a typical complication from vitrectomies. When I told a friend, she said, "Isn't that a good sign? Doesn't that mean he can see?" And I had to explain the ironic truth that cataracts could easily happen to blind people, that they were completely independent of sight.

More surgery was called for to remove both the cataract and the lens. At the same time, Dr. Chang urged a vitrectomy on the right eye. The sixty-forty odds had turned and the right eye would need salvaging as well. Thirty percent range of vision— that was the most we could hope for.

I spent the days before the surgery with one palm clamped over my left eye and my right hand circled over my right eye, hoping to envision what Evan might see. It wasn't much.

Just before Evan's third and final surgery, a beautiful full-term baby arrived in the NICU. In this hospital of tough cases, I immediately wondered what could have brought this seemingly healthy baby and her parents, Carolyn Bessette and John F. Kennedy Jr. look-alikes who seemed to have their terrific genes and incredible poise, to this terrible place. The very first time I saw the mother, I was shocked to find someone so thin and blond and beautiful in this dismal spot. Then her husband joined her, with his thick dark hair and tall good looks, and I thought I had surely entered a dream world. Parents like this didn't belong in the NICU at Central, and babies like theirs were unimaginable. I had come to terms with the fact that Evan had always been at risk for preemie complications—that in a way I was simply getting what I should have expected when I found myself at his crib and staring yet again at a tube snaking down his throat. I hardly remembered anymore what it felt like to imagine Evan coming home; the days in the NICU at Hampton, holding him and giving him a bottle, felt years away. This other baby was all rosy skin and good health, nothing like the other NICU kids, those with shunts and chest tubes. A sign at the end of her crib told me that her name was Alexandra and that she had been born two weeks earlier, weighing eight pounds, eleven ounces, at a hospital nearby.

The first time I saw Alexandra, it was at night and she was asleep in her crib, her mouth a perfect newborn pout. That night, as I left, I said to her mother, "Your daughter is so beautiful," and she looked up with tears in her eyes and said, "Thank you." The next time I saw Alexandra, it was broad daylight and her fists were pumping the air and she was crying and turning blue, and her mother was by her bedside, crying, "It's happening again, where *is* everyone?" and that was when I understood how Alexandra belonged at Central, just like Evan—that despite her healthy good looks, she had something wrong with her too. I had never seen a seizure before, but over the next few days, I began to understand that this was what was happening to Alexandra and that the doctors had no real sense of how to stop them. In the midst of Alexandra's seizures, her mother's poise naturally began to erode, and finally in the hall one afternoon, I walked up to this young, beautiful woman and, surprising even myself, said, "I don't know you, but I feel like I should give you a hug." She began to cry and said, "We just met with the neurologist who said it was time to face the fact that Alexandra is never going to walk or talk. 'This girl's not going to her high school prom,' he said."

I started to cry with her. "He can't know that!" I had heard so many prognoses by this point (and wanted, I suppose, my own hope, my own thing with feathers) that I felt outraged by this one doctor's statement. "If they can't figure out what's wrong with her, how do they have the right to say anything about how she'll turn out? I'm sorry, that just makes me so mad."

I wasn't much of a friend to people in those days; my time with Evan had shut me off. Throughout the hospital stays, I had resisted any kind of connection to other parents. The very fact of having a chronically ill child set me apart from others. Years later I would hear two women in a coffee shop talking about how someone they knew was sick. "She got better, then she got worse again . . ." More hushed tones, then a sense that this person was now in the hospital, possibly again? And I remembered all at once what it was like, those long hospital days and nights, and what I had forgotten: dreading hospital visits, making them anyway, giving myself permission to take a break, feeling guilty about that. Just the daily grind of that life.

I remember driving to Central Hospital one morning around Christmastime and telling my dad on the phone that Evan had come down with some new mysterious fever and that they had already started him on hard-core antibiotics to bring it down. "What kind of infection do they suspect?" he asked, and I said, "I have no idea. They say he started running a fever last night, but he was okay yesterday." And how many days and weeks were like that—just things changing all the time, and yet never changing, how tiring and hard it was to witness those days, and how much harder it was to stay away. This daily grind was why NICU parents smiled at one another and asked polite questions about one another's babies but did not sit and chat or get to know one another—partly because there was so little time, partly because we never knew when a person was going to leave, abandoning the others to a fate unchanged, and partly because it was so clear to us that each baby turned out so differently. All we really had in common were our sick children, and most of the time I had very little interest in knowing more than that. At no other time had I felt compelled to give another parent a hug.

What disarmed me about Alexandra's mother, whose name, I learned, was Holly, was her determination to help her daughter. I knew I had a similar determination but mine was always so clouded with avoidance and fear. Holly was beautiful and strong and smart and not at all passive or desperate. It was clear that she loved her child and was not afraid of her, and that however things turned out she would always love her child. She dressed her up and put bows in her hair and never lied to herself or anyone else about her daughter's condition. Since my own connection to Evan had been so tenuous for so long—not knowing if he'd survive at first, then not knowing how it would all turn out—I marveled at this ability to bond no matter the circumstances.

Right away, I wanted to think I knew more than Holly, being the NICU veteran that I was. When I gave her advice from my seasoned post ("Invite a friend, a good friend, to come visit; try not to do this alone") and she took it, and did so much better than I ever had in the same situation, I began to accept another layer of my own humility. From Holly I was to learn there was a lot I didn't know, and a lot I still feared.

There was the question, for example, of when and how to repair Evan's hernia. The doctors at Central wanted to do it immediately, while he was still on the vent from his second eye surgery. To me, that made sense only from a medical standpoint. Sure, it would be efficient to keep Evan intubated and put him back under anesthesia, but what about giving him time to get off the vent and heal? He'd gone from one surgery to another in fewer than ten days. Wasn't the more compassionate route one that allowed him time to recover? I belabored the decision, torn between doing the right thing from a medical standpoint and doing what I knew was probably better for my son. When I told Holly about what the nurse practitioner and the resident had planned, her outrage at this proposition outweighed even my own. "Let him get better first. Jesus, what are these kids to them, just a bunch of numbers? Vicki, you know the right thing to do here."

Holly did research and brought in studies for the doctors to read. She had outside doctors come in and sit by Alexandra's Isolette and give second opinions. She interviewed other neurologists to see if they would follow similar protocols to the ones the doctors at Central advised. I had always thought I was knowledgeable and proactive; Holly put me to shame. I'd suggested we bring in food for Thanksgiving and have a small gathering, but the day came and I couldn't bring myself to buy even a bag of potato chips, so demoralized was I by having to come to the NICU at all. Holly was there with crudités and soda and a bottle of champagne, all for the other parents and the nurses. She bought presents for Josie and gave me books to read. Holly was the one who told me it was perfectly fine not to wash my hands with the harsh soap and gave me permission not to remove my jewelry in the unit ever again after my wedding band fell out of my pants' pocket and went forever missing.

At one point, the neurologists, having failed to curb Alexandra's seizures with medication, decided they would try inducing a coma in her to see if perhaps shutting down her brain would also shut down the seizures. They moved Alexandra to one of the beds reserved for isolation cases. Typically, kids undergoing open-heart surgery or those who were at similarly high risk for complications occupied these beds. The isolation rooms were also used for kids with infections to prevent the spread to other patients. I arrived in the NICU one morning to see Alexandra in an isolation room, with Holly by her side. Immediately, I was concerned. "What's going on?" I asked. "Does she have an infection?"

"You're not going to believe this, Vicki. They're giving her sedatives and inducing a coma."

Even I was shocked at the seemingly crude, downright rudimentary protocol. "What is this, the nineteenth century? That's insane."

"I know," she said. "It's something they use in adult seizure patients and sometimes it actually works. No one's ever tried it on a baby before. They told us it's the last resort. After this, they don't know what to do."

And so I watched as the drugs slowed down Alexandra's heart and they intubated her and put her on a vent. I watched as Holly held her own vigil by Alexandra's bedside, the way I had done for so many months for Evan. Soon, Alexandra was on all the same kind of life support that had kept Evan going for so long, and soon, too, Holly was as helpless as I had been.

My parents arrived in mid-December and were there for Evan's third—and final—eye surgery. In the same way that I recognized my own weariness only when I saw it mirrored in my husband, the other NICU parents, or Holly and Brad, I knew my own worry only when it appeared in my own parents' eyes. My mother and father wandered the NICU halls at Central the way I did that winter season, adrift, not resting long in any one place, going between the waiting room and Evan's bedside. My dad spent a few hours one afternoon in a secluded room, reserved for the most bereaved parents or mothers pumping their milk, watching college football on TV with Brad. The morning of Evan's last eye surgery, while Cliff and my father roamed the hospital, my mother and I sat by his Isolette, taking turns comforting him in his presurgery hunger. "I'm so sorry you have to go through this," my mother said, holding him in her arms. "You're such a beautiful boy, I don't know what else to say."

Afterward, my parents were there to listen as Dr. Chang reported on her last bout with Evan's eyes. "The traction is still there on the right side," she said. "It's stable but it's not improving either. I'm guessing he'll have some peripheral vision in that eye but not a lot of central vision."

"And the left?" I asked.

"I went in and cleaned out the scar tissue," she said. "But the retina is completely detached."

"So nothing."

"Nothing," Dr. Chang said.

I tried to look at my mom and dad but couldn't. My father thanked the doctor. "I'm sorry," she said. We exchanged a few final words about the next exam and how often she'd be checking him and then we went down to a fast-food restaurant on the ground floor and tried to eat. My mother has a picture of us taken at this lunch, the only one of Cliff and me from this time in our lives. My husband and I have our arms around each other, and we are actually smiling—Cliff his standard open-mouth grin, me a more careful, impish one. I remember trying hard to smile even as I knew full well that behind the smile was the sadness I felt for my husband and my parents, being there for the news we had all just heard.

I have a Polaroid of Evan taken on December 15, 2000, after his final eye surgery. He lies in bed, a respirator tube down his throat, a feeding tube in his nose. An IV block and bandage covers one hand. A stubby finger of his other hand is wedged into his ear. A caption to the photograph reads, *Will someone tell Alexander to be quiet? I'm trying to sleep.*

This was our baby, our life. The kid with the tubes (back) down his throat and into his nose, the kid with the finger in his ear, trying to drown out the noise of the machines and the crying babies next to him, of Alexander, whose neurological impairments left him inconsolable; of Alexandra and her induced coma; of Debbie and her shunt and her G-tube; of the boy in the corner with the chest tube whose machine looked and sounded like nothing less than an aquarium. I often forget what Evan looked like in those days; my memories are so caught up with my own fears and accommodations. But Evan, poor Evan: his face is swollen, his chin thick and fleshy. I don't recognize him as the boy I came to know, the boy with the low laugh and the morning smile. This Evan is naked except for a diaper, the leads on his puffy chest bigger around than his belly button. He is suffering, and even the beginnings of his personality (that finger in his ear, so deliberate, this I can make sense of as the child I came to know) barely emerged beneath everything that was done to him in those months.

We moved in then, aware we weren't going home any time soon. They would fix Evan's other problems too, his hernia and his circumcision. There would be more surgeries, more days on the respirator, more tubes and intervention. I brought in more clothes, aside from that first pair of pajamas, and labeled them with his name. When he was awake, I let myself believe my son could see the black-and-white banners I'd strung across his crib, that the shapes would engage him. For the long hours he slept, I brought in a cassette player and music. "He pays such close attention," a nurse told me, "when that friend of yours—his Auntie Maria?—comes on and speaks." I came to know the nurses, gave them chocolate at Christmas. I actually smiled some days, no longer just angry about my lot, no longer just praying for Evan.

This was how we spent Christmas and the New Year: still waiting to go home.

5

THE YEAR 2000, along with being the turn of the millennium, was also, in the Chinese astrological cycle, the year of the golden dragon. According to Chinese astrology, those born in the year of the golden dragon are especially gifted and fortunate, since these two aspects—gold and dragon—appear together only once every sixty years. At the time of his birth and in the months and years that followed, I didn't think of Evan as particularly gifted or fortunate, but I did see and come to know his dragon power—to roar upon birth, to spit fire when angry, to be both strong and unpredictable. Today, when I read that dragon people are healthy, energetic, excitable, short-tempered, and stubborn, and that they are also honest, sensitive, brave, and inspire confidence and trust, I know this as my son.

At the time, as the year 2000 gave way to 2001, as Evan's hospital course dragged into twice as long as originally planned and the presidential election went unresolved, the year of the golden dragon also turned into the year of the golden snake, and I met the fortunes the snake often brings with it, that is, a cycle of upheaval and revolution, as if the inherent unpredictability of the dragon's actions caused a necessary chaos in its wake.

In Evan's case, the unpredictability gave way to the uncertainty of Evan's future hospital course, the question we'd been asking since August: when would he come home? It was the first week in January; he'd been in the hospital for five months, two months past his original due date. When the nurses rounded with the residents they recited the valuable stats of each case, which included the baby's age and length of stay. In Evan's case these numbers were mind-numbingly large. One hundred and fifty days old, each one of them spent in a hospital.

The doctors at Central had told us that they would eventually discharge Evan from their care to home. I asked that they consider letting him return to Hampton instead, once his hernia had been repaired and he was stable. At three and a half pounds, Evan still didn't weigh enough to come home, nor was he taking enough by mouth. His eyes required weekly exams. Since Dr. Chang had to do those exams, Central insisted he stay there until discharge.

"Why can't Dr. Chang get privileges at Hampton?" I asked.

"That's just not done," a nurse practitioner in charge of Evan's case told me.

As the daughter of a doctor, I knew she was wrong. "It's done all the time," I said.

I had spent more than two months making the half-hour drive back and forth to Central. Hampton was a five-minute walk from our house. Central was a hectic, chaotic place; I'd had enough of the self-important nurses and absent doctors and awkward residents, the parade of medical students passing by Evan's Isolette on their way to more significant or interesting or successful cases. It seemed like a simple thing—let us return to where they knew us and Evan, let us ride out the rest of his sentence in more comfortable surroundings.

Well, fine seemed to be the answer. If I could get Dr. Chang to agree to examine Evan at Hampton, and if I could get her privileges there, they would allow us to leave. Each morning,

I passed by the patient's bill of rights posted prominently on the wall outside the unit, and each morning my eyes stopped at number 14 ("You have the right to be treated with dignity and compassion"); number 19 ("You have the right to refuse medical care"); and, my favorite, number 25 ("You have the right to leave the hospital at any time, with the understanding that you might be leaving against medical advice"). This bill of rights, framed and sometimes printed in a comforting, cursive font, exists in every hospital, posted in Admissions and on every floor. It shows up in multiple languages, and at every turn it is intended to bring humanity to the process of medical care. When all I wanted was to leave Central, I heard myself reading those words aloud and, as they sounded in my ears, using them as the refrain I needed to push me forward in getting Evan first back to Hampton, and then home.

By early January, Evan had had his hernia repair and circumcision and was off the ventilator. It was time, finally, for us to meet with the doctors to talk about how and when he would be going home. Typically, discharge meetings held few surprises. Both the parents and the doctors knew the status of the patient; the meeting was simply a means to document that same status in the patient's chart and prove to everyone concerned that there was a plan for getting the patient home. In this meeting, we knew the doctors would tell us that with Evan relatively stable, the only forces keeping him at Central were his low weight and his inadequate feeding. That until he weighed five pounds and could take two ounces of formula by mouth every three hours, for a total of twenty-four ounces a day, he wasn't going home. What the doctors didn't know about this particular discharge meeting was that I planned to announce that Evan was leaving Central and heading to Hampton. I'd worked the phones all day Tuesday and Wednesday morning, speaking to Dr. Lamb's and

Dr. Chang's secretaries, getting the information I needed to find out how and when Dr. Chang could get privileges.

I was in the unit on Wednesday, the day before the discharge meeting, when I was called to the nurses' station by Dr. Prang, the head neonatologist at Central. "Dr. Lamb is on the phone for you," she said. I found it odd that Dr. Prang was not speaking to Dr. Lamb herself, since I had heard that Dr. Prang had actually trained with Dr. Lamb. It seemed even odder that Dr. Prang, having known Dr. Lamb, wasn't willing to negotiate Evan's transfer herself. I went to the phone to hear Dr. Lamb's soft, familiar lilt. We hadn't spoken since Evan had left Hampton, and it was a relief to hear a familiar, welcoming voice. Dr. Lamb informed me that he had been in touch with his medical director about Dr. Chang and that the hospital had agreed to grant her privileges. "If you need to come back to Hampton," he said, "we will take you gladly. Please tell Dr. Prang I said so."

"She's right here," I said. "You can tell her yourself."

I handed Dr. Prang the phone and stepped back into the unit, very aware that my golden dragon had given me both the strength and the diplomacy to make happen what he and I so sorely needed. In a minute or so, Dr. Prang returned to Evan's bedside. "Dr. Lamb would like to speak with you again," she said, divulging nothing of what they might have said to each other.

"Simply have Dr. Chang's office contact the medical director," Dr. Lamb said when I got back on the phone. "There is a form to fill out. Dr. Chang's secretary can take care of it." And suddenly the thing that was not done was that simply done.

"Thank you, Dr. Lamb," I said. "You don't know how grateful I am."

"Mrs. Forman, it is my pleasure," he said. "We will be happy to see you and your son again."

· · ·

The day of Evan's discharge meeting, in the same conference room where Dr. Chang had given me the hard news about Evan's eyes, I met the gaze of the on-call neonatologist, Dr. Thrum. If I had been a hardened NICU veteran when I arrived at Central, I was an even more hardened one now. I'd learned how to tell the nurses, in no uncertain terms, not to ask me about Evan's twin. "She is not relevant to Evan's care." When a new crop of nurses came along and started to ask me again, I'd met with the social worker and told her to document this same request on his chart. I'd accompanied my son to four successive surgeries, put off doctors when they wanted surgeries to take place before I thought Evan was ready. I'd accepted that my son was visually impaired. And, finally, I'd gained the strength, thanks to the bond with my golden dragon, to fight the doctors about transferring Evan to another hospital. Now, in this meeting, I stared down Dr. Thrum, a known force of nature on the unit; this was the doctor that most parents wanted to oversee their child's care, but at the same time they feared his intensity. I had seen Dr. Thrum stay by more than one very sick child's bedside well into the night, hoping for the numbers to improve. I had also seen him deep in conversation with Holly over Alexandra's seizures. I liked and respected Dr. Thrum and I was also very grateful to be able to say to him, before he could even begin the meeting, "Dr. Lamb has agreed to transfer Evan back to Hampton. Dr. Prang spoke with him herself, yesterday."

Dr. Thrum sat back in his chair. His clear blue eyes took me in and he said, "Well, there's no need to discuss our discharge plan then, is there?"

"Actually, I'm curious to know how you planned to handle his feeding issues, if Evan were to have stayed here," I said.

"I called this meeting because the baby is hemodynamically

stable," Dr. Thrum said. "In my opinion he could be discharged from here as early as this month with an NG tube in place to handle his nutritional needs."

An NG, or nasogastric, tube was put in place in patients who were unable to take food by mouth. These tubes snaked through the nostril, down the back of the throat, and into the stomach. Even when we were trying him out on feeds by mouth, Evan still had an NG tube for all of his supplemental feedings.

"You'd discharge him with an NG tube?" I asked.

"He can't stay here until he's taking full feeds by mouth," Dr. Thrum said. "Once he gains enough weight, he's otherwise stable enough to go home. If you were to remain at Central, the plan would be to discharge him with an NG."

This was news to me. It nearly felt as though Dr. Thrum were making a last-ditch effort to keep Evan as his patient. Certainly the protocol he suggested was different from anything Dr. Lamb had brought up. I had seen enough nurses place nasogastric tubes to know they were not easy to insert. The procedure was painful, and tricky, and required a little more than just a set of hands and faith. After the tube was inserted, the nurse had to make sure its placement was correct, otherwise the formula could end up in the lungs, rather than in the stomach. Placing an NG tube required the accurate use of a stethoscope, and some pretty good expertise. This did not sound like something I'd want to do at home, by myself. I expressed my concerns to Dr. Thrum, who dismissed them with a wave of his hand.

"Parents learn how to put them in all the time. Or you can take him to your pediatrician and they can put the tube in and check placement. It's your choice," Dr. Thrum said. "We can transfer him to Hampton, or he can be discharged from here with an NG tube. You decide."

Dr. Thrum stood up, his task complete. The room cleared, and I was alone with this new bit of information. So much for a discharge meeting that didn't contain surprises. Downstairs, I called Cliff to tell him about Dr. Thrum's plan. "I'm not comfortable with him coming home with an NG tube," he said.

"We could learn to check placement," I said. "It would mean he could come home." I thought of what my friend Susan had said just the day before: "He needs to hear the birds sing and feel the fresh air." I thought of my son, my golden dragon, knowing what it felt like to have the warm sun on his face. I would do anything for this to happen, after the journey we'd endured.

"It sounds like they're just trying to get rid of him," Cliff said. "An NG tube isn't a long-term solution. Learning how to eat is a long-term solution."

It was January 4. Evan had been at Central since November 7, Election Day. On the television in the lobby downstairs, I had watched over the past several weeks as the Supreme Court took up the unresolved election, and I had hoped that Evan's course would follow suit. The Court had voted to stop any recounting, and Al Gore had conceded the election. Congress was on the verge of certifying the vote, paving the way for George Bush to be inaugurated. In my mind, the election and Evan's hospital course had always been inextricably bound. Since Bush was about to be inaugurated, didn't that mean that my son should be able to come home?

Upstairs in the unit, I held Evan while he slept, watched the milk snake from a syringe above his bed and into the NG tube, and thought to myself, *How do you make a decision when neither answer is wrong?* Could I take care of my medically fragile son with a tube going from his nose, down his throat, and into his stomach? There were real risks to home care in this kind of situation. Was I ready? Did I have what it took? Should I push the decision through, past my husband and my instincts? I had no way of knowing at the time that this would be an impasse at which I would find myself again and again where Evan was concerned: how to discover maternal instincts in a situation so beyond the ordinary that only new and stronger instincts applied.

At two o'clock a nurse came by Evan's bedside. "They called from Hampton," she said. "They're sending a transport ambulance. They're on their way." She told me to pack Evan's crib and belongings and get him ready for transport. In arranging for the ambulance, Dr. Lamb had made the decision for me.

Within fifteen minutes I had stripped my son's crib of the toys I'd brought to Central and had packed his few simple belongings: the preemie-size clothes that finally fit, the classical music cassettes, tape player, and extra batteries. After two months and four surgeries, the artifacts of this journey fit into two plastic bags. I took the bags, left Evan in the care of the nurse, and went searching for Holly to say goodbye.

On Holly's birthday, December 31, a nurse had put together a card and signed Alexandra's name to it. *Happy birthday, Mommy,* the card read. *I love you.* Alexandra was still in a coma and had developed an infection in her lungs from being intubated. This same nurse who'd gotten the card had at one point said to Holly, "You know, maybe it would be better if Alexandra didn't make it." The nurse herself had a child with severe cerebral palsy and was trying to tell Holly, in her own way, that children like Alexandra often became more of a burden than a parent could handle. Perhaps I too had had the same thoughts about Alexandra and Evan, but losing Ellie had also shown me that once a child was born, that child's death was nothing close to a solution. With Evan leaving, I couldn't help but feel I was abandoning Holly—to this nurse, to Central, to Alexandra in a coma. I looked for Holly all over the unit and finally accepted that I might not find her in time to say goodbye, when I walked out into the waiting room and saw her sitting there, beside her father. Her head rested on his shoulder and they had both been crying. I had my bags of Evan's patient belongings and was headed for the elevator.

"Vicki," she said. "Where are you going?"

"Evan's leaving. They're transferring him back to Hampton. The ambulance is on its way."

"Now? Today?" Holly started crying again.

"I'm so sorry." I pulled her into my arms.

"I don't know if I'm going to make it out of here," she said.

"You will," I said, and I started to cry too. "If Evan can make it out of here, so can Alexandra." I had left my phone number for Holly with the nurse who had charge of Alexandra's care. "Jenny has my number," I said. "Call me. Please."

I got into the elevator with my bag of Evan's belongings, turned, and watched the doors close before me. The last image I have of Central and our time there is of Holly standing in the middle of the hallway, the giraffe-pattern linoleum we'd never forget beneath her feet, crying as she said goodbye.

Evan had been at Central for two months. When he and I returned to Hampton, neither of us was the same. Even Annalise, the occupational therapist, would say to me later, "When you came back, it was so clear that Evan was your baby and that you were his mother and that you, more than anyone else, knew how to care for him." And so it was clear, even to others, that those two months at Central had transformed me from the mother who thought *They say it's your baby, but until you're home, it's not your baby, it's theirs* to the mother who alone knew how to handle the visually impaired, oxygen-dependent poor feeder that was my son. Our time at Central had been nothing less than a crucible. When we left Hampton, Evan was still a boy who might turn out fine; when we came back, I knew otherwise.

The night Evan came back to Hampton, January 4, the nurses saw us through intake, asked about his surgeries, and set him up with a real crib in Nursery C with the "feeders and growers." I had never spent much time in this, the least critical room in the unit. Here, classical music played on a CD player and the nurses ribbed one another about their charges, comparing the babies' chunky legs and unparalleled abilities at breathing, sucking, and swallowing. There were no ventilators here, only oxygen and heart-rate monitors. Nursery C comprised a baby's last stop on his journey out of the NICU and many stayed no more than a few days. This was where the barely premature kids hung out while they learned to regulate their body temperatures, or where a twin or triplet might improve feeding skills before going home. Nursery C was the most normal and least stressful hospital experience Evan had ever had, and I relished it. The nurses encouraged me to indulge myself—"You're going to be home soon enough and he's going to be a lot of work. Don't sit around here; have lunch with a friend"—and I took their advice. During Evan's time in Nursery C, I splurged on the most expensive item of clothing I'd ever bought: a full-length denim coat that cost more than a hundred and fifty dollars. To this day, whenever I wear that coat, I remember hanging it on a hook in Nursery C for the first time and hearing every nurse there admire my purchase. "You went shopping!" Joanna said. "Just like we told you to!"

"Yes, Joanna, I went shopping," I said. "And I spent a lot of money. I feel very guilty right now."

"Don't feel guilty. You deserve it," Joanna said. "Now listen to this dream I had about your son. . . ."

In his short time there, my golden dragon had quickly charmed Joanna and Sandra, the women of Nursery C. Together, they were convinced they would get Evan feeding. We divvied up the daytime feeds and made sure that the nighttime nurses assigned to Evan were the best available. Joanna and Sandra called me from the unit if Evan seemed hungry early, and I'd rush to the hospital in my new denim coat, ready to do battle.

Many parents of super-preemies can speak of their troubling experiences with feeding. Owing to a host of issues, including poor muscle tone, difficulty swallowing, neurological deficits in coordinating suck and swallow, and, sometimes, little or no sensation inside the throat and esophagus because of prolonged intubations, preemies are particularly vulnerable to feeding problems. Like many of the subtle challenges facing preemies, the possibility that Evan might not ever get it when it came to taking a bottle had not been discussed much. Before his transfer to Central, Evan had been taking more than an ounce at each feeding; subsequent surgeries and intubations seemed to have impeded any ability to eat he might have once had. Over the next four weeks, Annalise, the occupational therapist, and I worked to solve Evan's feeding problems. We added rice cereal to his formula to thicken it and make it easier to swallow. When the cereal made the formula too hard to suck, we sliced the tip of his bottle's nipple open with a razor blade to allow the milk to flow better. We gave him chin support and squeezed his cheeks to help him suck. Eliza, a German nurse, swaddled him so tightly he couldn't move and didn't give up until she'd gotten him to suck down two ounces. Joanna cajoled him with her singing. Sandra rocked him and twirled the nipple in his mouth to stimulate his tongue. I came to the hospital every three hours, hoping that among all of us we'd find the magic formula. In an effort to wean Evan off oxygen, Dr. Lamb turned it down. Evan's feeding slumped; I mentioned this to him and suggested we turn the oxygen back up. And every morning he was on duty, Dr. Lamb checked Evan's chart for the elusive, miracle combination of oral intake and weight gain. Some days my son was up, some days he was down. Mostly he was down.

We spent three weeks on these tactics. One afternoon toward the end of January, I was at Evan's bedside when the social worker came by to announce that Dr. Lamb wanted to meet with us to go over Evan's treatment and discharge plan. "You haven't had a head-to-toe since you got back," Sharon explained. "Dr. Lamb wants to make sure you're aware of all the issues."

Immediately, my guard went up. It was rare to have a head-to-toe unless there was some outstanding issue—or something new. "No surprises, right?"

Sharon hesitated. "He wants to discuss placement of a gastrostomy tube. Because of the feeding issues."

"Dr. Lamb wants to do a gastrostomy?" I said. I'd seen these G-tubes on kids at Central and knew they meant the surgical implantation of a rubber hose into Evan's stomach, through which we'd feed him his formula. "Not even an NG?" I asked, referring to Dr. Thrum's proposed solution at Central.

"You'll have to speak to Dr. Lamb."

Cliff and I met with Dr. Lamb the following afternoon. After running down the list of Evan's ongoing issues, he ended by bringing up the gastrostomy. "The only thing preventing your son from going home are his feeding issues," he said. "If we place a permanent feeding tube, once he is healed, he'll be able to go home."

"At Central, Dr. Thrum had suggested Evan could go home with an NG tube," I said. "Why isn't that an option rather than surgery and a gastrostomy?"

"I don't consider it safe for a child to have an NG long term," Dr. Lamb said. "There is wear and tear on the esophagus, which is very unhealthy over time. A child's speech can be affected. As you can imagine, it's challenging to feed orally with a tube down your throat. An NG tube is not a long-term solution for a baby like Evan."

"Say we do the G-tube surgery," Cliff said. "How long before he feeds enough by mouth that we can take it out?"

"It's hard to tell," Dr. Lamb said. "It could be as soon as six months."

"Or as long as?"

"Eighteen?" he suggested.

"Eighteen months!" I said.

"The baby needs to go home," Dr. Lamb said.

Evan had been in the hospital for six months, nearly twice as long as the original prediction. Six months of going back and forth from the hospital to home, of trying to negotiate his life, my family's, mine. My daughter would be turning four that spring, and nearly her entire third year had been marked by these events. My husband's job provided the security of insurance and enough money that I could afford this time off, but more and more, balancing that work with the stress of Evan's hospitalization caused us all to be frustrated, irritable. This had gone on long enough. While there was something profoundly unnatural about surgically implanting a feeding tube into my son's stomach in order for him to develop and grow, and something even more unnatural about seeing this as a solution, it was nonetheless one that would bring us closer to home. In the same way that my maternal instincts had been pushed to their limit, nothing was particularly natural at this point when it came to Evan. I thought of the sun and the birds and the world outside and knew this would be the only way. This was my son, and he had to come home, even if his imperfections were now further complicated by a permanent feeding tube implanted into his stomach. "If this is the only way," I said, "then this is what we have to do." After the meeting, I called my dad to tell him the news.

"Oh God," he said, the same phrase he'd used when I told him about Evan's eyes.

"It's the only way," I said. "He needs to come home. He won't gain weight or grow otherwise and he can't stay in the hospital his whole life."

"I know," he said. "But this whole thing is just incredible."

"Yes, it is," I said. "It's all rather incredible, isn't it? The baby who would turn out to be just fine. That's who he is, right?"

"I guess so, if you include a G-tube in the category of just fine."

It seemed pointless to tell my dad yet again that I was sorry, and that he should try not to worry, but I did anyway, finishing the conversation by telling him I loved him.

Four weeks after my golden dragon's transfer back to Hampton, I followed his crib as a nurse wheeled him up to the fourth floor for what was to be his fifth surgery, this one to place a permanent gastrostomy tube. The nurse who accompanied us turned to me as we waited for the elevator and said, "This can't be easy for you, seeing your baby into surgery."

"I've done this four times before," I reminded her.

"Even so," she said.

"I'm a pro," I said. "Just take good care of my baby."

I walked with them down the hall to the surgery room, right up to the yellow stripes in the floor that marked the place beyond which parents were not allowed. I watched the doors to the surgery center close behind them, then took the same elevator back down, walked through the hospital's front doors, and went outside to wait in the cool January morning. There, in a small patio by the maternity ward, when no one was looking, the pro broke down.

Part Three

6

M Y SON'S DISCHARGE summary from Hampton Hospital consisted of nine single-spaced pages listing fifteen different diagnoses operative at discharge, including: chronic lung disease; peripheral pulmonic stenosis; thrush; anemia of prematurity (twenty-three transfusions); bilateral inguinal hernias; retinopathy of prematurity (surgically treated); twenty-four-week prematurity; G-tube—Nissen, other; need for nutritional support; poor feeder. The summary also included prior diagnoses such as: respiratory distress syndrome; patent ductus arteriosus; hypotension; hypertension; heart murmur; sepsis; enterobacterial pneumonia; isoimmunization; thrombocytopenia; IVH grade 0; hyperkalemia; hyperglycemia; hypoalbuminemia; and failure to thrive. It concluded as follows:

DISPOSITION: The patient was discharged home on 2/12/01. The primary care physician following discharge will be Gaffney, M.D. Problems at the time included S/P 24-week twin A, chronic lung disease, diuretic and O_2 dependency, monitor, stage 4 ROP on right, probably no vision in left eye, feeding problems and GT placement and pulmonic stenosis.

MEDICATIONS: Aldactazide, lysine chloride, Vi-Daylin, and Fer-In-Sol

EQUIPMENT: apnea monitor, home oxygen, feeding pump

FOLLOW-UP: outpatient appointments include pediatrician
in 3–4 days, pulmonary clinic in 2 weeks, cardiology in
3–4 weeks, and regional center, surgeon, one month.
Ophthalmology 2–3 weeks. Other recommended follow-
up includes Synagis, due 2/20.

There was a bulletin board in the NICU where they posted
Polaroids of parents and graduates taken the day the babies finally left the unit. I'd spent six months waiting for my picture
and Evan's to be up on that wall: me in the wheelchair they'd
bring in for the discharge, as if to mimic the way the new
mothers and full-term babies left, Evan in my lap, dressed in
his going-home clothes. I'd picked out his outfit, a matching,
striped fleece jacket and pants I'd been given at a baby shower
in November, when we'd thought Evan would be home by
Christmas. I'd planned the moment: I'd be the proud, smiling
mother; he'd be the miracle, sleeping in my arms. We'd hide
the G-tube inside his clothes and except for the oxygen cannula
taped to his face, he'd look like any other newborn.

When the time finally came for us to leave Hampton, the
doctors and nurses spent so many hours explaining all the details of Evan's care—medications, settings for the pump, how to
advance his feeds as the swelling in his abdomen from the surgery decreased, maintenance of the G-tube site, which follow-
up appointments to make and when—and loaded us down with
so many syringes and devices and extra formula and bottles and
nipples, Cliff and I were too overwhelmed to think of taking a
picture. The planned forty-five-minute discharge lasted more
than two hours. Cliff had a sinus infection, and it was pouring
outside. By four o'clock, I just wanted to take my seven-pound
baby with his fifteen diagnoses, nine-page discharge summary,
oxygen, feeding pump, and monitor and go home.

That night, while my husband struggled in the bedroom to set up the pump that would deliver formula into Evan's stomach during the night, I answered the phone to hear Holly at the other end, crying in distress. Alexandra was in the pediatric intensive care unit at University Medical Center; she'd been airlifted there from home after she'd had a seizure that lasted for several hours. They'd been home from Central for all of two days. Even with all her tough mother love and protection, Holly, herself a pro, had fallen apart. "I don't know if I can do this, Vicki. There's another little girl here who has severe cerebral palsy, and they're telling me this could be Alexandra. I'm looking at this girl and all she does is cry. Her parents aren't around, she can't hold up her head or eat or do anything, and all I can think of is how scared I am. I'm so scared." The words just tumbled from her. "I'm sorry to call you like this but you're the only person I know who understands."

I listened to the familiar hospital sounds in the background, the pages over the intercom and the bells going off, and I did understand. I understood what it was like to be in the presence of some version of your life you'd rather not see. I'd felt that way when Evan was in a room at Central with a child who'd recently gotten a G-tube. The sight of the rubber hose coming from the baby's stomach, of the bag of formula hanging next to him, of the syringes of liquid being shot into his tube—none of that was pleasant to watch, and yet here I was with the same set of circumstances.

Holly and I had not spoken to each other since Evan had left Central. We had left messages, and then, when the messages stopped because neither of us had the strength to report on her stay, we began to trade faxes instead. In the middle of the night the fax machine would come to life, and page after page would emerge with Holly's dense cursive, reporting to me on Alexandra's case. She'd had a G-tube placement as well—the doctors thought this might curb the seizures—and feeding difficulties too. I wrote back to Holly, faxing my replies about Evan, his progress, the G-tube. In this way I came to learn more about her: how she'd quit her job as an attorney; her love of poetry; that her grandmother practiced automatic writing and was something of a clairvoyant. In the time since Evan had left Central, in this way we had become friends.

That night, I told Holly that she couldn't know when she looked at that other child she was looking at her future; no one could know that. And then I told her to walk away, not forever, but at least for that night. To sleep in her own bed rather than a cot by Alexandra's side. To see her husband and eat a meal in her own kitchen. By now it was February, and Holly had been sitting by Alexandra's beside since November. Four months of going back and forth between her house and the hospital, of eating cafeteria food and seeing only other sick kids and their parents. Four months of being a hospital-parent specter.

"Holly, I know you don't want to hear this," I said. "But you need to go home."

"If I'm not here, no one's here," she said. "They're not even charting her seizures. They leave the kids alone all night. It's incredible. If I'm not there, she's all by herself."

I couldn't know that in three short months I'd say those same words to Holly, this time about Evan, in response to our own journey back to the hospital, our own episode with complications.

"You need to take care of yourself," I said now.

"That's what everyone keeps telling me."

"It's good to hear your voice," I said. "I've missed your faxes. They were my only way of keeping up with you."

She laughed. "I could say the same. How is Evan? How are you?"

"Evan just came home."

"What? Today?"

"Today," I said. "About three hours ago. They sent us home with enough supplies to start our own NICU." I told her about the diagnoses and doctors' appointments and the nine-page discharge summary, and about the fight Cliff and I had just had over the location of the bags for the feeding pump (Him: "If it weren't for your incessant need to put everything away." Me: "If it weren't for your utter disregard for the logistics of this household"). "We've been fighting all day," I said. Cliff's sinus infection and the stress of the discharge had made me cranky and mean. I'd even suggested during the discharge process that if he didn't feel well enough to stick around the hospital, he was free to walk home. "It's pouring outside and I have a sinus infection and you're telling me to walk home in the rain?" Cliff had said. "I guess I am" came my reply. I told Holly about the arrival earlier in the day of the torpedo-size oxygen canister, and the equipment surrounding Evan in his crib, and about the subtle shifts too—how Evan seemed to have developed a tightness in his neck that twisted his head permanently to the right, that his left eye was now noticeably shrunken, especially when compared to the right, which continued to grow.

"They didn't even take a picture of us as we were leaving," I said. "It took them two hours to discharge us but no one thought to take a picture when we finally left."

"But you're *home*," she said.

"Yes," I said. "We're home."

Holly and I knew it was all you ever wanted when your child had been in the hospital for prolonged periods of time: to be home. But what was this home we'd come to? Not the one we had known before. That first month Evan was home, and the second, were a blur of responsibilities and phone calls and chores. When my dad came to visit, a week after

Evan left the hospital, his comment—"You've got your own little ICU here"—said it all. Feeding pump, oxygen tank, apnea monitor. Five meds into the G-tube round the clock, attempts at feeding him by mouth, then the rest with a syringe into the tube. I typed up Evan's schedule and taped it to the kitchen cabinet:

> 7 a.m.
>> Inderal—1.5 ml
>> Lysine—1 ml
>
> 8 a.m.
>> Aldactazide—3.5 mg
>> 2 oz formula mixed w/ 1 tsp rice cereal
>> Linum B_6—½ capsule
>
> 10 a.m.
>> Vi-Daylin—1 ml
>
> 11 a.m.
>> 2 oz formula mixed w/ 1 tsp rice cereal
>
> 1 p.m.
>> Inderal—1.5 ml
>> Lysine—1 ml
>
> 2 p.m.
>> 2 oz formula mixed w/ 1 tsp rice cereal
>
> 6 p.m.
>> 2 oz formula mixed w/ 1 tsp rice cereal
>
> 8 p.m.
>> Aldactazide—3.5 mg
>> Linum B_6—½ capsule

9 p.m.
    Set up pump: 45 ccs over 1 hour
    Check O_2
    Turn on apnea monitor

11 p.m.
    Inderal—1.5 ml
    Lysine—1 ml

The round-the-clock care that had once been the purview of a team of nurses and doctors had now become our job, mine and Cliff's. I took the morning shift; Cliff had the nighttime routine. My last task for the evening was to turn on the feeding pump Cliff had filled. He handled the last round of medications at eleven, and in the morning, at seven, it all began again. When Evan needed antibiotics a few weeks later, the pediatrician looked at the list and asked, "Is this for real?"

"Well, yes," I said, thinking to myself, *What did you think it meant to have a child like Evan at home, on five meds, oxygen, a feeding tube?* On the countertop below the list, I lined up the meds with their labels clearly marked, along with a box containing the appropriate syringes and various other supplies: monitor leads, cannula tubing, medical tape, a synthetic material called DuoDERM that we used to keep Evan's oxygen cannula taped to his face.

Along with giving the charted meds and feeding duties, being home also meant the daily routine of Evan's care, and very little of this care was without complications. In the morning, I sometimes discovered that the plastic adapter that connected the pump to Evan's G-tube had come undone. Instead of dispensing the formula into Evan's stomach during the night, the pump had flooded his crib. Evan slept on, a pool of formula at his feet, and the pump kept going, with its *whoosh-whoosh-whoosh* sound. I never knew if I'd wake up to a baby who had been fed all night or a crib full of formula. Sometimes, the apnea monitor undid me. If Evan moved in the wrong way in his sleep, or took too deep a breath, the leads to the monitor slipped and the alarm went off, waking everyone, including Josie. Every time the alarm sounded I had to unsnap Evan's pajamas, reset the leads, and try to get him back to sleep. This could happen six or seven times a night.

I especially resented the monitor since all the studies of ex-preemies clearly established that after thirty-nine weeks' gestational age they were not prey to the apnea (not breathing) and bradycardia (slow heartbeat) episodes that were truly serious. Even in his time in the NICU, Evan had had very few of these incidents. He'd come home with the prescribed apnea monitor only because one of the rules of going home on oxygen was that the baby also required a monitor. Since I knew Evan was unlikely to stop breathing or have his heart arrest, I finally gave up and unplugged the damn monitor.

One afternoon, about six weeks after Evan came home, the technician from the medical supply company who had come to download the data from the monitor sat at my dining room table, puzzling over the lack of information.

"There's nothing here," he said.

"Really?"

"Mrs. Forman, have you been using this monitor?"

"Now, Chip," I said. "You know I've been using the monitor."

"There's no data here. If you'd been using it, there would be information for me to download."

"Well, that's just strange, isn't it?"

"Are you sure you've been using it?"

"Would I lie to you?"

"Some parents find the false alarms annoying and turn it off," he said. "If this were my child and I knew he was at risk for his heart or breathing to stop, I can assure you I'd be using it. I tell all my parents: it's for the safety of the child. You don't want to endanger your child, do you?"

Evan lay on the sheepskin rug next to the fireplace. I'd put him in clean pajamas, with toys next to him. The oxygen was taped to his face, and there was a bolus syringe next to him, ready for his next tube feeding. I'd even placed a baby gym above him in the hopes of stimulating what little vision he might have. The baby was fed, clean, and clearly well cared for. "Does that look like a child I would endanger?" I asked. "I mean, really."

Of course Chip knew I was lying. The next time I took Evan to see Dr. Gaffney, she came into the examining room and announced, "I got a call from the medical supply company."

"And they want to know why I'm not using the monitor."

She looked at me and said, "Why aren't you using the monitor?"

"Do you really want to know?"

"Yes, I do," she said.

"I'm not using the monitor because half the time I use the monitor it goes off eight times a night for no reason. I showed you the study about preemies and monitors after thirty-nine weeks' gestation. Even Dr. Lamb will tell you Evan came home with the monitor only because he's on oxygen. So no, I'm not using the monitor. And until one of you is in my house at three in the morning to fix the leads when the alarms go off, I won't be using the monitor. Does that answer your question?"

"I guess it does," Dr. Gaffney said.

• • •

Being home meant learning how to makes these decisions about my son and risking the opprobrium of his medical team. Being home also meant entering the world of social services and therapists that quickly became another daily fact of our lives. On his discharge from Hampton, Evan was referred to our local regional center, a state-funded program that assessed and provided social services. A caseworker arrived to take Evan's history, and a few weeks later we received a call from his service coordinator. "Your son has been approved for therapy based on his medical history," she said. "That one was a no-brainer." She then went on to explain to us the various services for which Evan qualified: occupational, physical, and vision therapy; respite care; entry into the state-run medical plan; sibling programs for Josie; and so on. Our state, it turned out, was remarkably generous when it came to help for a child like Evan. The service coordinator referred us to a program that provided nursing care for medically fragile children. When I expressed concern to the nursing supervisor who came to approve our case, telling her that I didn't need an actual nurse in the house caring for my son—despite the med charts, the equipment, and all else—the supervisor answered, "You realize that if you couldn't care for Evan, he would be in an institution, and that would cost the state even more money?" "I guess so," I said, unconvinced that if it weren't for me my son would be institutionalized. When I told the service coordinator who staffed Evan's therapists that I didn't think we needed all those services, she said to me, "You realize that Early Intervention is the key to your son's future." When I suggested to the pediatrician that maybe Evan was stable enough for us to see her once a month rather than once a week, she said, "You realize that if this child doesn't gain weight, he will be back in the hospital?" Being home meant being reminded, in all these ways, of what caring for a child like Evan involved. Therapies, doctors' appointments, nurses, and social services. The specter of institutionalization should I somehow not be up to the task.

I'd been asked to go back to teaching that spring but had declined the position, since I didn't know when Evan would be home. I'd hoped to start writing again, to begin crafting a story, any story, any writing other than the plaints and intentions in my journal. The rules of our new home made it impossible to do anything more than attend to the doctors and therapists and the round-the-clock routine of Evan's care. And yet, despite all these challenges, if someone had asked, What was it like to be home? I would have said this: It was hard, and it was wonderful. The joy I felt the day we left the hospital—my son was, at last, my own—carried me through the chores and the trials. When I wasn't tending to his feeding and his meds, I piled Evan and his supplies in the car, oxygen tank and all, and took him with me to Josie's ballet class. I sat beside my son as he slept in his car seat and watched Josie's three-year-old legs twirl her around with the other girls; no more calling the hospital to get the report on Evan while standing outside the dance studio in the rain. I took both my kids to the park and as I swung Josie, giving her the blastoffs on the swing she loved so much, I carried Evan in a Snugli, warm against my chest. Sure, there was a portable oxygen tank strapped over my shoulder, and yes, this was a heavy burden, but we were together at last.

I was so proud of my son when he came home, of his rapid weight gain, his ability to sleep through the night, of what a good baby he was. "This is such a good baby," I told my brother, my parents, and my friends. "Look at how sweet he is," I said. Asleep, Evan was fat cheeks; the same thick, pouty mouth as Josie's; tender slanted eyes like his dad's. The connection I had with my son, forged out of the crucible of his early birth and long hospitalization, only became stronger once he was home. At night, I lay in bed next to Evan in his portacrib and watched him sleep, that incomparable rise and fall of his chest beneath his blue pajama top, breaths on his own I would never take for granted. During the day, I fed and changed and bathed him like the proudest mother: put him in new, clean clothes; gave him massages at diaper-changing time; held him tight against me and took in his sweet-sour baby smell as I tried to feed him a bottle. I watched him gain weight like a champ, cleaned under the growing folds on his neck, pointed out to Cliff his slender, tiny feet. "They're just like your dad's," I said, remembering my father-in-law's size 9 shoes. "Remember what delicate feet your father had?" Even though my son could not look me in the eyes, and did not smile or laugh for months, I grew to recognize each of his subtle expressions: the raising of an eyebrow at the sound of music, a fist under his chin as he slept, the response of that same slender foot in my hand as I counted his toes.

I slept with his crib by my side; knew when the monitor was giving false alarms; understood that I would learn how to make the decisions about his care and find a way to be his mother. I'd determine the challenges of raising a child like him and I'd rise to them all. The fears I'd had at Central and beyond faded in the light of being home, and being Evan's mother. We had been through so much together; I could now reap the rewards of my devotion.

In coming home, I surprised myself. I fell in love with my son.

The bonds of love were strong. I called every doctor I'd been told to call, made every appointment. I had Evan at the pediatrician for his scheduled visits and weight checks—first every few days, then once a week, then once every two weeks. In between, I took him on the other rounds: the pulmonologist to check his lungs; Dr. Chang for his eyes; the neuro-ophthalmologist to examine his optic nerves; the ocularist to fit him for a prosthetic shell that would allow his left eye to grow at a pace equal to his right, despite the detached retina. I got to know the pharmacist by name, came to recognize the voices of the receptionists at our pediatrician's office and the eye doctor's. I learned where to find his medications and how to get the insurance company to authorize more than thirty days' worth of drugs so that we could buy them at reduced rates. I negotiated Medi-Cal forms, made sure to be home for the growing list of people who came to evaluate Evan and provide his services, called the insurance company's risk-management agent when our medical supply company went south on us. In turn, these providers all came to know me as the competent, organized, list-making mother of a super-preemie. I turned into a person who had preferences about not only medical tape and monitor leads but also which types of syringes were best (60 cc slip tip! Give that woman a slip-tip syringe!); one who could teach the nurses at various hospitals and doctors' offices how to administer medication through a G-tube; one who would even refuse certain syringes as not being appropriate—"I said, *Slip tip*. This is not a slip tip!"—and get results.

My husband stood in respectful awe of these newfound skills. After the first night Evan came home, and our fight over the bags and the feeding pump, Cliff and I had successfully divvied up the tasks in a seemingly natural way, not unlike any new set of parents. I organized the day; he went to work to support his family. Being home meant learning how to be a family in this way too—the triangle that had been Josie, Cliff, and I became a rectangle, with Evan and I more and more in a sort of parallel universe of doctors, appointments, therapists, and medical care. Since I was better at the details, and since I was home with Evan while Cliff was at work, many of the nuances of Evan's care fell to me. I made the appointments, digested the information, ordered the supplies, and taped the list to the cabinet.

During the day, as I took care of my son, I also worked hard to keep my daughter in her own routine, which now included a sibling unlike any of her friends'. I bought Josie a book called *Views from Our Shoes: On Having a Sibling with Special Needs,* and this became her own book of consolation, in much the same way that my Buddhist book had been mine. We read the sibling narratives and Josie came to know a world very different from that of her friends. Her three-year-old vocabulary now included words like *cerebral palsy* and *epilepsy* and *autism* and *Down syndrome* and *fragile X*. She bookmarked her favorite sections: Kate, whose brother J.T. had autism; Amy and her sister Jeannie, who'd been diagnosed with mental retardation; Sarah, whose brother Jeff had epilepsy. These I read over and over to her until she nearly had them memorized.

Apart from these stories and the occasional photo opportunity, my daughter showed little interest in being Evan's sister. Instead, she wanted to play "you be the sick patient, and I'll be the doctor," tying me up with strings to various machines in her room, the air conditioner doubling as an oxygen tank in her three-year-old mind. "Now I'm going to give you a shot," she'd say, using a toothpick to poke me in the arm. "Say ow!" "Ow!" I'd oblige. "Now tell me not to give you any more shots." "No more shots, please!" "Okay, now go to sleep, but just pretend, okay?" "Okay." If Evan needed me in the midst of this play, she begrudgingly allowed me to change a diaper or squirt a bit of formula, but only if it took "two minutes"—no more, no less, two minutes being the standard unit of measurement to a three-year-old.

I asked my own mother if I should be worried about Josie now that Evan was home, if some kind of delayed reaction to the twins' birth and Evan's condition might be coming my way. She reassured me that as long as I was doing a good job of taking care of Evan, Josie would feel confident that her world was held together too. I took the advice to heart and did everything I could to make it happen.

Through it all, in these beginning stages of being home, I believed. I believed my (blind) son could see, that my extremely premature son, my one-pound baby, would be okay. That the oxygen and the feeding tube and the medications were a temporary bump on the road to having a child who had problems but who would still be able to do the things children were meant to do, including walk and talk and play. I believed in all this because I didn't want to consider the alternative: a child who could not.

I told a social worker that Evan seemed a bit floppy. He didn't hold a position well, and needed me to control his arms and legs—more than I remember being the case with my daughter or other newborns and infants I'd held. His arms and legs were soft, pliable. It wasn't something specific I could describe, merely something I felt was different.

"Have you mentioned this to his therapists?" the social worker asked.

"No? Why?" Immediately I sensed that the insight must be significant.

"That seems like important information," she said, confirming my fears. "Not that I would know anything about it, of course. . . ."

I reported this conversation to Holly. We mulled over the words *important information*.

"She said that seems like important information?" Holly asked.

"Yes," I said. "Those were her words. *Important information.*"

"Important how?"

"Important as in tell someone, I think."

When I did reveal this information, the therapist who evaluated Evan couched its significance in vague terms that ruled out any clear prognosis. She said that owing to his extended time in the hospital, Evan had low muscle tone. She ordered a big blue foam seat that would hold him upright—the hope being that with this added support in sitting, his muscles would learn how to do it themselves. When I went to look up *low muscle tone* and *supported adaptive equipment* in the book on prematurity by my bedside, the words took me straight to a chapter on cerebral palsy. And there, on the same page, I was dismayed to see a picture of a child in this same blue seat. One afternoon when we were all in a bookstore, I found another picture in a book on cerebral palsy. Josie was in the kids' section, parsing out picture books. Cliff sat next to her with his own collection of martial arts magazines and Buddhist texts. I parked Evan beside us and showed Cliff the picture of the big blue seat. "It says here that some kids with cerebral palsy can have low tone, not high," I said. "Do you think that's Evan?" Cliff glanced at the pages, then back at me. "Those are just words," he said. "I hope you realize that."

I understood Cliff's point, the same one we had made many times over—that the words didn't mean a thing when it came to our son, they didn't dictate who Evan was or what he could do—but even so I wondered, holding this book in my lap. Was the therapist trying to tell us, by way of this blue foam seat, *Your son has cerebral palsy?* I was too afraid to ask; it was enough to know that my son, with his rapidly shrinking left eye, his feeding tube, and his oxygen, now sat in a piece of adaptive equipment reserved for yet another peer group that might be his: kids with cerebral palsy.

I now know that Evan's low muscle tone was in fact not the result of his extended hospital stay but of brain damage due to oxygen deprivation during birth, and that this low muscle tone did in fact correspond to certain types of cerebral palsy. Low muscle tone explained why it took my son until he was two to sit up, and until three to crawl, and why he couldn't hold his head up on his own until he was nearly a year old. Low muscle tone also makes it hard for intestines and bowels to work, and it impairs speaking and swallowing. Like every other diagnosis I would receive about my son, the words didn't change what Evan might or might not do. Even so, this was another case of hoping that if I worked hard enough, the story I secretly knew to be true—my son was disabled, he was impaired, he was imperfect—would not be true.

The absence of any obvious development in our son was another truth I wished I did not have to face. By the time he came home, Evan was nearly six months old and had yet to smile. A therapist in the NICU reminded me that the newborn smile was very tied to sight, and that because of his blindness, Evan's smile would surely be delayed. But no smile by six months? At the suggestion of our occupational therapist, I surrounded Evan with soft, silky items, hoping they would be pleasurable. I rubbed a satin blanket over the backs of his hands; he stared into the distance, content, but unresponsive. I put him under a baby gym and rattled the noisy toys. I moved his hands to touch the toys. He showed no interest in them at all. I rolled squeaky toys along his tummy. They didn't register. I put him in a swing, a jumper, a bouncy seat. He tolerated each fresh attempt and remained most comfortable lying by the fireplace on his sheepskin rug, his arms out to the sides, quietly listening to the classical music I played on the stereo. If I put a toy in his hand, Evan didn't even have the skill to put it to his mouth, an act typical babies mastered by four months of age. In those first weeks and months after he came home, it became difficult to ignore this lack of progress. "When will he hold a toy?" I asked. "Hard to say" came the reply. Even amid the bonds of my newfound love, these truths were disturbing. Cliff began to call him our Buddha baby. "We just have to see him as our Zen master," he said, "and let him lead the way." With that image in mind, we tried to put the worries about his development aside.

The absolute reality of how difficult our situation was came in the form of a visit to the cardiologist when Evan had been home a month. We had situated ourselves with his therapies and his floppy body and the absence of a smile. I'd gotten the tape to work on the feeding pump and survived the fight with the pediatrician over my nonuse of the apnea monitor. But it was the cardiologist who threw me back into the world of suffering like no one else.

While he was still in the hospital, Evan had been diagnosed with several congenital heart conditions, including pulmonary valve stenosis (which essentially meant that one of his heart valves didn't open and close all the way) and hypertrophic myocardiopathy (which meant that there was a thickening of the heart muscle). Both conditions were mysterious in origin; together they caused a pretty significant murmur (the same murmur that had had the anesthesiologists scratching their heads at Central for each and every surgery). I hadn't paid much attention to the heart issues. It was enough to worry about Evan's medications and therapy appointments, his feeding and oxygen dependency, his visual impairment and developmental delays.

In the office, Dr. Vance, an experienced cardiologist who had been in the business of looking at children's hearts for many years, ran a few tests on Evan. We began with an electrocardiogram in which no less than thirty leads were hooked up to my son's bare chest. Evan tolerated the trial the way he tolerated most things those days: quietly, patiently. No screaming, not from this child. When that test proved inconclusive, Dr. Vance shuffled us to a dark room and moved an ultrasound wand across Evan's breastbone, examining his heart function. These echocardiograms had been done multiple times on Evan in the hospital, but I had never witnessed one. Watching the monitor, I could see the blood flow through my son's heart, the pulsing waves of blue and red as the muscle pumped the blood along. Dr. Vance studied the monitor, moved the wand, pulled in for some close-ups. Finally, he turned the echocardiogram machine off and the lights back on and told me to dress my son. Once Evan was safely back in his car seat, Dr. Vance looked at me and said, "I examined your son in the NICU several times. I had hoped things would improve with this baby but that is not the case. His myocardiopathy is worse than before and the stenosis is putting enormous pressure on the valve."

"What are you saying?" I asked.

"Cases like this never turn out well," Dr. Vance said. "Babies with this condition grow up to be children who have open-heart surgery; they have pacemakers as teenagers. They rarely survive into middle age. It's a terrible condition, one of the worst you can have in cardiology."

In the chapter on fear in my Buddhist book, the writer tells the story of the man who discovered a snake in his mountain cabin: gripped with fear, he stays awake all night, staring at the snake, neither one of them moving. This is pure fear: the snake in the corner, the inability to move because by moving you will break the spell. With these words from Dr. Vance, I slipped right into that spell.

"What you're telling me is that this baby will never live to be your age, or even my age, and will probably not see thirty?"

"That's right."

"That I'm raising this deeply imperfect child so that he will die?"

"It's very bad to start where we're starting. The situation just becomes more dismal as time goes on," Dr. Vance concluded. "We'll put him on an additional beta-blocker to remove some of the pressure off his heart. I want to see you back here in six months. He'll need to be followed very closely."

Outside, after I'd received the prescription for yet another medication and made the requisite follow-up appointment, a drizzle came down. Evan was asleep now, bundled in a blue hooded sweatshirt, his thick cheeks taped to hold the cannula in place. I stood and watched the sidewalk go slick with the rain and had no idea where to go or what to do. Years later, when Evan turned three and school-district personnel came to evaluate him for placement in special education, I could tell the speech therapist to take her coffee cup off the top of my piano and I could point at the occupational therapist and tell her the words she used to describe my son were inaccurate and loaded and didn't belong in the report she was about to write. I could question diagnoses and shrug my shoulders when asked to put my finger on what made my nonverbal, nonambulatory blind son tick. I had developed those new and necessary instincts about my son, those that gave me confidence in what I knew to be true—and not—about him. Standing in the rain outside Dr. Vance's office, I had none of this capacity. Despite all we had been through, I had yet to become Evan's mother in a way that allowed me to think *What does that man know?* or *Time to get a second opinion.* Later, I would hear the father of an ex-preemie remark in an interview, "I don't know what made doctors and nurses think they could say anything and everything to us, but they did," and I would recognize our experience in his words.

I found myself walking toward Hampton, like a homing pigeon, to the place where others had been able to tell me things about Evan and where they had, seemingly, understood me. I entered through the emergency room, navigated my way into an elevator, and went up to the NICU. I asked to be buzzed in. I wasn't visiting Evan; I was bringing him to them. I have no idea what took me back to the hospital that rainy morning, other than the feeling that there wasn't a real home for Evan or me—that our new home wasn't equipped for this news, and that our old home, the NICU, could help bridge the gap between where we were before and where we were now. Later, when Evan started having seizures, I brought him back to this same hospital, this same home.

I tracked down Annalise, the occupational therapist, and told her about the appointment with Dr. Vance. She flagged down the social worker, since, as she put it, "Sharon is better at this stuff than I am." They took me into the same waiting room where we'd spoken to Dr. Masters and Dr. Vine about Ellie, more than six months earlier. "So this is it?" I said to Sharon when she arrived. "This is how it ends? With me burying two children?"

"Dr. Vance is a very good doctor," Sharon said. "I doubt he would exaggerate the problem."

"Sometimes I just want to throttle this baby," I said. "After everything he's put me through, I'd like to pick him up and throw him against the wall and walk away."

"You might not want to say those things out loud," Sharon said. "Some people might get the wrong idea."

"Oh, please. You know me. You know I'm not going to do that."

"Even so," she said, giving me her professional-social-worker look, the one that said *Be careful. Not everyone is your friend when it comes to honesty.*

"Are you getting help?" she asked. "You can't do all this by yourself. I'm sure that's why you are feeling so overwhelmed."

"I've just been told that my son won't live to be forty," I said. "So, yes, I am a bit overwhelmed. And, no, I'm not getting help." I thought of the med sheets, the pump, the oxygen, and all else. The therapies and the nursing care that had yet to arrive. "Who would you trust with a baby like this?" I asked her.

"Have you tried one of the nurses here?" she suggested. "They work for our patients' parents sometimes. I'll get you some numbers."

"Thanks, Sharon. I appreciate that. Really I do."

"Call one," she said. "You really need to have help."

At that moment, sitting in the room with Sharon and Evan, the same room where I'd argued months earlier about Ellie's future, her prognosis and outcome, the last thing I wanted was to censor myself and my reaction to Dr. Vance's news, or to hear Sharon's suggestions and platitudes. The NICU wasn't going to save me, even if one of the nurses came to my house to help. It was never your baby in the unit, but when you brought him home, it was your baby alone. Their job was done and mine had begun.

That night, I called my parents to tell them this new development. "What can I tell you, Vicki," my mother said. "The doctors who resuscitated those babies should be shot. They've left you with a severely disabled child and ruined your life and his. That's all there is to say."

I wanted to argue with my mother. I wanted to say, *You're*

wrong, he's not severely disabled. Maybe my life is ruined, and maybe his is too. But he is not disabled. Years later, it seems incredible to me that this was the point I wanted to argue. Yes, he was blind. Yes, he had a G-tube and oxygen. But nowhere in my heart or mind did I think of Evan as disabled. Just hearing the word aloud was enough to make me want to say the word *no* and keep saying it until it was true.

7

UNTIL I MOVED to Southern California I had no idea how much I disliked camellias. Some consider these finicky bushes with their waxy leaves and annual flowering to be a rare seasonal treat; I myself would much rather have an azalea or a lilac growing in my yard any day. I dislike the blooms the camellias offer, am disappointed that they don't smell, and find that they appear wilted within seconds of blossoming on the tree. Even their waxy leaves annoy me; the way they collect grime reminds me of how much pollution there is in the air. In my backyard there is a camellia I have tried, unsuccessfully, to yank out of the ground on a yearly basis; every spring, when it blooms, I can see the flowers just outside my dining room window and am reminded yet again that I shouldn't be so cruel. This plant has nothing against me, and so I allow it its barely tended life.

It seems fitting, then, that I live a mile away from gardens famous worldwide for their camellias, as if the plants are there to convince me, just as my own camellia tree has done, that they are just fine and that I need to let go of my irrational distaste. Visitors flock to the gardens during camellia season to see the array of white, pink, and red bouquets; on our own trips there, my daughter loves to pick up the blossoms where they have fallen and give them to me. The spring Evan came home, we went to the gardens with friends on Mother's Day, and Josie collected dozens of fallen camellias, handing each one to me as she picked it up. "I don't want this," I kept saying, and she kept giving them to me anyway. Eventually, I began to pile them on Evan's lap until his whole blanket was covered in them.

I was particularly irritated about the camellias—and everything else—that morning because our lives in the past several weeks had taken on further complications from the ordinary G-tube, oxygen, doctors' appointments, potential-heart-transplant-and-probable-not-living-past-forty concerns. At the end of April, just before Josie's fourth birthday, I'd awakened in the middle of the night to the sound of Evan crying, not a typical baby cry but one that was sharp, rhythmic, and intense. With each cry he also bent at the stomach, clenching his fists to his side. This happened five or six times. Immediately, I picked him up and tried to console him, and yet the cries and the jerking were beyond my comfort or anything Evan himself could control. Even he seemed shocked, somehow possessed. Eventually, the cries returned to normal and, finally, he went back to sleep. I settled him back in his crib and mentioned it to Cliff the next morning. "What do you think it is?" he asked. "I'm not sure," I said. "Maybe a bad dream?" With Evan it was impossible to know. The next day all was quiet, then he did it again that night, this time as he was falling asleep: the same sharp cry, the twitching in his body. I'd seen seizures before, but the behavior was so different from what I'd observed in Alexandra and in one other child in the NICU back at Hampton, I couldn't be sure.

Over the next several days I kept a close eye on Evan, hoping to catch an episode while Cliff was around. As if to foil me, Evan did not oblige, saving the cries and movements for me and me alone. Sometimes he'd start in with a telltale jerk as soon as Cliff left the room. By the time Cliff had returned, no matter how quickly I called him, the event had passed. My husband believed me when I said something was wrong; he just didn't witness with his own eyes what I described.

At Josie's fourth-birthday party, I parked Evan in his car seat right next to me and turned my back to him only when it was time to cut the cake. Later, when we were packing up, I said the words out loud to my brother: "I think Evan might be having seizures." I described the cries and the movements, then backpedaled a bit. "I don't know, maybe I'm wrong."

"What makes you think you're wrong?"

"What makes you think I'm right?"

He shrugged. "Usually when you think something is happening, it is."

I don't know what I was expecting him to say—maybe that I was prone to exaggeration or making things up. That Evan had enough wrong with him, I didn't need to be inventing seizures; that my reality had been permanently skewed by what I'd seen in the NICU. But his simple bit of advice was enough to make me consider the potential truth. Having said the words aloud, I had also admitted to myself they might be true, that my instincts might be right. The next day I held Evan in my arms and was on the phone with my friend Maria when he started doing it again. This time, there was someone else on the other end to listen.

"You need to call the doctor," Maria said after Evan's jerking and crying had ended. I had already mentioned my fears about seizures. "There's nothing normal about what I just heard."

I knew Maria was right and yet even as I made the appointment I hoped both she and I were wrong. I urged the pediatrician to fit me in that day, while Josie was still at preschool. "This is serious," I said.

Evan's regular pediatrician, Dr. Gaffney, wasn't available, and so we saw Dr. Strand, another doctor in the practice—the same doctor who had examined Josie at birth and whom I saw occasionally for Evan's appointments. I described what I had seen. Dr. Strand asked a few questions, then went to wash his hands. In between, he barely touched Evan (who was asleep in his car seat) except to examine his ankle joints. I now know that Dr. Strand was performing Step One of the Post-Seizure Physical Exam he'd learned in medical school—the examination purportedly offering information about the effect of the seizure on muscle tone and joint flexibility—just as I know that examining the ankle joints is not unlike putting leeches on the back of a febrile patient: it says nothing, does nothing, and means nothing. Even so, for Dr. Strand the information was conclusive.

"I saw a lot of seizures during Evan's time in the NICU," I said, hedging my bets. "None of them looked like this."

"There are a lot of different kinds of seizures," he said. "I'm sorry. You were right. This is slam-dunk seizure activity from everything you've described."

Afterward, Dr. Strand gave me the numbers of some neurologists and recommended I call them as soon as possible to start medication. He stressed that I needed to call right away, since it was hard to get an appointment, and I asked him, through my tears, if maybe he couldn't call the neurologist, if maybe that wouldn't get us in sooner. He couldn't. I wiped my tears, picked Evan up, and stowed him back in his car seat for our drive home. Then Dr. Strand showed me out of the office by the back door, a route that didn't involve my walking through the waiting room where other mothers and their children would see what a mess I was. I left through that back door to somehow find my way to the car, pick up my daughter, make dinner, tell my husband this news, and pretend to myself I was okay with this news, that I would find a way to handle it. After all this, after I was gone, Dr. Strand wrote in Evan's chart, *Dx: Seizure disorder. Consult neuro. Recommend psychological counseling for mother.*

Evan was readmitted to Hampton on May 8, 2001, and discharged on May 10. His one-page discharge summary stated the following:

REASON FOR ADMISSION: new-onset seizures

HOSPITAL COURSE: Patient was admitted to the pediatric ward and loaded on phenobarbital via G-tube. Patient subsequently placed on maintenance phenobarbital. EEG was done, which was abnormal. Head CT done, which was normal. Patient had no further seizures on phenobarbital.

TREATMENT: Patient was continued on home meds.

CONDITION ON DISCHARGE: Stable

PROCEDURES: EEG—bilateral sharp wave activity, right greater than left, mostly in the temporal region; Head CT—normal

FINAL DIAGNOSES: (1) new-onset seizures; (2) history of extreme prematurity; (3) bronchopulmonary dysplasia; (4) retinopathy of prematurity

Patient discharged to home; see Dr. Imus in two weeks, Dr. Gaffney in four days. Dated 5/10/01 by Dr. Montaldo.

No less than a week later, my daughter took a pair of scissors in the bath with her and cut off all her hair. I was on the phone with Evan's service coordinator, telling her about the seizures and the rehospitalization, when Josie called out to me that she wanted a pair of scissors. "To cut the bubbles," she explained. I was too preoccupied to question her and handed over a pair of baby scissors, then left the room to continue my conversation. When Josie paged me again, I got off the phone and walked into the bathroom to find her surrounded by mounds of hair—her hair.

"Josie! What did you do?"

"I just started cutting," she said, "and it was only a little bit at first, but then I liked the way the hair looked floating around in the tub and I just kept going."

The image of Josie's long brown locks on the surface of the water amid the white bubbles was stark, as stark as Ophelia must have been to Hamlet when he found her drowned. Even starker: the sight of her now very short hair, with only a tail in the back, a ringlet of hair she had not been able to reach. She'd done a good job, in fact, and later when we told friends the story, many of them wanted their own version of Josie's half-Twiggy, half-mullet hairstyle, but my heart broke when I realized how badly things were going. What kind of mother gives her child a pair of scissors in the bathtub? A mother with a very sick baby and a four-year-old who was trying to get her attention in the midst of it all, clearly.

"You know your hair isn't going to grow back right away, don't you?" It was the most consoling thing I could think of to say.

She nodded. "I'm sorry, Mommy."

"Don't be sorry," I said. "*I'm* sorry."

The haircut, along with the games we'd been playing since Evan came home—the "you be the patient" games—told me I did need to be worried about Josie. Not as worried as her preschool teachers, who offered editorials on the haircut and all else, but worried nonetheless. There was no denying that these pleas for attention came from a child under duress. The next day I bought Josie a can of colored hairspray and covered her short hair in sparkly green. She thought she looked very cool ("like Tinker Bell," she said) when she went off to school, and I felt only a little better about what had happened. That night I offered to let her cut my hair so that it looked like hers, if she wanted. She took the scissors and cut my bangs to within an inch of my head.

And so the picture of us on Mother's Day: Josie on Cliff's shoulders, smiling, with her Twiggy haircut; me kneeling by Evan's stroller, my bangs crisp and very short, to match her own. And there is Evan, a pile of wilted, brown-tipped camellias on his lap, passed out in a phenobarbital haze.

Within a few weeks of Mother's Day, Evan's seizures returned. Dr. Imus, the neurologist to whom we'd taken Evan, increased the medications' dosages; Evan got worse. We still had no words to put to what was happening, no real diagnosis. The CT scan of his head was normal, the test of his brain's electrical activity abnormal. This time when I asked the questions—of the neurologist and our pediatrician—I got shrugs, avoidance, general statements on the mysteries of the brain, as if I hadn't been sitting by his hospital bed for the past months doing everything right and didn't know how to keep asking the questions until I got answers. "Are these ex-preemie seizures?" I asked. "Why the late onset? How can you have a normal CT scan and an abnormal EEG?" There were no answers from the doctors, nothing more than "We'll just have to wait for the medication to kick in" and "Seizures are tricky." I remembered all the head-shaking and confusion over Alexandra. All the misleading tests, the trial and error. Cliff's work took him out of town often that spring and early summer, leaving me mostly alone to cope. The uncertainty of our son's medical course until now was nothing compared to watching a dozen seizures a day and not being able to do anything about them, not having any real answers from the doctors. I remembered the days I'd watched Alexandra's seizures and thought to myself, *That is much worse than what I have to deal with,* and now here I was, doing it myself, counting them, paying attention, asking the questions, getting the same vague answers.

The textbook definition of seizures, one Dr. Strand surely must have read in medical school, went something like this:

Temporary abnormal electrophysiologic phenomena of the brain, resulting in abnormal synchronization of electrical neuronal activity. Seizures can manifest as an alteration in mental state, tonic or clonic movements, and various other symptoms. They are due to temporary abnormal electrical activity of a group of brain cells. The medical syndrome of recurrent, unprovoked seizures is termed *epilepsy,* but some seizures may occur in people who do not have epilepsy.

In layman's terms, a seizure was essentially a misfiring of the brain's electrical energy that resulted in the cries and movements I'd seen with Evan and Alexandra. Seizure activity could almost always be traced to some type of abnormal brain activity. In Alexandra's case, there was an abnormality in the functioning of her basal ganglia, one of the deepest regions of the brain. In Evan's case, the EEG appeared to describe a focal point for the seizures within the temporal lobe, an area that controlled speech and auditory processing. Whether or not this abnormal brain activity spoke of actual brain damage was a chicken-and-egg kind of proposition. I had always considered Evan's seizures to be idiopathic, that is, "of unknown origin"; later, a doctor would tell me that owing to the circumstances surrounding his delivery—the four hours of labor without fetal monitoring, the fact that he had been blue and clearly oxygen-deprived at birth—that these all added up to a probable fact-finding of injury to the brain.

Beyond the definition and the science, though, was this: a seizure, when it arose, sent a parent into profound helplessness. Hence Holly's cries back at Central: "It's happening again. Why isn't anyone helping?" Watching Evan have a seizure was more sobering than seeing him hooked up to a ventilator, more frightening than holding my breath as a doctor searched for a vein to start an IV. At first, his eyes began to twitch. Then they rolled back in his head. Then the cries, one after another, as he shot forward at the waist, his fists clenching by his side, his legs stiff and unmoving. The area around his lips turned blue, then his whole face. His whole body jerked like this, sometimes twenty or thirty times. Finally, eventually, the seizure would end, his body would relax, and the cries would stop. A short while afterward, he'd fall asleep, exhausted from the effort.

One afternoon five people from the school district's special-education office sat on my couch and watched as Evan had a seizure that lasted for more than three minutes. Ten, then twenty, then thirty times he jerked at the waist, hands fisted, eyes rolled back, lips and face blue. None of them said a word; when I looked up at them from where I sat on the floor, holding Evan in my lap, they all seemed not to have noticed a thing.

Evan's occupational therapist came for a session and witnessed a bout. "You need to call the doctor," she said. "You need to stress that he is cluster seizing."

Cluster seizing. It certainly sounded serious when put that way.

In a previous conversation I'd had with Dr. Imus, he'd mentioned that we might be adding yet another medication to his regimen, one that came as a sprinkle to put on his food. "But he isn't taking solids by mouth yet," I said.

"He's ten months old and he's not taking solids," Dr. Imus said. "What's wrong with him?"

Um, he's G-tube fed, has no suck or swallow, and can't tolerate anything being near his mouth. . . .

"He's a super-preemie," I said. "We haven't started him on solids yet. Is there any other form the drug comes in? The baby has a G-tube."

"If he doesn't improve after next week, we'll start him on Topamax," he said. "I'll be away on vacation until a week from Monday. Get in touch with me when I get back."

A Friday, four o'clock: Evan's condition had deteriorated further. He'd had twenty seizures that day, in clusters of fifteen, twenty, sometimes thirty spasms. All day I'd been on seizure watch; all day I'd charted them. I called the pediatrician and asked for Evan to be readmitted to the hospital. My husband was out of town on business and I had to pick my daughter up from preschool by five. "I can't spend the weekend with him like this," I said. When I gave the doctor on call Evan's history and told him he was a super-preemie with newly diagnosed seizure disorder, the man corrected me. "He's an *ex*–super-preemie," he stated, as if to say: *And yes, I'll humor you. We'll go ahead and readmit.*

If the doctors had lined up at Evan and Ellie's birth to do the impossible, to prove all that medical science could do to save one-pound babies, I was to learn how little those medical professionals on the other side of that accomplishment could or would do to help. Already I had hardly any faith in the neurologist who had left on vacation. I had had a glimpse of the unwillingness of the pediatrician to assist us without giving his own bit of editorializing. When we arrived upstairs on the pediatric unit at Hampton for the second time in as many months, the house pediatrician said to me, "I don't know why you're here," meaning, I think, that there was no reason for a child with uncontrollable seizures to be in the hospital getting care. "You've never had control of the seizures," she said, as if this were news to me.

In Admissions, the intake person, upon learning that Evan was an ex-preemie, stopped typing for a moment to ask if I would be going to the NICU reunion that was scheduled for the next day.

Evan was beside me in his car seat. I hadn't taken my eyes off him, seizure patrol being a twenty-four-hour watch. I turned my gaze for a moment to look the clerk in the eye. "Excuse me?" I asked.

"Well, my son was a preemie too," she said, starting to type again. "My husband and I are going. I was just wondering if you're planning to attend. I know they like to see the babies—"

Her earnestness stunned me. "I'm sorry. Was your son born at twenty-three weeks? Is he blind? Does he have a G-tube? Did he go home on oxygen and a million medications?" I couldn't believe what I was saying; the words just kept spilling out. "Is he about to be readmitted to this hospital for uncontrolled seizures?"

The woman had stopped typing and looked at me directly. "Well, no," she said.

"Well, then, you and I have very little in common, really," I told her. "And no, we won't be going to the reunion."

The next day, the irony of the NICU reunion was not lost on me. Evan lay in a large pediatric crib with thick, tall bars on each side. The crib dwarfed him, and given his phenobarbital haze, the picture was even less rosy. There on the lawn below me were doctors and nurses I recognized, babies dressed up, their proud parents bouncing them on their knees. I thought for a moment about joining them, telling Dr. Lamb and Dr. Tam and Annalise and the others about this latest complication, gaining their pity or at least their recognition that Evan's future seemed bleak right now. I looked down from Evan's hospital room to the lawn and saw the balloons and the tables of food and the magicians and the face-painting. I saw parents milling around, the success stories of healthy NICU graduates in their arms and running across the grass. I turned back to Evan; he lay in the hospital crib, dressed in the standard blue pajamas handed out on the pediatric unit, and I knew I couldn't go downstairs, not then and probably not ever. I would say only mean things, awful things. I would list all that was imperfect with my own ex–super-preemie, and I'd dismiss every positive step Evan had taken. I didn't need to remind the doctors about all they hadn't told me. There were so many truths. The reality of the healthy NICU graduates there on the lawn didn't cancel out mine, nor did mine cancel out theirs.

A week later I called the hospital and asked for Evan's name to be taken off the mailing list of NICU grads so that in the future I would not know about these reunions, the parties, the celebrations.

I had often been warned of the various reasons why Evan might be readmitted to the hospital: pneumonia, infection, failure to thrive. *These preemies are unpredictable*, I'd been told. *You think they're doing fine and then one day, poof, they just stop breathing.* If I lived moment to moment in those days, it was for this very reason, that Evan could be a walking time bomb of complications, and that the next time around, or with each successive admission, the situation could get worse.

You think the NICU is bad, I'd heard. *Try peds.*

Every parent who graduates from the NICU only to be read-mitted to a hospital's pediatric unit will tell you how different the two experiences can be. In the NICU there was one nurse for every three babies, and parents were considered auxiliary. *They say it's your baby but until you go home, it's not your baby.* Parents were frequently kept out of important decisions un-less their consent was needed, and they were rarely apprised of their child's condition voluntarily, nor were they allowed to read the chart or question dosages or medications. I once sug-gested that Evan's worsening lung condition might be a func-tion of decreased dosages of a steroid, only to be told, "Interest-ing . . . ," and then ignored.

In peds (rhyming, not inappropriately, with *needs*), the NICU world of doctor-parent-patient interaction was turned upside down. One nurse covered a whole wing of the unit, sometimes ten or fifteen beds. My first night on peds, in Evan's first hospitalization, I discovered that the lights went out at ten o'clock at night and that when a child cried he or she kept cry-ing until the nurse arrived, sometimes half an hour later. I had heard such a child in that first readmission, heard him cry on and off most of the night. "What's wrong with him?" I finally asked the nurse at the desk. "He's got pneumonia and his par-ents went home," she said, shaking her head. "What can you do? They said they needed to sleep. . . ." In peds, the nurses and doctors not only wanted a parent to stay the night, they expected it. "You'll be staying the night, of course," the nurse said to me that Friday when she showed us to our room. She pointed out the chair that became a bed. "There are directions on how to open it," she said. "And we'll give you fresh sheets." My mother told me I shouldn't wear myself out by spending the night at Evan's bedside, but I remembered Holly's experience with Alexandra on peds and knew that if I were to go home I'd have no idea of what his night was like. Seizures weren't charted unless I mentioned them—the time came when I simply held on to the seizure chart myself rather than rely on the nurse to document them—and medications often arrived late. If Evan experienced pain, I asked for Tylenol and administered it with my own syringe rather than wait for the nurse to bring one. When it was time to change the tape on his cannula, I borrowed a pair of scissors, used my own tape, and did it myself.

The Friday Evan was readmitted to Hampton for breakthrough seizures, the doctor covering for Dr. Imus during his vacation appeared in the examining room as I provided Evan's history. "I'm Dr. Kalnan," she introduced herself. "I guess I should be listening to this. Do any of you have a pen?"

Clearly Dr. Kalnan would not inspire confidence; Dr. Heaver, the house pediatrician, dismissed Evan's seizures as "nothing more than he was already doing," and suggested a loading dose of phenobarbital. They did a blood test and found the levels of seizure medication in his bloodstream were low; Dr. Kalnan increased the dose. Nothing else was suggested. "I wish I could help you," Dr. Heaver said when I sought her out at the nurses' station. "Frankly the baby is stable, and I really think we've done everything we can." I happened to run into Joanna, a nurse from Nursery C in the NICU, as I left the hospital that night. I told her about Evan's seizures and the medications and how we had forgone the reunion after being readmitted to peds. "Well, think of it this way," she said, giving me a hug. "Now you really do have something to write about."

I called Holly that night to give her the news about Evan's readmission. Holly would know what to do; Holly would help. Holly was the one person who understood about seizures and medications and what it was like when a child took a mother beyond all the doctors. Cliff cut short a business trip after this new hospitalization and took over Josie's care, but the strain of the seizures affected him as well as me. We were both lost, upset, and distraught. "I'm going to call Holly," I told him as I left the house that night, *calling Holly* having become code for "I'm going to get help from someone who understands." I stood in the supermarket parking lot, across the street from the hospital, and told Holly about Evan's seizures, the abnormal EEG and the normal CT scan, and the vacationing neurologist and the unhelpful house pediatrician, the one who had told me she didn't know why we were there and then had gone on to lecture me about learning the dosages of Evan's medications in milligrams rather than milliliters—"You're smart enough to figure this out," Dr. Heaver had said. "The volume of medication is irrelevant. What we need is the actual *dosage.*"

"She said she didn't know what you were doing there?" Holly said. "How about trying to get help for your sick child? Oh my God, Vicki. I'm so sorry."

"They always warned us the NICU was nothing compared to peds," I said. "I know it's in his chart, but I doubt they would even remember to give him his medication."

"Or the right *dosage,*" Holly said. "Vicki, six seizures a day is not in control."

"The neurologist said we might have to get used to the fact that we won't be able to control them. He told us some kids just have seizures."

"That's ridiculous." Holly went on to tell me that in three weeks at University Medical Center, Alexandra had gone from thirty seizures a day to none.

The news came as if through a haze. "Alexandra's seizures are under control?" I said.

"She's been in control since March," Holly said. "After I called you that night, things changed fast. They upped her dosages and it took a while, but after three weeks she was seizure free."

Seizure free? Alexandra?

"Forget that stupid doctor with her dosages—"

"Wait a minute," I said. "Let's go back to the part where Alexandra is seizure free. The same girl they put into a coma at Central? That girl has stopped having seizures?"

Holly laughed. She sounded like a different person, the person I wanted to be. "I know, it's crazy. I never thought it was possible."

I looked out at the half-empty parking lot. It was now nearly eleven. Evan was in the hospital across the street, waiting for me. My internal medication clock reminded me that he would need his Inderal in a few minutes. Who knew how many seizures he'd had since I had left him at dinnertime? I thought back to the image of Dr. Heaver at the nurses' station telling me that she had done everything she could and that she didn't see any point in Evan staying more than one night. "There's not much more we can do for him," she'd said.

"We need to get you out of there," Holly said. "First thing Monday, I'm calling Dr. Steele at University Medical Center."

"What do I do between now and then?" I asked.

"Remember rule number twenty-five?" she said, referring to the patient's bill of rights. "They can't keep you there against your wishes. Take him home."

Once again, home had become something very different. Home was where we returned when the doctors couldn't help, where it became easier to watch Evan have a seizure in his own bed, next to me, than it was for me to chart it for some nurse who might or might not appear. Home included all the supplies I needed without my having to ask for them, and the right syringes too. "I realized we couldn't solve every last one of Evan's problems in the hospital," I told my friend Maria when she asked me how it was we had come home after only one night. "It's not going to be that simple."

Home was where I now hung tight and waited: for the increased doses of medication to kick in, for doctors to call me back. For my son to get better, or worse.

Believing in the impossible.

Years later, when I went to write about this time, this one phrase came to mind again and again. By then, Evan had actually started walking and no longer resembled the drugged, distressed baby we'd nursed along that spring. When the words came to me, I'd been able through force of will and instinct and a fierce attachment to my son to see him to a place no one would have predicted for him, the place where he laughed and smiled and felt his way around the house, where he learned to take steps despite not being able to see a thing. Where he had a walker and a cane and ten team members who all loved him and, to their credit, also believed. I was different, changed. I became the person who could tell the occupational therapist which words not to include in her report. I could meet her professional gaze and say, "You were in my son's room for all of ten seconds. I doubt you even touched him. He sees a world-renowned neurologist. I'm going to save those diagnostic words for him." I was no longer afraid or in denial; I could sit in a waiting room and engage in all sorts of black humor about the world of disability. I had advice for others. I knit and did not cry.

The person I had become, the one who stood firm and loved her son, was also someone remarkably detached from who she'd been—the person I was before Evan was born, and even the person I was when Evan first came home. Eventually, I had no investment in Evan doing anything, didn't trust he'd keep it up, had to tell the others, "He's going to do what he's going to do when he's going to do it," and let them feel their own way to that same detachment. This was my balance: fearsome attachment and strength when called for, combined with the utter compassionate distance from all outcome. It was a balance I worked on every day of my life. I spoke to a friend to tell her that Evan had started walking and I said, "It's inconceivable to me. You put in the time, the therapy, the doctors' appointments, the tests and the drugs and all else and then, wow, he actually gets up and does it. I had no idea it would turn out this way." By then, I had reached the point, finally, where I did not ask for much when it came to Evan. Yes, during that terrible spring, I wanted relief from the seizures, for his sake and mine, but I never put him on a list to have his retinas transplanted, didn't force-feed him or even make him wear the leg braces the physical therapist recommended. A friend later said to me, "You're really good at accepting what comes and not expecting anything else." Truthfully, I didn't know how to do anything else.

Later, Dr. Steele himself would write to me, after seeing a video of Evan taking steps, "What a determined kid and how fortunate to have a mom to help him get to this point. Parents clearly make all the difference in the world." The differences I made? Getting him to Dr. Steele in the first place. Standing by him while his head was hooked up to electrodes for a second EEG, this one at the University Medical Center. Telling medical professionals not to call me Mom but to use my real name instead. Insisting on dignity rather than pity for my family. Loving Evan, no matter who he was. Is that what cured his seizures, eventually, or had him taking steps at the age of five and a half? Was it, somewhere along the line, believing in the impossible? I suppose I must have held on to some animistic belief deep down beneath my grief and suffering. So often I was reminded of Piaget's theory of assimilation and accommodation and how they swing back and forth in a perfect pendulum whose ideal state is equilibrium. Eventually, my equilibrium became this compassionate detachment. During the days of Evan's seizures, the state of grace and balance was much more hard-won. In those days of seizures and NICU reunions and rehospitalizations, I was very aware of all that Evan had taught me from the day he was born, and that was quite the opposite of believing in the impossible: expect nothing; take whatever comes; live in the moment. Put one foot in front of the other. When things get bad, keep your head down and try not to look people in the eye. They won't like what they see. Believing in the impossible would have meant: cure the seizures; bring me back my (already imperfect) child; release me from the misery of another hospital, another team of doctors.

If my faith in the medical had been sorely tested in my time with Evan, there still resided, in its deepest reaches, a profound belief not only in the impossible, but also, perhaps even more important, in the power of a specialist. When Holly spoke of Dr. Steele and his miraculous abilities, this was the equivalent of a medical sweet spot: the guy who would make all the others look like fools. If Dr. Steele had brought Alexandra from the place where she'd been in a coma and still seizing uncontrollably, then surely he could help Evan. Men like Dr. Steele gave medicine a good name; they were the guys who kept us believing. They made swift decisions and didn't feign ignorance. I didn't expect a miracle where Evan was concerned, but after

Drs. Heaver, Imus, and Kalnan, it was a relief to consider putting myself in the hands of someone who would see the problem as a problem—and not an unsolvable mystery—and come up with a plan. And so, a week after Evan's readmission to Hampton, my husband and I drove with Evan into the deepest San Fernando Valley to meet with Dr. Steele, Alexandra's brilliant neurologist, at a satellite office of the world-renowned University Medical Center. I had shared with Cliff my research on the man and informed him that Dr. Steele was, indeed, respected all over the globe for his research into pediatric epilepsy. He wasn't just a specialist, in other words, he was *The Man*. Like me, Cliff was hopeful.

We arrived early and were waiting outside the office when Dr. Steele's nurse appeared. Charlotte was warm and affable, knew our names, had a chart ready and waiting for us. There was no paperwork to fill out, no annoying medical history questionnaires, just plain talk. We sat in a quiet waiting room, the only patients. Eventually, I heard the soft, kind voice of Dr. Steele as he asked about the morning's appointments. Then Charlotte called us in.

"I hear you're having some problems with your boy," Dr. Steele said, shaking first my hand, then Cliff's. "Why don't you tell me what's going on?"

The gaze in his blue eyes was kind, gentle. I recited the history of Evan's seizures and listed the medications he was on, the frequency and dosage.

"Let's have a look."

I took Evan out of his car seat and laid him down on the examination table. Dr. Steele handled my son gently, and with great tenderness. I realized that it was the first time since Evan had come home that we were in the presence of a doctor who didn't seem afraid of my son or reluctant to become involved.

"I'm concerned about his muscle tone," I said to him. "I feel like he's a bit floppy."

Dr. Steele touched Evan's legs and hips and tested his range of motion. Evan was quiet, calm. "His tone is a little on the low side," he said. "But it's not too bad. Low tone is still better than high tone."

I knew from my research into muscle tone that high tone spoke of severe cerebral palsy, but low tone indicated a milder condition. "So no severe cerebral palsy?" I asked.

Dr. Steele shook his head. "I don't think so. Did he have any kind of intraventricular bleeding after he was born?"

"No."

"You realize that at his gestational age that's a miracle, right? Ninety-five percent of kids born that early have some kind of brain bleed. Is it your sense that since he's been having these seizures the baby's development has stopped?" he asked.

Cliff and I looked at each other. Before Mother's Day, Evan had seemed on the verge of rolling. Now he could hardly even hold up his head. "I would say so," I said.

Cliff agreed. "Is it the seizures? Do they stop development?"

He and I had already debated the chicken-and-egg aspect of seizures, of whether or not brain damage caused seizures—and stalled development—or if the seizures themselves caused brain damage. Either way, Dr. Steele had just confirmed the fact that Evan's lack of development was problematic, and definitely connected to the seizures.

"When a kid is busy seizing all day," Dr. Steele said, "it's pretty much impossible for him to develop and grow. Okay, kiddo," he said to Evan, putting him back in his stroller. "Let's go talk in my office."

I strapped Evan in and wheeled him into an adjacent office behind Cliff and Dr. Steele. Once we were all sitting down,

Dr. Steele placed his hands on his desk and said to us, "Based on your description of Evan's seizures, and the fact that he had stopped developing since the onset of the seizures, I suspect Evan might have a condition called infantile spasms. I need you to know that this is potentially a very serious seizure disorder. It's imperative that we confirm with another EEG and start treatment immediately. Can you get to UMC this afternoon for a repeat EEG?"

"You can't confirm the diagnosis with the EEG they did at Hampton?" I asked.

"I like to do my own tests," he said. "Besides, things may have changed since that last EEG. It would be better if you could come to UMC."

"I can do that," I said. "If that's what we need to do."

"I want to see you back in my office Monday morning," Dr. Steele said. "I'll have the results of the test by then and we can discuss our options."

Three hours later, I navigated the warren of corridors and dead ends that led me to the EEG lab at University Medical Center. In the car ride home from Dr. Steele's office, Cliff and I had shared our relief over the appointment. We weren't waiting, we were taking action. Dr. Steele believed this was serious. Cliff returned to work and I took the next bargaining step with my son.

Perhaps it was believing in the impossible, perhaps it was my faith in the world of the specialists. Between the two, my confidence in Dr. Steele and his decisiveness was enough to carry me through to another hospital, another procedure, more (potentially) bad news. In the EEG lab, I laid Evan down on a gurney and the EEG tech began the slow, laborious process of applying twenty-one electrodes to strategic locations on Evan's scalp.

"I'm sorry about this paste," he said, indicating the thick white stuff that would transmit electrical activity from Evan's brain to the probes and on into the machine. "Usually it washes off with shampoo." When he was done, he wrapped Evan's head in so many layers of gauze, my son looked like a cross between Frankenstein's monster and the Mummy. Except that his eyes, peering out from under the gauze, were a lovely warm brown, and his mouth, beneath the oxygen cannula, formed itself into that same thick pout I had come to love. "I feel like I should take a picture," I said. "Have you ever seen a cuter mummy?"

The tech smiled. "I can see why you'd want to," he said. "He is pretty cute."

As the tech left the room to sit at a computer terminal just outside, I held my son's hand and thought about how off the definition of *cute* had become in our world. *Cute* was a smile, a laugh, a funny burp. *Cute* was not a bandaged head with EEG probes emerging from it. The tech leaned back inside and said, "I'm getting started now. Let me know if you notice a seizure during the test. It's actually better if he has a seizure while we're running the test. That way we can compare the observed seizure with the brain activity we're measuring."

Better. Just like *cute*, the definitions were changing all the time.

Of all the tests done to Evan over the years, the EEG had to be the most inscrutable. Even neurologists have a hard time decoding those mysterious waves and electrical activity of the brain, their frequency and amplitude. In an EEG, the probes connected to the scalp pick up the activity of the brain's neurons and then translate that activity into a picture of how, at that moment, the brain's electrical activity—specifically its voltage—functioned. Compared to the EEG at Hampton, this procedure at UMC was the height of technology. The Hampton

EEG had been the old-fashioned kind, with needles skittering across a roll of paper, not unlike a lie-detector test. That test looked positively medieval compared to the computerized rendering of Evan's brain waves now being recorded, charted, and measured. There was no margin for error here; whatever we found on this test was going to tell the truth in the way the previous one had not.

After all I had witnessed with Evan—intubations and extubations, twenty-three blood transfusions, countless IV sticks, one particularly bad afternoon in the NICU where they were trying to get arterial access and had to cut into both his ankles and wrists before they succeeded—this was the first procedure I actually turned away from, since the information on the screen meant absolutely nothing to me. Even the tech told me he had no ability to translate the wave patterns he observed.

As the test ran, my eyes went back and forth between the screen and Evan, and sure enough, as if to oblige the EEG gods, the neurologist, and everyone else, Evan had a nifty little spasm right there in the office. The tech didn't notice, but I did. "He's having one," I said. "Right now."

Mother notes seizure activity at 1418 hours and 1425.

Did the brain waves notice? Did something magical take place on the screen? It hardly mattered, except that it *helped* the neurologist and was *better* for Evan to have a seizure while the test was running. Ten minutes later the test ended. As I unwrapped the gauze and then wiped the thick white paste from his hair, I actually kissed Evan and thanked him for cooperating.

That Monday I sat in Dr. Steele's office to hear his interpretation of that same EEG and its results. "There's been a significant deterioration in the baby's EEG," he said. "He most definitely has infantile spasms and we have to change his treatment plan immediately."

Between the Friday of the EEG and that Monday's appointment, I'd done enough research to know that the rare and significant seizure disorder Dr. Steele had suspected in our original consult also had potentially devastating outcomes. Infantile spasms. An innocent-sounding diagnosis, one I'd gone on to discover described one of the worst seizure disorders a child could have: up to 80 percent of children with infantile spasms developed severe mental retardation or autism or both. The news stunned me. *This? This was what we'd now been given?* In our first days and weeks in the hospital after the twins were born a doctor had said to us, "I don't think about the statistics, I don't discuss them. They don't mean anything when it's happening to your baby." For the first time I understood how true this was. So 40 to 80 percent of kids with infantile spasms turned out to be severely retarded—what did that mean to us or to Evan? We had a blind child, a child on oxygen and a feeding tube. I'd accustomed myself to the world of multiple disabilities. And now would this be our future too? An autistic child, one with severe mental retardation?

My father was with me during that appointment with Dr. Steele. Later he would tell me that even as I'd described the symptoms of Evan's seizures to him over the phone, he'd known without seeing them that they were spasms, and he'd planned this trip, without my knowing it, to help bring this news to light. My father has always been considered a terrific diagnostician, but this news, his knowing from three thousand miles away what was wrong with my son when the doctors looking right at Evan didn't, this ability elevated him to the role of psychic.

In the examination room, Evan lay in his car seat on the table. Before the seizures, he had loved the crinkly paper covering the examination tables, had rolled around and grabbed at it and smiled at the sound it made. Now, he was so sedated he didn't even wake up enough for me to take him out of his car seat. Dr. Steele sat across from me. My dad was in the only other chair, next to the examination table. I stood, using the wall to hold me up.

My father took notes as Dr. Steele outlined his plan. The definitive diagnosis of infantile spasms lay there between us and weighed especially heavy on my father, the only one brave enough at Evan's birth to maintain, "These kids do not turn out just fine," and equally compassionate enough never to say, "I told you so." I hadn't even shared with Cliff the information I'd read about spasms. Until there was an official diagnosis, I saw no reason to worry him too. It was my father then who bore the brunt of this news, who was there to witness it with me. After Dr. Steele explained prognosis and treatment plans, he presented us with a choice. "I have a study we're conducting that has room for a few more patients, patients like Evan who have just been diagnosed with infantile spasms and who have not had any other treatments," he said. "We're doing research on whether or not this drug, Vigabatrin, is useful in spasms." He paused. "The drug isn't FDA approved—I think I'm probably one of the only guys around who can prescribe it, thanks to the study." He went on to outline the terms of the study and what it would mean for Evan to participate.

"Vigabatrin?" I said. In my desperate weekend of research, I'd learned that this was the most hopeful drug for kids with infantile spasms, but that due to potentially dangerous side effects, the FDA had not approved its use in the United States. I'd read stories of parents obtaining Vigabatrin from Canada and Mexico, of black markets and bartering. There were also miraculous stories of the Vigabatrin stopping the seizures cold, even in kids who'd been having dozens of spasms a day. I had actually seen Dr. Steele's name associated with the very study he now described, a study clearly labeled Closed to New Participants on a website I'd stumbled upon over the weekend. Was it believing in the impossible to think that the one person in the country who might help my child was the person I had somehow found? Was this my golden dragon working his magic yet again?

"You can prescribe Vigabatrin for the baby?" I asked. "I thought the study was closed."

Dr. Steele smiled. "So you've heard of it."

"Vigabatrin is like a miracle cure when it comes to spasms."

"I wouldn't go that far," he said. "We've had success, and it's certainly far less invasive than other treatment options. But the drug is still not FDA approved. We've been unable to adequately prove its efficacy. Evan is only eligible for the study because he's not been diagnosed before now, and because he has not been treated for the spasms with any other drug protocol. Plus, we caught it early. Studies have shown that when Vigabatrin is the first course of treatment and you're able to start within six to eight weeks of the spasms appearing, you've got a better chance. After that, the seizures become fairly intractable. You see much worse results the longer you wait."

Dr. Steele paused and looked directly at me with the candor of a person who, like Dr. Chang at Central, delivered hard news every day as part of his job.

"I'm not going to pull any punches here," he said. "Kids with this seizure disorder used to end up profoundly autistic, retarded, completely shut off. Their seizures were so intractable there was nothing to be done, no hope whatsoever. More recently, we came to treat these kids with an army of drugs, including steroids, which often made them very sick. Some of them died. But the Vigabatrin gives us another option, a very good option. I'd say you were pretty lucky you came to me when you did. This slot I want to hold for Evan is one of the last ones available."

Dr. Steele warned us of side effects and gave us a schedule for stopping the old drugs and starting the new. "The Tegretol he's on," he said. "We've learned that in the case of spasms it makes the seizures worse, not better. That's probably why his seizures increased when you upped the dose. And the pheno-barb. I don't like to use it. It's an old drug, one of the first gen-eration of anti-epileptics, and it's got disastrous consequences for cognitive development. Have you noticed any changes in the baby's awareness since he's been on it?"

We all looked at Evan, still slumped in his car seat, asleep.

"He's pretty sedated," my dad said.

"It's unorthodox to wean him so quickly and start the new drugs so fast," Dr. Steele said. "Typically we like to go a lot slower. Because we're going so fast, you may see him get a lot worse before he gets better."

"Should we have Valium on hand?" my dad asked. "In case we need to stop the seizures?"

Dr. Steele gave my dad a long look. "Just how is it that you're aware of Valium for seizures? That's not exactly common knowledge."

"I'm a retired child psychiatrist specializing in kids with de-velopmental disabilities," my dad said. "I've seen my share of seizures."

"Well then, you probably know a lot more about what's go-ing on here than you'd care to," Dr. Steele said quietly.

The two of them exchanged a look, doctor to doctor, and that was when I started to cry. Dr. Steele was right. My dad did know too much about what was going on. He'd known too much from the day the twins were born. Dr. Steele turned to me and asked, "And how are *you* with all this?"

"I'm okay," I said. And I was. That one question, amid all the hard news I'd just heard, was enough to make me, at that moment, some new version of okay, one where *okay* meant *I can take this, I can do this, I can walk out of here with all this news and figure out how to go on.*

> *I want him to be 100 percent seizure free.*
> *I want him to develop and grow.*
> *I want the Vigabatrin and Topamax to work*
> *For his good and the good of all concerned.*
> *I want him to develop and grow.*
> *I want the Vigabatrin and Topamax to work.*
> *I want him to be 100 percent seizure free*
> *For his good and the good of all concerned.*

It was impossible to know how to phrase the intentions this time around. What exactly did I want? Nothing less than what I knew I could not handle: *Please, not me, not that child, not the forever-disabled child, the nonambulatory nonverbal child. Let that be another mother's fate. Please.* In our new world, in the division of pediatric neurology at the University Medical Center, there were many other children in worse shape than Evan, kids who would most definitely be nonambulatory and nonverbal. Why did Evan deserve to escape that fate? And what right did I have to want that for him, a cure?

My husband took the news about the diagnosis of spasms the way he took most news about Evan: if there was no way to change what was happening, he worked his way toward some new adjustment. Not me. I bargained and begged, looked for new words and with them new faith or hope. *Chance* became a word I used, then avoided, then used again. *Should we chance it?* I asked myself when I learned that while the Vigabatrin could cure his seizures it might also impair what little eyesight he had left. Dr. Chang didn't recommend taking the chance. Dr. Steele said it was up to us, but in my mind, we really had no choice. "He seems to think your chances are good," my dad said after our first meeting with Dr. Steele. This idea of chance went beyond religion or faith, beyond the days of invocations at Central or the moments of samsara when Evan was at Hampton the first time around. It was both palpable and visceral. *Chance.* A nice word, a good word, not something you would be smote down for believing.

I read about the kids with infantile spasms, read their parents' appeals on message boards and websites, and felt my chances ebb and flow. What worked for you? What made a difference? Did anyone know about Dr. X at Hospital Y? *We've just had our thirtieth seizure of the day and we've been through ACTH, Vigabatrin, Topamax, Zonegran, the ketogenic diet, and vagal nerve stimulation. Nothing works. Does anyone have any advice for us at all?* This was desperation beyond NICU-parent desperation. The news here was, if possible, worse than any I had read about before. More than half of all children with infantile spasms developed intractable seizures—those that would never be controlled. Whether or not the seizures were controlled, almost 80 percent of those with the disease went on to become permanently disabled. *By all accounts the majority of patients with infantile spasms suffer a poor outcome with respect to chronic epilepsy, mental retardation, and other neurodevelopmental disabilities.*

On the afternoon I drove back from University Medical Center after Evan's EEG and before we started in the Vigabatrin study, I asked my dad about Evan's prognosis. I had read about a future of mental retardation and developmental disabilities. "I don't know, Vicki," my dad said. "The baby might end up with mental retardation. It's possible." Before he'd said those words, I'd lived in a world in which many of Evan's complications could be cured, a world where he might, in the end, make a reasonable recovery. With stem-cell research and other technologies, his blindness could someday be reversed. The other demands of taking care of a chronically ill child might recede—he could learn how to eat, walk, maybe even talk. The oxygen would be gone, certainly, and probably the feeding tube too. When I told Holly that Evan had West syndrome, another term for the disorder, she was shocked. Evan's seizures were potentially worse than Alexandra's. "Years ago kids like these always ended up in institutions," Dr. Steele had said. "You'd never get control of their seizures and they'd just get worse and worse until they were profoundly autistic and mentally retarded and there was no hope for them whatsoever."

I could not conceive of this as our future, nor could I believe we had gone through two hundred days in a hospital to end up here. Somehow the steps from Evan's drugged haze to life in an institution seemed too dramatic for me to believe in. Perhaps I was foolish; perhaps my system of denial had kicked in wholeheartedly. I suppose any doctor looking at me with this child would not identify him as a "well, wonderful baby," as I'd actually heard myself telling his first neurologist. Even reading the diagnostic descriptions of the seizures themselves came like salve on my wounds. Now I had a reference point when I read that kids with infantile spasms had salaam seizures, so called because the child bent over at the waist and raised his or her fisted hands out to the sides. Immediately, from the description, I recognized my son's movements and understood why they were so atypical of the various seizures I'd seen before. Or that the Tegretol actually made them worse. And that the combination of drugs he was on now was the safest and most effective treatment. I read that Evan's chances were better (that word again) because his seizure disorder was of idiopathic, or unknown, origin. For some reason, I focused on only the good news.

Today I marvel not only at my naiveté but also at just how deep my denial went. Today, when I research the statistics on infantile spasms and see the disorder described as catastrophic, the news is more than sobering. At the time, I was so caught up in the dynamics of Evan's care and drugs, so relieved to have a name for what was happening, a description and a diagnosis, I never allowed myself to contemplate the outcome. The fear that had encapsulated my life with Evan in the hospital, at his birth, with the eye surgeries—it was gone. Taking its place: a state of absolute suspended animation. I walked more slowly, tried to drive safely, took my time in every gesture so as not to see and know what was actually going on around me. And I thought about chance.

I think we have a chance, Dr. Steele had said.
We got to this early, that helps our chances.
There's a chance.

Compared with the days of waiting at Central, and the days of praying over Evan's eyes, and even the first days and weeks after he was born, the days of his seizures were far worse. I was so very far away from a place where my fix-it fingers could operate that all I could do was wait for the seizures to strike and hope the aftermath would offer some release until the next time around. I lived minute to minute, hour to hour. Maybe this is why I never stood back to contemplate the long-term consequences or outcomes. I didn't have the capacity.

I say *I* because, although Cliff was there, and Josie, and my mother and father, increasingly this became my own journey, or my journey with Evan. The bonds of love, forged in the NICU and made even stronger in his homecoming, had grown ever tighter, so entrenched now as to become nearly visceral. This intensity left little room for anyone else. Only I was strong or daring or brave enough to go where Evan now went, to witness and become part of his haywire brain. I took Evan to the clinical-trial appointments; I saw him through EEGs and examinations. Somewhere during this time, my daughter's hair grew back and a new preschool year began. My husband went off to work every day and came home at night, and while those lives carried on, I sat beside my son, sunk into his big blue chair, contemplating the word *chance*. One night I reached into the cabinet above the kitchen sink where we kept Evan's medicines and took out the phenobarbital.

"Want some?" I asked Cliff. I'd already had two glasses of wine and was looking for a deeper buzz.

"Seriously?"

"Why not? It was good enough for jazzmen, right?"

Another husband might have called in the psychiatrists. My husband knew me well enough—and loved me strongly enough—not to judge. Instead, he joined me. We each downed a medicine cup full, then compared notes.

"Nasty taste," he said, commenting on the bitter flavor.

"I'm a little sleepy," I said. "But not much else."

"Me neither."

I decided the phenobarbital wasn't the high I was looking for. The next night I reached for the Topamax. This time, I kept it to myself, aware that even Cliff might think I'd gone too far. Phenobarb was one thing, but Topamax? Where was the kick in that?

It wasn't so much that I wanted to get high—though I did—it was more that I wanted to know what the drugs did, how Evan felt with them in his system. Once the Topamax kicked in, I understood all too well why my son was so woozy and unresponsive. I felt like I was on LSD, only in a slow motion, tripping and wanting to fall asleep at the same time, with a little bit of a speedy edge to the whole thing. All in all, there was nothing fun about it. The next night I stuck to the drugs my own doctor had prescribed, those that kept me awake when I needed to be awake and asleep when that was the proper state.

My connection to Evan, so deep that I found myself taking his drugs instead of my own, eventually reached a point where I knew when a seizure was about to happen—I'd open his diaper and Evan would pee all over my hand and I'd think, *Here it comes,* and sure enough, he'd start to seize. Or I'd be in the front seat of the car and hear something off about his voice and I'd know, *He's having one.* Once, driving with my dad, I said, "Check on Evan, something's going on," and he turned around and remarked that he seemed fine, and I knew, with dead certainty, that he'd had another seizure, despite the absence of the cry or the movements. In the world of seizures, many parents describe an aura that appears before the child is struck, a sense of something amiss that is nearly visible. I came to know this aura, just as eventually I could hear one of Evan's seizures even if I was in the other room—I'd just get it right away, I'd know, I'd be right there.

According to all the reports, the Vigabatrin, if it succeeded, would work within the first two weeks of treatment. Only then would Evan be considered a responder. Now that we were in the hands of the best neurologist in the country, the only man who could prescribe the very drug that would help my son—and now that Evan, my master brinksman and golden dragon, could list both *seizure disorder* and *drug-study participant* on his medical CV—I was more determined than ever to be a success. Not just for Evan's sake, but for my own as well. I crushed the drug, said a prayer, squirted it into his G-tube. And I waited.

> *I want the Vigabatrin to work.*
> *I want his seizures to be under control.*
> *I want him to develop.*
> *Please let the Vigabatrin work.*
> *Please let the seizures be under control—100 percent.*

The seizure diary we kept at the time tells the hard facts, the tapering-off of the seizures—seven the first day of treatment, then five, then four and two and one—and then, incredibly, a day on which they stopped: July 17. Nothing. The morning passed. None. Then the afternoon. The note I wrote in the seizure diary read, *Very drowsy, awake only from 12–4 p.m.* But no seizures. I'd take a sleepy baby over one with ten or twenty or thirty spasms a day. That night, as I put Evan down in his crib, I held my breath. Nothing. Just an ordinary baby, falling into an ordinary sleep.

The next day, July 18: *More wakeful.* No seizures.

Dare I hope? I sent an e-mail to our contact at the University Medical Center, who wrote back to say, *Dr. Steele is smiling.* I called my dad. "Evan went a whole day without a seizure."

"That's incredible."

"Do you think it's working? Do you think he'll be a responder?"

"I don't know, Vicki," he said. "But this is a very good sign."

Maybe we had a chance.

That morning, I looked at my boy with new eyes, allowed myself to notice the day was sunny. I dressed Evan up for his scheduled study visit at the University Medical Center, picking out a matching blue outfit and the striped fleece jacket I liked so much. Yet again I could envision a day so simple my only task would be to pick out the clothes my son might wear. I dropped Josie off at daycare, my eyes still on Evan, sleeping in his fleece. My responder. I imagined the look on Dr. Steele's face, a smile. I would brag about our two days spent "seizure free!" By ten a.m., I stood outside the medical building in the bright sunlight, ready to head inside. There, under the blue skies, I saw it—the eyes first, then the fists, then the cry.

No, I heard myself thinking. *No.* No.

The seizures were back. Evan was not a responder.

8

ON EVAN'S FIRST BIRTHDAY, I bought a cake and took pictures. *Our Boy, One Year Old Today,* I wrote for the caption. Can't hold up his head, totally zonked from meds, had five seizures before this picture was taken. Blind. Delayed. Maybe cognitively impaired. Definitely not a responder. Evan screamed as I put the cake in his lap; his hands swept across the white frosting and he flung the stuff from his fingers as if even butter cream were an insult to his system. He was still on oxygen, and some of the frosting caught on the cannula. That is the picture I have of him on that day: his face red with rage, Josie with her pixie haircut patiently looking on.

"How's my boy?" a friend asked over the phone after extending birthday greetings.

"I don't know what to say. You really have to see him to understand. He's a year old, he can't sit up, barely even holds his head up, doesn't eat, still on oxygen, can't get control of the seizures. It's a mess."

There was a pause. "That sounds so . . . hard. Have you thought about a support group?"

Did this person have any idea what she was saying? *No, she doesn't, that's why she just said it.* And I learned then the art of the phrase *I have to go.*

Which is what I did a lot in those days—I left. For work,

the supermarket, the drugstore, a night out with a friend. For lunch with Holly or a trip to the mall. I left Evan in the care of a nurse, went to Wal-Mart to buy a pair of sunglasses I'd have for the next six years. I left our pediatrician, Dr. Gaffney, for another. "I'm sorry," I said as I took Evan's chart from her hand. "I just don't trust you anymore. Both you and Dr. Imus missed the diagnosis. I just can't stay with this practice." If I couldn't change the situation or make it any better, the next best option was to flee.

Sometimes I even left my son. One night, when Evan's labored breathing next to me kept me awake, I went to sleep in Josie's room. I could lie next to him all night and listen for his every breath and cry and seizure, or I could abandon him and sleep. He didn't wear the monitor, and Cliff might not wake up. That night, I left my son's side knowing I also left him to his fate.

On a flight home from Hawaii with Josie and Cliff, long before the twins were born, I remember noticing a developmentally disabled boy in the row in front of us. He was fifteen or so, traveling with his mother and siblings. The boy played with a fire truck during the entire flight; he did not speak except in unintelligible sounds. His mother yelled at him often about some frustration or annoyance, and I felt for her: how hard it was, how angry she seemed. And yet she could not turn her back on this boy.

Surely she had felt the way I did that night I left Evan's bedside: if something was going to happen, so be it. I had done my job for that day. I had given him his meds, charted his seizures, and checked in with the doctor to see if there was anything more we could do. There wasn't. Whatever might come along to relieve me of this burden I would accept.

• • •

In the weeks before Evan and Ellie's first birthday, Cliff and I talked about making plans for a grave for our daughter. It had been more than a year since Curt and I had visited the ancient and beautiful cemetery east of town and I'd wondered, hearing the noise of the children on the hillside below, *Do the dead really notice, do they care about the living?* By now I had lost the list of cemeteries the social worker had given me and recognized the effort to bury Ellie for what it was: something profound and internal and not to be resolved with cemetery-shopping trips. I started a story I titled, not ironically, "The Twelve Times We Tried to Bury Our Daughter."

I asked my parents to help me fill in the pieces with their recollections of the visit they'd made to the funeral home the Thursday after Ellie died. "The young man who helped us had just had a baby six weeks earlier," my mother told me. "He looked like this was the worst day of his life. He showed us urns with ABC blocks on them, another with angels and butterflies. We asked him for something plainer."

I tried to picture the scene but could not.

"We paid for the cremation and ordered the death certificates and told him you'd be back the next day to sit with her ashes. The whole visit took less than an hour."

So there were numbers two and three and four—*my parents picking out the urn, plans for the cremation, death certificates*—made at a funeral home not half a mile from the hospital. CHURCHILL & SONS, MORTUARY. A place barely five minutes from my house, one I had driven by so many times and never even noticed until the day we went to sit with Ellie's ashes.

The last day, I would write much later. *We held you again then, four hands on that box, two hearts that dreamed of a girl coasting to the sky on a swing, trailing feet in the dirt, dropping from the monkey bars into the arms of a sister, a mother, a friend.*

To the list of imagined attempts to bury my daughter I might have added my trip to the accountant seven months after the twins were born. It was March, and Evan had just come home. He was there with me for my appointment with Jim, the accountant. He lay in his car seat, the oxygen tank in the basket underneath, the cannula fastened to his cheeks with medical tape stretched tight across his cheeks. "Doesn't that hurt?" Jim asked. "The tape? It looks so uncomfortable."

"I think it must," I said. "He tries to pull it off all the time." Always the pragmatist, I added, "I keep having to come up with new methods."

We paused a moment, taking in the reality of Evan: the tape, the G-tube, the blindness, the uncertain future. I rattled a toy against his hands. Briefly, just for a moment, I thought I saw his fingers reach for it. Jim returned to the papers on his desk and I took out my list of various deductions. "You know, we could probably claim Ellie on our tax form," I said. "Evan had a twin sister. She died."

Jim's eyes grew bright. "We'd need a Social Security number," he said, tapping his pencil.

"I have one." The nurses at Hampton had made sure we filled out this form as well as the birth certificates.

"You do? That's great!" Jim rubbed his hands together, contemplating the extra seventy-five-hundred-dollar allowance on our tax form, then looked up at me and said, "I'm sorry."

"For what?" I asked.

"For getting so excited about the deduction."

"Don't feel bad. I'm the one who brought it up."

There was no etiquette for a baby who'd lived for four days and was now ash on a bedroom radiator. Shortly after Ellie died, I'd submitted a death benefit to the insurance company, and six weeks later, I'd deposited their five-hundred-dollar check into our savings account. That would have been attempt number nine, then, before "use her Social Security number to obtain tax deduction."

I had Ellie's death certificate in a file behind the birth certificates of my living children; we had her urn on the radiator in my bedroom. Later I would hear the story of a friend who had had a baby born at twenty weeks; he'd died in her arms after an hour of life. Less than a week after the baby died, this friend had a funeral with a coffin and family and friends. She found a spot and placed a marker and interred her son publicly. I listened to the story and wondered, *How?* How did this mother have the strength to face so directly her loss? How could she manage to ask others to experience the loss with her? Everything about Ellie's birth and death had been private for us; a year later her memorial, the one we kept hoping we would plan, had yet to take place.

When it came to Evan and trying to move forward, we had somehow begun to figure out our lives as the parents of a disabled son. When it came to Ellie and knowing how to incorporate a dead daughter or her burial into our lives, we were stalled, unable to move past step ten. My journal tells me that we planned to scatter Ellie's ashes on July 30, Evan and Ellie's birthday. The event never took place. There is nothing that tells me why it didn't, and now, years later, I still do not remember what stopped us.

We did not have a ceremony of any kind on the anniversary of Ellie's death, August 3. We did not buy balloons and let them go into the sky as I had once considered, nor did we invite friends over to eat a meal or light candles or share our grief with us. Friends had asked, on Evan and Ellie's birthday, "What about Ellie? Will you be doing something for her?," gently calling attention to the unfinished business that lay between us. I am not one to judge the means and ways others have for funerals or memorials or interment of family members lost before their time, but even I had begun to feel a bit ashamed, aware that in not burying Ellie we had also somehow ignored her, not given her what she deserved.

Around Evan's birthday, our sitter Elizabeth asked me if I'd ever considered Forest Lawn Memorial Park for Ellie. The guru of Elizabeth's religion, the Self-Realization Fellowship, was buried there. Forest Lawn was no more than fifteen minutes from our house, and yet it was not a cemetery I remembered from the social worker's list of long ago. On a hot Saturday in August, I convinced Cliff that we should take the drive. As we made our way through the gates and into the cemetery's green, rolling hillsides, Cliff and I both noticed how peaceful and lovely a place it was. The hillsides were dotted with large California pines, and the gravestones were discrete, lying flat among the hills. "It's not as ugly as I thought it would be," I said.

"It's not ugly at all," he said.

The cemetery was on a rise that offered views of the surrounding valley. To the north and east lay Pasadena, where we lived; to the south, downtown Los Angeles. When we drove home that afternoon, I noticed the cemetery's green hillsides from the freeway. There was comfort to me in knowing this, that a route I often took from home to school or a friend's house or even Central Hospital, where Evan continued to see his specialists, would be a drive that might take me past the hillside that held Ellie's gravesite too. Before we'd left we stopped by the office to get a brochure about prices and availability and made an appointment with the woman who would finally help us sort out the details of the burial we had long delayed. *Shirley Darling* read the name on her card. *Like a song*, I thought.

• • •

My first thought about Shirley Darling, eighty years old, half-blind, and even more deaf, was that she ought to have been put out to pasture long ago. In our first appointment, a week after that exploratory visit to Forest Lawn on our own, it was I who decoded the prices in her binder, I who sorted through and pointed out to her the available options. I had to shout my every desire and instruction, only to repeat myself and help her when she dropped the binder containing the graveyard's map and price list into the gutter. In that first meeting, Shirley so frustrated me that when we were done I was ready to call her boss and demand her retirement. "How can you have someone selling plots who is halfway there herself?"

But if Shirley was deaf and half-blind, my son Evan was fully blind. If Shirley had trouble walking and could probably have used a cane, my son, with his uncontrolled seizures and failure to hold up his head at a year old, might never walk. In this first year as Evan's mother, I had been repeatedly humbled by death and disability, and so I drew in a breath and found patience I'd never needed before for white-haired Shirley in her orthopedic sandals. Cliff, Josie, Evan, and I followed Shirley in our car as she led the way around the cemetery, driving her small copper sedan no more than five miles an hour. She stopped to show us a niche in a gated area called the Triumphant Fate Terraces—popular for its privacy—and then another in an enclosed area, the Freedom Mausoleum, that smelled and looked, with its beige tile, like nothing less than a janitor's closet.

"If this isn't where I'd want to go to my last reward," I told Cliff, apropos of the janitor's closet, "I'm certainly not going to put Ellie here."

No doubt sensing our disappointment, Shirley drove us up the road to a last option, an open area called the Columbarium of Harmony. Cliff put Evan in his stroller, and Josie and I walked behind Shirley up the short path to a small, closed-in collection of niches where there was an opening to the sky. Looking up, I could feel the fresh air and hear the birds. Inside this place were walls of niches on three sides, arranged in rows twenty wide by thirty high. Each niche was no more than eight inches wide by twelve inches tall. Large enough, she told me, to hold four separate urns. We'd have enough room for everyone but Josie. Or Evan.

Josie skipped in and out of the space, her red sequined shoes tapping a rhythm on the marble surface. Evan had started crying and Cliff pushed him back and forth in the stroller.

"How much are these?" I asked Shirley. The other niches we'd seen had ranged in price from a thousand dollars, for the one in the wide open, to three thousand, for the gated, private spots.

"It depends on where you want to be," Shirley said. She fumbled with her binder of prices and nearly dropped it again, for the third time. "Let me see what's available."

Using the schematic in her binder as a guide, I searched for the corresponding niches as she read some numbers aloud. One was up nearly at the top, another way down below, nearly at ground level. "There's one about eight rows up," she said. "Fifty-four ten."

I spotted the niche and saw it was nearly eye level and visible. We could reach it to place flowers when we visited. We would be able to read, without straining our necks, the plaque we planned to have engraved. "I like it," I said. "It's in a good spot."

"That one is two thousand and ninety," she said. "Plus the endowment care and tablet, witness to placement, vase placement—"

"Vase placement?"

"Those knobs you see for the vases," Shirley explained, pointing out something the size of a drawer pull cemented to the front of a niche.

"The niche doesn't come with one?"

"Unfortunately not."

"How much?"

"I'd have to check," she said. "I think it's no more than thirty dollars."

"So how much altogether?" I asked.

Shirley added up the costs on her memo pad, taking a long time to write each item, crossing some out and rewriting them again with different, hopefully correct, amounts. "Roughly thirty-six hundred dollars, if you want a Saturday interment. That's an extra two hundred and eighty-five."

"Thirty-six hundred dollars," I said. "That's a lot of money."

Next to me, Cliff pushed Evan back and forth in the stroller, clearly annoyed that I was looking for bargains when it came to our daughter's memorial care.

"Sometimes you can find people selling plots—"

"Selling them?"

"—in the newspaper," Shirley explained.

I looked askance, and skeptical.

"Well, they have *value*, you know," she said. "And if someone moves or changes their mind, they own them, and they're allowed to resell them."

"Are you telling me we might find a niche for resale in the classifieds for less?"

"You might," she said. "But you won't have much choice of location. Remember, this is a lifelong investment."

Cliff remained silent during this discussion. I could see on his face the humiliation of being married to a bargain cemetery shopper and yet I could not find a way to stop myself from going into these details. Nor did I see how a niche in a cemetery constituted a "lifelong investment." And then I remembered the urn on our radiator. It wasn't respectful to keep Ellie's ashes in such a temporary spot for the rest of our lives either. By now Evan was crying inconsolably and Josie pulled at my hand, dragging me back to the car. "We'll be in touch," I said.

"That's fine," Shirley said. "Remember, though. Once the niche is gone, it's gone. And this is a very nice spot for the money."

"Of course," I said. "Of course you're right."

We drove away then, with Shirley calling out after us, "Bye-bye, Mr. Tomato."

"Did she just call you Mr. Tomato?" I asked Cliff.

"I think so," he said. "But what do you expect from a woman whose name is Shirley Darling?"

Pages and pages of my journal still held invocations for Evan and his seizures—*I want him to develop and grow. I want the seizures to stop. I want him to be cured.* The seizure diary still reported six, ten, sometimes twenty spasms a day. The drugs hadn't taken hold and I no longer considered myself particularly lucky for having found Dr. Steele or Vigabatrin. When I mentioned to Evan's eye doctor his Vigabatrin dose, the man said, "That's a lot of Vigabatrin," telling me what I'd already suspected: if the drug hadn't worked in that amount, our chances were no very longer good.

One night, as we lay in bed in the dark, I heard Cliff say, "I want to talk about Ellie. It's time, I'm ready," and I could hear past the words all his sadness and resignation. I had begun to wonder myself—mystically, irrationally—if Evan would only get better once Ellie was buried. I told Cliff my theory. He concurred. "They have some kind of pact with one another," he said. "They have to, they're twins."

"So if we bury her . . ."

"It's official—he's survived."

And so it was agreed: we would find a way—find it necessary—to bury Ellie, and let her spirit go.

Before we could formally inter Ellie's ashes, there was one more visit with Shirley Darling I had to endure, and that was our meeting to pay for niche 5410 in the Columbarium of Harmony and order a plaque. The day before Labor Day I went back to Forest Lawn and sat across a desk from Shirley in a designated "need-counselor" cubicle, filled out the necessary forms, and wrote a check for $3623.80, which amount we had taken out of our savings account. Shirley and I struggled over every part of the three-page, carbon-copy form. She made a mistake in each box; I had to guide her hand to the proper space for our names, address, and phone numbers. "Maybe I should fill it out myself?" I asked.

"Unfortunately I can't let you do that," Shirley said. "The laws of the State of California require that I complete the form."

Forty-five minutes later, Shirley discovered she had made some irreversible mistake and we would have to start all over. "I won't take long," she said. She lifted her briefcase to find a fresh, blank form and managed to spill its entire contents on the desk. "Oh dear, I'm so sorry," she said. "Just give me a minute to pick up these papers."

If this were a comedy of manners, the pile of papers on the floor might elicit the biggest laugh of the day. But I had seen Shirley drop too many papers already and I cringed at the thought of spending one more minute in this need-counselor cubicle with Shirley Darling. We had been at it for nearly an hour. I was tired and thirsty and ready to go home. We still had not picked out a design for the plaque on Ellie's grave and I knew I did not want to return and do this all over again. I took a deep breath and waited for her to copy over the infor-

mation, working with such concentration she was the definition of *laborious*.

My father tells the story of purchasing a plot for his uncle,
shortly after the man had died. My father and his aunt and his
cousin sat in the need counselor's office, discussing their various options. The counselor explained that the gravesite they
had in mind would hold two coffins. "Are there other family
members who might require plots?" the counselor asked.

"My cousin," my father responded.

"Is he with us?" the counselor asked.

"Yes, he's with us."

"And where is he?"

"He's *with* us—" My father tried to stress the *with*, because,
in fact, his cousin Melvin sat in a chair behind them in the
same office.

"So he's with us?" the man repeated.

"Yes," my father finally said. "He's *with* us. That's him, sitting right there."

I remembered that story yet again as Shirley applied herself
the second time around to this all-important form, aware that
humor and death are often not far apart. Finally, she came to
the end of her task and we could finish the job of discussing
the plaque.

"Here are your choices of styles," Shirley said, handing me
a laminated page of bronze plaques. "These are the images that
are also available. You could have an angel engraved, or a heart
if you like."

"I think I'll pass. How big a plaque can the space accommo-
date?" The tablets I saw before me ranged in size from eight-by-
ten to much bigger. I wanted enough room to engrave a message
like the one on Ellie's urn, which read *Forever in Our Hearts*.

"We have a display across the hall," Shirley said. "Let's go
have a look."

The display room held dozens of plaques, in all sizes, with all sorts of phrasing. There were bronzed profiles engraved into the markers of deceased, along with images of crosses and the angels and hearts Shirley had mentioned. The plaque that would fit on Ellie's niche was small—no bigger than six inches wide by eight inches high—and could hold only four lines of text, with sixteen letters per line. I added up the lines in my head. One for my daughter's last name, another for her first, then her birthday, and the date of her death. The writer in me wanted more room. "Are you sure we can't add another line?" I asked. "Or use a bigger plaque?"

Shirley was sure. "I'm afraid that's the only option," she said. "Remember, you'll want to keep a few lines free for your names, when you pass."

The idea that I would add my name, or Cliff's, to this plaque was beyond me. On the sketch I would later receive of Ellie's inscription, I saw those two extra lines Shirley had urged me to keep free for other family members and I wondered, *Why did I listen to her? Why didn't I add* Forever in Our Hearts? At the time, I was too tired from the hour I'd already spent in her office to argue. I didn't question the determination, nor did I press about fonts, or lower- and uppercase lettering. I wanted to be done with Shirley and done with this task and so I left her with the following inscription:

KAMIDA

ELEANOR ANNE

JULY 30TH–

AUGUST 3RD, 2000

Afterward I would call Shirley and ask for the wording to be changed. I did not want the *th* or the *rd*. These abbreviations sounded too informal, somehow not right. In the world of words and language that still held me so powerfully in its sway, these tiny details made a difference. We had a disabled son and a dead daughter, and somehow I still believed that if I could get the wording right, we would also in some way be fine, in the end.

Two weeks before Ellie's interment, I received a note from Shirley along with my copy of the form she'd so laboriously completed.

> Dear Vicki & Clifford,
>
> So very nice to meet you both and my thoughts are with you in making arrangements for Eleanor Anne. I'm so glad you have your little boy.
>
> Here is a copy of the vase order—and a map.
>
> On Saturday, Sept. 22, if you wish, you can stop by the Information Booth and verify as we list every service and where they will meet. I'm sure everything will go very smoothly.
>
> It will take approximately 6–8 weeks for the tablet to be placed. You will be notified but the vase service will be on 9-22-01.
>
> > Sincerely,
> > Shirley Darling

We arrived at Forest Lawn to inter Ellie's ashes early in the day on September 22, a Saturday. I had the urn, the permit to hold the ashes at home, and the death certificate, all of which Shirley had instructed us to bring. Together with Cliff and Josie, I had picked out photographs to put inside the niche with the ashes. We had a picture of Evan and of us as a family and a note from Josie that read *I love you Ellie*. Here we were, then, at steps eleven and twelve.

The niche was open when we arrived, a small aluminum stepping stool in front. There was a single witness from the cemetery, a young man with close-cropped hair who wore a blue blazer and khaki slacks. He ran his hands through his hair, and when he saw the four of us—Cliff, Josie, myself, Evan in his stroller—he asked, "Are there more to your party?"

"No," I said. "Just us."

Until that moment it had felt necessary that we do this alone, as a family of four that had once, briefly, been five. Cliff and I had agreed on this point, on the privacy and simplicity. Now, in exposing ourselves, so few, to the young man with the blue blazer and groomed hair, I wondered if once again I had hoped to escape the true meaning of this by not telling anyone, as if in keeping it to ourselves I had also, somehow, neglected to acknowledge the reality of what we were about to do. It was too late, on this September morning, to quickly call friends or family. We had decided to perform this interment alone, and so here we were, just the four of us.

The young man reached for the urn in my hand. "Well, we can get started, then." He climbed the step stool and put the urn inside the niche.

"We have pictures too," I said, handing them to him.

The day was cool, fall-like. Up on the hillside, a few trees had started to change color. The young man leaned the pictures against the urn and descended the stool. "Take as long as you like to say your words," he said, removing himself a step or two.

I lit candles and incense. Cliff and I each stood in front of the exposed niche. In the same way that I had not wanted to give up Ellie's body on the morning she died, I could not bring myself to think that this would be the last time I would see the urn that held her ashes. This letting-go had been taking place over such a long time, and still I was not ready. I had asked Shirley if we could open the niche if we wanted to see the urn again. "You can open it any time," she said. "But it's rather expensive."

"How expensive?"

"A thousand dollars," she said. "Typically a family only opens the niche if they plan to move the cremains." *And sell the niche in the newspaper,* I thought.

So that was it, then. Ellie's ashes, once interred, were going to stay inside the niche. There would be no holding the urn or touching it again. One by one, the steps in her burial were becoming more and more final, complete.

In time, I would learn to accept this distance and detachment. Despite our not being able to hold her urn, this niche of Ellie's at Forest Lawn would come to feel like another part of our lives, a place we would know to be as meaningful as any other important site—a former apartment, a park my children loved. In time, I would come to think of Ellie as more than a missing piece in our lives, something forever lost and gone. But the day we put her ashes in the niche, I had no sense that this would ever be true, or that her gravesite would ever become a place of comfort. Instead, I said what I thought was goodbye.

I held my breath as the nameless young man slid the cover on the niche, and we saw Ellie's urn and the photos and the note for the last time. Today, I can't remember what is inside the niche other than Ellie's ashes. I cannot picture any of the tokens we put there. When the niche was sealed I'd simply thought to myself, *Is that it, then? Is this better, an improvement?*

9

I TOOK TO THE ROAD that October, Evan in the back seat, a pound of red licorice in my lap, and an audio book of Dominick Dunne's *Another City, Not My Own,* his narrative of the O.J. Simpson trial, on my tape player. I was on Interstate 40 on my way to Albuquerque, New Mexico, where Evan was scheduled for eight hours of alternative touch-therapy sessions spanning two days.

Over that summer, a good friend of mine with a chronic illness had convinced me to try the therapy—which had given her remarkable results with her own disease, its pain and symptoms—on Evan. Western medicine, with its drugs and procedures, had not cured my son; perhaps the alternative might help. The particular system had been developed by a woman who was herself a physical therapist; it focused on functional body processes, using therapeutic touch to help the body heal itself on a cellular level. The underlying premise of the therapy was that the body was a series of integrated systems that didn't always function together, and that touch, applied in the right places with the right amount of intensity and with the proper attention to the body's response, could help reintegrate bodily function and, by doing so, heal illness and disease. I'd found a practitioner out by the airport who had begun the long, slow process of teasing apart congestion—all by touch—in Evan's nerves, tendons, arteries, veins, and muscles. Before the seizures had begun, I took Evan to Ginger, the therapist, to address tightness in his neck that had caused Evan's head to tilt permanently to one side. Ginger diagnosed the condition as torticollis—sustained contraction of the muscles around the neck—and established the condition as being connected to his G-tube surgery. "His neck is reacting to the insult on his stomach," Ginger said, pointing to a chart of the human body in her office and explaining the anatomical basis for her theory. I marveled at the diagnosis. I had taken Evan to both a physical therapist and a chiropractor for his torticollis. Neither of them had suggested a connection to the G-tube. And yet I somehow knew Ginger, who herself had been a physical therapist, was right. "He didn't have a problem with his neck until his G-tube surgery," I said. "The tightness appeared immediately afterward."

"And probably everyone just tells you to keep stretching it," she said.

"Yes, but it goes right back."

"Precisely. That's because you're not treating the underlying source. I used to see this all the time as a physical therapist. You treat bursitis, for example, by applying heat and working to increase range of motion at the joint. But if you never work on addressing the source of the bursitis, which could be an old injury around which the body has defended itself, you'll never get rid of the pain. With this therapy, we work to identify and treat the underlying source, allowing the body to heal at the source, rather than focusing entirely on symptoms."

Evan's torticollis had become so acute his neck tilted permanently at an angle. This in turn placed pressure on the back of his skull, causing his head to become misshapen. At our first appointment with Dr. Steele, he'd mentioned what he called the "major minor" issue of Evan's positional plagiocephaly and recommended helmet therapy. So in addition to taking his long list of medications and going to his therapies, my son now also wore a helmet, night and day, to reshape his still-malleable skull. If Ginger thought the misshapen head and the tight, twisted neck were all connected to the insult of his G-tube, of course I was willing to consider the possibility. And if she also thought that a trip to Albuquerque that fall to meet with the therapy's founder might help us find an underlying cause for the far worse conditions we now faced, the seizures and the lack of response to the Vigabatrin, I would find a way to get him to Albuquerque too. In our journey together, Evan had led me to three different hospitals, inside CT scans and MRIs, deep into the recesses of his brain, on detours through drugs and therapies. The path had me taking his drugs to see what they might do for me. Of course I'd take to the road to see if that might change things for him, and for me. Perhaps Albuquerque would help when all else had failed: the drugs, the prayers, the invocations.

By October, Evan's original list of medications had morphed into something even more complicated than the one that accompanied him home that February:

> 7 a.m.
>   Inderal—1.5 ml
>
> 8 a.m.
>   TPM—125 mg
>   (one large 100 mg tab, one small 25 mg tab)
>   Solids
>   Linum B_6—½ capsule
>
> 10 a.m.
>   9 oz formula
>   VGB—2 tabs
>
> 11 a.m.
>   Solids

1 p.m.
  Inderal—1.5 ml
  9 oz formula
  Zonegran—35 mg (14 ccs)

6 p.m.
  Solids
  9 oz formula

8 p.m.
  TPM—125 mg
  (one large 100 mg tab, one small 25 mg tab)

9 p.m.
  VGB—2 tabs

11 p.m.
  Inderal—1.5 ml

We'd gone from the springtime cocktail of phenobarbital and Tegretol to a new concoction of Topamax, Vigabatrin, and Zonegran. Evan's seizures had evolved into a combination of spasms and partial and breakthrough seizures. One Saturday morning, while I shopped at a toy store for a birthday present for my nephew, Evan collapsed into a full-blown grand mal. I raced from the store, Josie at my heels, and threw my son into his car seat, his face blue, his arms and legs thrashing, spit at his lips. There, in the parking lot, a light fall drizzle coming down, my mind traveled immediately to the totemic seizures I'd read about and seen, the epileptics throughout history: Caesar, Bonaparte, Molière. Now it was my son foaming at the mouth, now my son with the purple lips, the jerking limbs. I counted out the seconds the way one might count the moments of an earthquake while it happened, to judge its seriousness—five, ten, fifteen—my hand on Evan's chest to make sure his heart kept beating. "It's okay, it's okay," I said to him. "He's okay," I told Josie. "Don't be scared." Once Evan was breathing again and his color had returned, I drove us home and called the neurologist. "Sounds like a grand mal," Dr. Steele's assistant told me, and then prescribed Zonegran, a third anti-epileptic for Evan's arsenal, in the hopes it would prevent a grand mal from happening again.

My parents came to town the weekend before I was scheduled to leave for Albuquerque. I had made a point of not telling them about my trip; anything remotely alternative was not something I wanted to advertise. A plan to drive Evan a thousand miles—and spend nearly a thousand dollars—to have people put their hands on my son and hope to heal him was about as far from a medical solution as one could get. As I said goodbye to my parents in their hotel room, my father said, "Someone from the Desert Health Center in Albuquerque called the house while you were out. They wanted to confirm Evan's appointments for next Tuesday and Wednesday?"

That was my dad. No matter where I hid, he found me.

"What's Albuquerque?" he asked.

I explained the touch therapy and my plan to drive Evan to Albuquerque to meet with the founder and have her diagnose and treat Evan. "I know it sounds crazy," I said. "But I'm at the point where I feel like I have to try everything."

"Of course you do," my mother said. "How could you not?"

My mother's response surprised me. I could see in her eyes the same longing for help that I felt, and the acknowledgment of how far a mother must often go for her child.

Before my parents had arrived and before I'd decided to drive Evan to Albuquerque, I had asked my friend John, who also did massage and body work, to come over and visit, to see Evan and try to get a sense of whether or not he would respond to the intensive treatments—whether he could even handle three days of people's hands on him. When John arrived he pulled me into his arms and said, "How are you?" He and I had not seen each other since the twins were born.

"I'm okay," I said. "I've been better."

"You don't have to call me just when things are bad, you know," he said.

I first met John when he taught a yoga class I attended, before the twins were born. He walked into the studio on a wet Friday night and immediately the room warmed up. John had red hair and freckles and a soft, young voice. He looked to be in his late twenties, even though he was actually nearly forty. "It's the yoga," he liked to say.

I had Evan in his blue plastic seat, the one that denoted cerebral palsy. I showed John the G-tube and the oxygen cannula. "Oh, I've seen all this stuff before," John said. "I used to work with AIDS patients, remember? At least he doesn't have a chest tube or a trach."

"True," I said.

John knelt on the floor in front of Evan. "So what's going on?"

"I'm considering taking Evan to this clinic in Albuquerque," I said. "For intensive touch therapy. I wanted to know if you thought it would help."

John laughed. "If *I* thought it would help?"

"Well, of all the people I know, you're the most able to tune in to someone in an intuitive way," I said. "And no one else has done that with Evan."

"Except you."

"Except me," I acknowledged. "And I'm pretty out of touch these days."

He took Evan's hands in his, closed his eyes, and drew in

several deep breaths. My son remained in his now familiar semiconscious state, his head to one side, the helmet covering his eyes. I don't know what I'd hoped for from John, who was himself the subject of a story I'd started before the twins were born, a story called "Yoga Man," about a young woman who could not have children and fell in love with her yoga teacher. Not an autobiographical story, but definitely one that touched on the abstract longing I'd experienced before the twins. The kind of longing that now, with Evan's hands in John's, seemed distant and profoundly irrelevant. "When are you going to finish 'Yoga Man'?" a friend asked periodically. *When my life turns back into that story,* I wanted to say. In other words, never.

"I can't find him," John said, opening his eyes at last. "He's seems very far away."

"He's pretty sedated," I said, echoing my father's words in Dr. Steele's office.

"So I gathered. I can't tell if this trip will help him or not," John said, letting go of Evan's hands. "To be honest, I'm more worried about you."

"What about me?"

I'd called John shortly after the twins were born to tell him the news of Ellie's death, Evan's tentative survival. At the time, he'd told me that I would need help. "What I said then I still believe," he told me now. "You need someone to put their hands on *you.*"

"I'm sure you're right," I said. "But at the moment my priority is Evan."

How I was. Whether or not I needed what John said I did. Those questions were not admissible. Some days I held it together just fine. Others, I barely functioned. A freelance copywriting job I'd taken on had dissolved when I could no longer field what I felt were petty complaints—"Vicki, the protein bar is about *protein*, why do you keep ignoring that fact? Why do you keep writing about carbs and fat instead?"—while caring for my sick son. That September I'd gone back to teaching for the first time since the twins were born and was little more than a phantom in the classroom. Our first class I'd forgotten the regulation class-size cap and added three too many students. The first piece of student fiction I read was so polished I felt certain it had to be plagiarized and nearly confronted the student. Some students had names I knew and faces I recognized from week to week; others would approach me in the hall and I had no idea who they were. Most of what I did that fall was hold it together as best I could, grateful for a job and an escape. Even though I was certainly doing better than I had been a year before—I was finally working again, after all—I wouldn't say that I was fine, by any means. I couldn't even say what it would take for me to be fine. Find a way not to think I had ruined my family by bringing Evan into this world? Have another child in the hopes that might erase what had happened? Have Evan be cured of everything?

On a daily basis, small details told me how not fine I really was. My identification with the student who'd been in prison. Getting dressed up for appointments with Dr. Steele, as if by painting my nails and wearing a skirt I might also get him to pay attention in some new way that would cure Evan. Not giving credence to the neuro-ophthalmologist when it came to his opinion about the very high levels of Vigabatrin, and how if the drug hadn't worked by a thousand milligrams a day it might never work. "That's a lot of Vigabatrin," he'd said. Believing that by putting her hands on him, a stranger might cure my son. And, finally, waking up to the planes flying into the World Trade Center in September of that year. *Please protect the souls of those who have perished* went the first line of my incantations on 9/11/2001. As I watched the towers fall, I knew how far gone I truly was. *Now everyone else knows how I feel every day*. The most absurd tragedy had struck; there was no going back; grief had arrived in an awful and unexpected way to the innocent. A clear blue sky would never look the same. "Are the buildings in Los Angeles big enough for a plane to crash into them?" my own daughter asked. "Or Pasadena?" From the moment my twins were born, I saw a potential for tragedy wherever I turned. Now, after 9/11, the country would experience life in the same way, every day, as I.

In the years after the twins were born, some version of posttraumatic stress syndrome operated in my life on a regular basis. The need for others to know and understand the arbitrary nature of what had happened, along with the ability of ordinary life events to rattle me, meant that no reaction was ever ordinary. Josie was invited to a birthday party at the zoo the summer Evan came home. I left her in the hands of her friend's trustworthy father and drove away. Panic set in as soon as I was home: What if she was kidnapped? What if the father turned his back and she got lost? Clearly I had left my daughter, my perfect brilliant daughter, in an entirely unsafe situation. Before the twins, this would never have been my thinking. After the twins, this was always my thinking: the unsafe pool party, the sleepover that would end badly, the potential car accident. When Holly gave birth to a full-term healthy daughter several years later, I went to visit her and asked if I could hold the baby. Holly's husband, Brad, replied rather cryptically, "Can you wait?" *Wait for what?* I thought. They didn't want anyone else to hold the baby until they went home with her, he explained. And then I understood; I saw on his face the same posttraumatic stress that kept me company nearly every day. Something could happen. Someone might drop the baby.

The happiness and redemption embodied in this second child, this perfect baby girl, could vanish in an instant, the same way the happiness of Alexandra's birth had vanished into a haze of seizures and cerebral palsy, all those years before. Since Alexandra had continued to have seizures on and off—to be cured and then not—I could understand even better Brad's fear.

The brain responds to trauma with a set of fight-or-flight hormones centered in the amygdala. From there, the hippocampus takes over with the production of neurotransmitters that help process and organize memories. When a person experiences severe trauma, these neurotransmitters are heightened and increased. As a result, the raw emotions inspired by the fight-or-flight response in the amygdala, a part of the brain so ancient and original it's present even in lizards, are not processed or integrated but rather preserved and kept alive, only a moment's reach away. For me, the interconnection between trauma and the amygdala explained why the memories surrounding the twins' birth and Evan's hospitalization were so clear years later. These memories, kept isolated and miraculously free from integration, remained as vivid as the day they occurred. The operation of the amygdala in relation to trauma also explained why the raw emotions brought on by trauma and stress could be so easily reached and re-created: the brain is not sufficiently able to integrate and calm those emotions.

On the drive to Albuquerque I had not come to this place of rational understanding for why I felt the way I did, why the continued fear and anxiety, the sense that planes crashing into the World Trade Center explained things in a way that I could not. Instead, I focused on packing up my child, his supplies and medications, the books on tape to keep me company on the eight-hundred-mile drive, the bottles of water, that pound of licorice.

Here was the same route that had brought my husband and me to California almost fifteen years earlier, but in reverse this time. I have a picture of us standing in the middle of the Mojave Desert, on that trip west from New York City, the one where we'd kept the heater blasting in one-hundred-degree weather on the old Subaru we'd bought; someone had told us that if we kept the heater on, the car itself would not over-heat. I don't know if it was that advice that kept the car out of the red or just dumb luck but we passed at least two cars on our way to the top of the desert that had caught fire while our fifteen-year-old yellow wagon chugged along. I remember be-ing stunned—I had never seen a car fire before—and exhila-rated too at this omen of our new adventure. We were heading into uncharted territory for certain. In the picture, we stand in the rest area, the wind blowing dust around our heads, long-haired and young and smiling. The world was wide open, and so were we. Fifteen miles earlier, in the town of Mojave itself, I'd asked the gas station attendant, "Where's the desert?"

"The desert?" she'd said. "Why, honey, you're standing in it."

To my East Coast mind, the desert was meant to be a vast expanse, with dunes perhaps, no vegetation, just sand, empty landscape. Instead, I stood at a gas station where the fumes melded with the air, causing man-made mirages, and saw a dozen fast-food restaurants within walking distance, an office supply store, and a car wash, fenced off, under construction. And yet, apparently, the woman was right: the desert was all around me; I was standing in it.

This time, this trip, I recognized the desert as I drove through it, the low ridge of brown and purple mountains, the flat road that wound toward a mountain pass, beckoning a hundred miles ahead. This time, I drove a big red SUV we'd bought a year earlier, gas mileage be damned, in an effort to have a safe car. Compared with the Subaru of years past, this ride was luxurious: I rode high, there was no danger of over-heating, dual-zone air conditioning kept me comfortable without chilling Evan to the bone in the back seat. If I liked, I could even take advantage of my cruise control. The road to Albuquerque was familiar to me from that first trip with Cliff and from trips since then: to visit Cliff's middle brother when he lived in Phoenix; a drive with a friend to Boulder when I was still in graduate school. I listened to the Dominick Dunne audio book, read with gusto by the man himself, and remembered with nostalgia the time in my life when my biggest concern was whether or not I'd get to watch the O.J. Simpson trial that day.

I drove fast, stopping only for food and the restroom. I pulled over outside of Flagstaff for lunch at a spot I'd been to twice before, once with Cliff on our way to Phoenix, once with my graduate school friend. The place, set amid tall pines, smelling of fresh air and the nearby mountains, hadn't changed. I was glad to recognize it, glad for the familiar. Inside the restaurant, Evan and I drew stares, thanks to his oxygen and helmet and the syringe of formula in his lap, but I actually found myself relaxing over my lunch of hamburger, fries, and a Coke. "What do you think, Evan?" I said. "How do you like Arizona?" I refilled his syringe—it was Evan's lunchtime too—looked out upon the highway and the view to the mountains beyond, and discovered that even with my disabled son, a road trip still lifted my spirit like nothing else. The sky was blue, the air smelled of pines. Although I still carried my burden with me, it felt lighter in Flagstaff, among the trees.

Back on the road after lunch, I listened to Dominick Dunne describe the Simpson trial by day and dinners with illuminati by night and I ate red licorice and mastered the art of filling

Evan's syringes with one hand, then leaning over into the back seat to squirt formula into his G-tube. By eight thirty that night I was negotiating the freeways around Albuquerque. I had driven in a mad rush, eight hundred miles in ten hours.

I found the motel where I'd made a reservation, ordered a pizza, and opened a bottle of wine. I stretched out on one queen-size bed while Evan rolled around on the other. He'd been a good traveler, sleeping and waking, hardly fussing for most of the drive, and now he seemed thrilled to have some freedom, to be out of his car seat at last. At the foot of the bed stood the five canisters of oxygen I'd brought with me, big ones to keep in the room and smaller ones for traveling back and forth. I unpacked our supplies, loaded Evan up on his meds, and lay down on the bed next to my son. Before I fell asleep, my dad called to find out how I was. "I'm here," I told him. "I made it."

Our first day at Desert Health, Evan and I were assigned to a practitioner named Lisa. We had sessions scheduled for the afternoon with the brilliant founder, Susan, during which, I'd been told by Ginger, we'd determine a specific treatment plan, a triage of Evan's symptoms and appropriate strategies for addressing them. This morning session with Lisa had been planned for "mapping" Evan. Lisa would use her hands to unearth the blockages and dysfunction within Evan's nerves, arteries, muscles, and tendons. His organs would come under scrutiny too: his liver, kidneys, heart, and brain.

The clinic was a large, brightly lit room with six massage tables arranged in rows of three. By nine, the place was busy, a patient and practitioner taking up each table. Like me, patients had come from all across the country for these intensive sessions with Susan, Lisa, and the other experienced therapists. Lisa led us into a small cubicle off the main room and laid Evan down on a table. She had his chart before her and knew which areas Ginger had worked on to help resolve the torticollis. She had barely started her work when a voice called out from across the room.

"Tetralogy of Fallot." It was Susan, the founder of Desert Health. She had her hands on her own patient, and a phone at her ear. She didn't look up, but we all knew she was talking to Lisa about Evan.

"Tetralogy of Fallot?" I asked.

Lisa smiled, then took an anatomy book off a shelf next to me. She checked the index and then turned to the relevant page. "Susan knows a bit more about anatomy than I do," she said. "Sometimes even I have to look things up."

She handed me the book and I read the page to discover that without looking at Evan or putting her hands on him, Susan had diagnosed Evan's heart condition. Tetralogy of Fallot described "an anatomic abnormality with severe or total right ventricular outflow-tract obstruction and a ventricular septal defect allowing right ventricular unoxygenated blood to bypass the pulmonary artery and enter the aorta directly."

His heart? The same heart Dr. Vance had said would need to be replaced before he was five years old? After my first, terrible appointment with Dr. Vance, I had found a new cardiologist for Evan, one who told me the situation wasn't nearly as dire as Dr. Vance had first suggested. The new cardiologist, a compassionate man named Dr. Burton, listened and weighed each answer carefully, then told me that we would simply need to wait and see. "Sometimes these situations resolve themselves," he'd said. Here, at Desert Health, the heart was back to being center stage.

"He has a pulmonary valve stenosis," I told Lisa. "But I've never heard of this tetralogy of Fallot business before."

She flipped back a page in the anatomy book. "'Pulmonary valve stenosis is associated with right-to-left atrial shunting,'" she read. "'Usually the right ventricle is severely hypoplastic and an ejection murmur is clearly audible.'"

"That sounds right," I said, remembering what Dr. Burton and I had discussed. "He's on Inderal to ease the strain on his heart. We may need to put in a stent to open it up but for now he's stable."

Lisa and I spent the next two hours of our appointment holding points on Evan's body that would ease the strain on his heart. We talked a bit but mostly sat in silence while we worked. Evan tolerated the session like a pro, lying still and patient. We gave him breaks only to feed and change him, working steadily the whole time. By eleven o'clock, when the session ended, I was hungry, thirsty, and exhausted from the work. I drove back to the motel and called my dad. "They say it's his heart," I said.

"His heart? You can't be serious. It's not his heart that's causing his seizures," my dad said. "Surely you realize that."

"I know," I admitted. At Desert Health, like those first days after the twins were born, I found myself giving in to a kind of momentum, one I did not question. This time, the momentum was one of hands and instinct, of Susan, who could diagnose my son from across the room, and Lisa, who helped me understand which places to hold on Evan's body to maximize the effect of the therapy. That afternoon, I returned to the clinic to meet with Susan. Immediately, I brought up my dad's point about Evan's heart problem not being the root cause of his seizures.

Susan laughed. "No, you're right," she said. "This afternoon we're going to work on his brain."

Where Lisa was thin and slight and soft-spoken, Susan was large and brassy and all-knowing. Even as she held her hands at Evan's temples or moved them down, over time, to behind his ear or his neck, she fielded phone calls on a headset she wore, calls from clinics she managed all across the United States. Back in Los Angeles, several weeks later, Ginger would check in with Susan at a clinic in Connecticut. I could picture Susan taking the call while her hands were on some other client, solving his or her constriction or blockage or dysfunction. She worked for twenty minutes at a time on Evan, then got up, took another call or a long pull from a bottle of Perrier, and then returned to the task at hand, which was intuitively following my son's neural pathways, working her way through the lobes and glands, deep into his thalamus and hippocampus. She had an anatomy textbook next to her and used it for reference, but only occasionally. Mostly, she kept her hands moving and her eyes closed as her touch felt its way through Evan's brain. At one point, she had me remove his helmet. "We can't work on his brain when he's wearing this," she said. I placed the helmet in the basket under Evan's stroller and resumed my spot at his side, back to helping Susan deal with the inner workings of my son's neurotransmitters. She asked me to hold Evan's toe as she worked around his skull. "Can you feel that?" she asked.

"Feel what?" I began to say, and then I did. A jolt of energy, coming directly from his foot.

Susan must have noticed the surprised expression on my face. "Neurons in the brain are comprised of axons," she explained. "One of the longest axons in the human body runs from the big toe to the medulla oblongata of the brainstem. That's what you felt just now."

"Wow," I said.

Susan smiled. "Yep. Wow."

When the session was over, I went to put the helmet back on Evan's head. "I wouldn't do that if I were you," she said.

"You're saying he shouldn't wear the helmet?" I asked.

"We can easily reshape his head when all this is done. But if you put that back on, you're closing off all the work we just did. Energetically it just doesn't make sense."

So much of what Susan and Lisa and Susan's partner Timothy did at the clinic rested on assumptions: the assumptions of the medical profession, for example, that medications and tests and diagnoses would tell the truth and offer a cure; and their own assumptions, that a patient who gave himself over to the medical profession might lose the chance to connect to the deeper cure that could arise from tuning in to his or her own body. In the early days and weeks after Evan was born, I had spent much time by his side, trying to attune myself to his needs, who he was, what might cure him. I meditated on those needs, and when touching him had caused his oxygen levels to crash, I removed my touch and held my hand over his Isolette instead. At Central, when Dr. Thrum had wanted to send Evan home with an NG tube, I'd first learned about the deeper, subtler instincts I would need to be a mother to my son. Then came the days of seizures and drugs, CT scans and EEGs and MRIs, where, despite my newfound instincts and the bonds of love, I lost an ability to connect with my son, to grasp what was necessary. Instead, I'd said my prayers and offered up my invocations, and when those were done, I'd given up. By having me put my hands on my son in this way, Susan and Lisa and Timothy were also asking me to return to the place where I could touch my boy without being afraid, and where my own touch might help him heal. I allowed them their convictions and kept Evan's helmet off.

As I was leaving Desert Health that first day, after the two-hour session with Susan and Evan's brain, I saw a mother and child in the waiting room whom I immediately recognized as being in the same kind of distress as Evan and myself. The little girl had white-blond hair and blue eyes and looked to be about two years old. Her mother held her in her lap in much the same way I held Evan, uncomfortable, unable to control the loose arms and legs of her child. We glanced at each other—me with Evan in his stroller, the oxygen cannula taped to his cheeks, she with her daughter, who was all loose limbed and unable to sit up—and nodded and smiled. The mother waited with her daughter and a car seat by her side.

"Do you need a ride?" I asked.

"Oh no," she said. "I called a cab."

"Are you sure? My car's right outside."

The mother, young and blond herself, kissed the top of her daughter's head. "We'll be fine. Really. My husband said he'd meet us at the motel."

"If you're sure," I said.

"I'm sure."

I left the clinic and headed back to the motel, the mother and her daughter prominent in my mind. I had asked Susan and Lisa to recommend a restaurant in the area where I might have a nice dinner. Even as I drove to the restaurant, carried Evan inside the dining room, and ordered dinner, I kept thinking of the young woman, the haunted feeling I had from seeing another mother and child at this same spot, also looking for hope and help. I wondered if this was how Evan and I often appeared to others, with that same, vague air of loneliness and desperation surrounding us. I ordered a pitcher of margaritas and called my friend Sarah and left her a message. "The waiters here are really cute," I said. "I think you should consider a road trip."

The next morning, I arrived with Evan at Desert Health to find the young blond mother already there. "Did you get home okay yesterday?" I asked.

She shushed her daughter, who had started fussing, and said, "Oh yes, thank you."

"Listen, I know it's not my business—" To my shock I had started in on one of those very conversations I'd condemned early on in my life as Evan's mother, the ones that started "It's none of my business" and ended with "Do you mind if I ask you . . . ?" The conversations that crossed boundaries and made the other person, usually me, profoundly uncomfortable. And here I'd gone and done it myself, and I wasn't stopping either. "I was wondering. You're here for your daughter . . ."

"She has a seizure disorder," the mother said.

"So does my son," I said.

"My name is Allison. This is Jennifer."

More questions spilled from me then, about where she was from (Utah) and what kind of seizures her daughter had (spasms, like Evan) and what treatments they'd offered her here at Desert Health (nothing to do with her heart, mostly therapy for her brain), and, finally, what kind of other interventions her daughter had received back home.

"To tell you the truth," Allison said, "we have a hard time getting much of anything."

"That's ridiculous," I said. "You should be getting physical therapy and occupational therapy and—does she eat?"

Allison shook her head.

"Well, she should have feeding therapy too," I said. "And respite care and nursing assistance." I ran down in my mind all the help I now received with Evan. "Do you get those?" I asked.

"Services in Utah aren't the greatest," she said. "We have some physical therapy and a bit of occupational therapy. It's hard to get much else authorized." There was a pause. "Is your son still having seizures?" she asked.

After my dinner of tacos and margaritas the night before, I'd

awakened in the middle of that night to the sound of Evan seizing. "He had one last night," I said. "What about Jennifer?"

Allison nodded. "The neurologist said we might never get
them in control."

"That's ridiculous," I said, sounding not unlike Holly. "I
think you need a better neurologist."

"Probably." She paused. "Do you believe in this?" she asked,
her voice low, her gaze taking in the clinic, the tables inside,
the therapists waiting to treat their clients. "I mean, do you
think it works?"

"I have to believe in something," I said, the memory of Susan's work on my son the day before fresh in my mind. "What
other choice do I have?" It was nine o'clock, and the morning
sessions had started. "Maybe we can talk later," I said.

"Sure. I'd like that."

That morning, Susan continued to work on Evan's brain,
with the help of a visiting therapist named Wilma. At one
point, there were three of us on Evan's body, six hands warm-
ing him and healing him with therapeutic touch. We were far
away from EEG machines and drugs and everything Western
medicine had tried with my son. I asked Wilma about her practice in Germany, where she lived. "My practice is very busy,"
she said. "I see a lot of kids too. Not many like your son, but
some with cerebral palsy, seizure disorders."

"Wilma's a gifted therapist," Susan said. "And while she'd
never brag about it, she also makes all her own clothes."

I looked at the pressed lapels of Wilma's shirt, the perfect
buttonholes. The workmanship was impeccable.

After the first hour, Susan applied herself to Evan's heart
and lungs, following up on the work Lisa had done the day before. "Do we know that he needs the oxygen?" she asked. "Have
you tried him without it?"

"A few times." My parents had come a month earlier to baby-sit and had taken Evan off the oxygen for long periods of time—after his bath, in the early morning. Even Josie had remarked how normal Evan looked without a cannula taped to his face. My dad had insisted, after checking Evan's nail beds, which remained pink, that he was ready to be weaned. In Susan's care, I felt willing to try. I turned off the valve on the oxygen tank while Wilma and Susan held points on Evan's chest, lungs, and heart. We stayed that way for several long moments. Evan's breathing slowed, became more relaxed. His color remained pink. Like those first moments when he'd come off the ventilator, all those months ago, I marveled to see my boy flying solo.

"You can turn it back on again," Susan said ten minutes later. "He did great, but I don't want to put him in distress."

Before Evan could be taken off oxygen permanently, his pulmonologist had determined that my son would need to undergo an overnight sleep study, in which his breathing would be monitored for any signs of apnea. In that moment in Susan's office, I could see we might find another way, a path where I weaned him slowly, tuned in to my instincts about whether or not Evan was in distress. That my boy would tell me himself when he was ready, so long as I listened.

Susan addressed Evan's other problems too that morning, the stiffness in his neck, his undescended testicles. As I left for lunch, she explained the challenges I would face after we left Desert Health. "I know we make it seem easy. Just remember you're going to need to follow up on all of this," she said. "These aren't miracle cures. We've done a lot of work these past two days to ease up the various strains on your boy, but don't expect magic. He still has a long way to go."

"I understand."

"And I'd keep that helmet off him," she said. "I know it's

hard, but if you could even just keep it off for a little bit each day, it will help."

That afternoon, I treated myself to a real sit-down lunch in the restaurant next door. I sat Evan next to me in his car seat and wondered, looking at his bare head, the cannula, his sleeping body that was somehow more peaceful now, or so it seemed, if I could hope for him to get better. With Susan's and Lisa's help, I was back to believing in chances, the impossible. When I returned to the clinic for my afternoon appointment, a new client sat in the waiting room. I smiled and complimented the woman on her purse, an expensive name-brand one I'd recently seen myself on a shopping trip. "It's lovely," I said. "Really simple but lovely."

"Thanks," she said. "How is your therapy going?"

I explained what had been tried on Evan. "It's been a very positive experience," I said. "Everyone here is very knowledgeable."

"This is my first time," she said. "I came all the way from Boulder, for my back. It's been giving me trouble, and I thought I'd try an alternative approach before having surgery."

"Well, I've had a long road with my son," I said. "And believe me, this definitely beats surgery."

She smiled. "I'm glad to hear it. What's wrong with your boy?"

I briefly explained Evan's history—the prematurity, the blindness, the seizures.

"You seem to be very grounded with so much going on," she said.

I shrugged. "I don't really have much choice. To tell you the truth, compared to taking care of my son and my daughter together all day, this feels like a vacation. I'm a big fan of road trips."

A little while later, Ally arrived with Jennifer. Her worried expression showed me she did not share with her own child the optimism I'd felt during lunch with Evan by my side.

"Are you okay?" I asked.

"I don't know," she said. "I don't feel like any of this is going to help, you know. I just can't help but feel . . . I don't know. Desperate?"

I let Ally's words resonate and fill the room. The woman with the lovely, expensive purse returned to reading her magazine. "I still think you need help. You need a break, someone to come take care of Jennifer for you. You need respite care and you need a better neurologist."

"I guess. . . ." Ally sagged with Jennifer in her arms. "I don't know why I thought they'd be cured in two days. I mean, talk about ridiculous, right?"

During the afternoon session I watched Susan struggle as she worked on Jennifer. Ally cried on and off as her hands helped Susan with the therapy. Before I left, I gave her a piece of paper with my phone number and address. "Please write to me, okay?" I said. "I want to help."

I left Albuquerque later that day. Evan had a seizure while I waited in line for a drive-through coffee to keep me company on the way out of town. But I wasn't scared this time, and I didn't panic or descend into fear. Instead, I knew the moment for what it was: a challenge, one I could face.

I took my time on the drive back, letting the experience of Albuquerque, the hands on my son, the oxygen being turned down, the advice to keep the helmet off, the instructions on how to follow up with his treatment, letting it all sink in. I spent the night at a motel in Gallup, ate dinner in front of the TV watching reruns of *Thirtysomething*, a show I'd loved from my time before children, the loss and struggles of the twins.

Before I had to believe in experimental medical treatments or even knew what they were.

That fall, the early-morning noises of my house kept me company as I wrote, piecing together words and sentences for myself for the first time since the twins were born. I listened to Evan kicking in his bed, Josie in the bathroom, then back to sleep. We celebrated Thanksgiving that year grateful for Evan's neurologist and therapists, people we never knew until Evan. I received a three-line note from Forest Lawn notifying me that they had placed the plaque on Ellie's niche—the plaque whose wording I'd struggled over so long and hard with Shirley Darling—and thus entombed her publicly. No more anonymity in this regard. She was officially, and for all to see, a baby who'd lived four days. We were officially her parents, her family.

I continued to see Ginger for touch-therapy sessions and to apply the techniques Susan and Lisa had taught me in Albuquerque. I left Evan off the oxygen for longer periods, envisioning a time when he would not need it at all. A year earlier, our son had still been in the hospital at Central, intubated, undergoing surgeries, becoming blind. This year, I could begin to see the boy emerging beyond the disabilities. On a cool fall day in my friend Susan's backyard, my son gave me his first smile. It had been nine months since he'd been home, and when I saw his baby gums for the first time, his lips pressed open in a full grin, I cried.

"He's smiling," I said to my friend. "Will you look at that?"

I went to visit Holly and Alexandra that fall, and her baby Sydney, in the new house she and Brad had bought, hoping to start over in a new life. Holly had landscaped the backyard into a playground completely accessible for Alexandra, who now used a wheelchair due to her severe cerebral palsy. There was adapted equipment that would allow Alexandra to swing, spin on a merry-go-round, and ride in her wheelchair on paved paths that circled the yard. Once again, I stood in awe of my friend's will, an innate spirit that never allowed her to give up. She'd had a vision of a backyard in which Alexandra and all the neighborhood kids could play together, where no one would feel left out, and she'd made it happen.

In the corner of the yard, Holly showed me a hopscotch square made out of colored grids of cement. Each grid had in its center a colored tile. "Did I ever tell you about the poem my grandmother wrote?" She knelt and showed me a black-and-white tile in the center of the hopscotch grid. Words curled around the tile in a spiral. In one corner, the tile was chipped, broken. "Isn't that perfect?" she said. "It broke when we were setting it."

The lettering was small and I had trouble reading it. "What does it say?" I asked.

"'Ah, lovely life,'" Holly quoted, half reading the tile, half from memory.

> Come stay yet a while with me
> I am a beggar for your errant charms,
> although I know your sorrows many be
>
> I try to hold you prisoner in my arms
> I'll ever dread to see you go away
>
> Yet you are fickle as the
> restless sea
>
> Your trials are heavy
> let come what may
> The thrill of you is ever there
> for me.

Standing in Holly's marvel of a backyard and listening to her read the poem, I felt a chill. Holly and I had spoken a few times about her grandmother's clairvoyance—she had more or less predicted Alexandra's birth and future disabilities, that Holly and Brad would weather them, and that there would be another daughter too. We didn't dwell on the topic, but each time she mentioned her grandmother, I often felt her spirit close at hand, somehow looking out for both Evan and Alexandra, and probably Holly and myself as well. "Your grandmother wrote that?" I said.

"Isn't that wild? It's almost as if she knew what was going to happen to me," Holly said. "And that I'd survive, whatever it was. Because you know what? I do want to live this life, despite everything, because it really is lovely."

A day before Thanksgiving, one of the nurses from our stay in the NICU, the nurse who'd been Evan's most consistent caregiver in his first few weeks of life, walked into the local coffee shop while Josie and I were having a happy midmorning snack. Evan was home with the sitter, and Josie and I were enjoying some mother-daughter time. "There's Linda Lou," I said. "Remember her? Evan's nurse?"

"Say hi to her," Josie said.

"I'm not sure I feel like it." I imagined the conversation, and what I might say. *How's Evan?* she'd ask. *Fine,* I'd say. *Except he's got this devastating seizure disorder. He's doing a little better now—we're down to four or five spasms a day—but for a while we had no idea if he would walk or talk or even know who we were.* She'd blanch, and my honesty would have her rethink every hopeful comment she'd ever made. She'd walk back to work with a new perspective on all those lifesaving drugs and machines around her, the medical womb the technology created.

Maybe even tell the others, *We really need to remember what we're doing here. There are families involved, whole lives that are forever altered.*

"Talk to her, Mommy."

My friend Maria once said to me that even if the doctors were to come to me and say, *Everything you told us is true,* I still wouldn't be satisfied, and she was right. And so I didn't say hello to Linda Lou, in the same way I didn't go to the NICU re-union the morning after Evan had been readmitted for seizures. Instead, I told Josie we'd wait for Linda Lou to come to us.

Maybe Linda Lou didn't recognize us. Perhaps she did but chose to respect our privacy. She'd come for coffee, she'd get coffee. Linda Lou and the other nurses and doctors were al-ways good at this, maintaining purpose while offering only sideways eye contact, the theory here being that if you met a gaze full on, you might actually have to stop and have a conver-sation, reassure a patient, discuss the case and your decisions too. That morning in the coffee shop, Linda Lou gave us one of those sideways looks, collected her coffees, and left. I remem-ber being on the other side, seeing Linda Lou arrive with coffee for others; I'd even given her a coupon for a few lattes back at the beginning.

"Mommy, where's Linda Lou?" Josie asked a short while later, looking up from her scone.

"I think she's gone, honey."

"You didn't say hi."

"I guess I didn't feel like it."

I'd become skilled at what not to say, or knowing when I couldn't say what I truly felt. At Thanksgiving dinner the next day with my brother and his family, after the meal ended and we sat amid the empty plates, there came a pause in which my sister-in-law admired the sleeping Evan in my arms. "He looks so much like Cliff now," she said. "He'll be such a handsome man." And I stopped myself, as I did with Linda Lou, from saying what I felt: *It's such a shame, not having Ellie, Evan being so impaired. Wouldn't the alternative have been even more beautiful?*

That was the trick he played on me, this child. How every day, more and more, I learned to let go. Early on, I'd told my father, "I've never had something from which I couldn't walk away," and it was true, this was the reality. There was nowhere else to be taken, no world where I put three healthy kids in the car, where my twins were walking and talking and Josie had the sister she craved rather than a ghost. No place, as my mother had put it, where I didn't have a severely disabled son, because now I understood that the response to her statement after that ill-fated appointment with Dr. Vance was no longer "No, you're wrong," but rather "Yes, it's true."

The night after our Thanksgiving dinner, I reminded Cliff that there were pictures of Ellie, that the social worker at the hospital had them. "I know this is hard to talk about, but I can't remember what she looked like," I said.

"I can," he said. "I see it every day."

"Will this ever get easier?"

"It's never going away," he said. "It might recede. Sometimes when I think about my parents, I'm not quite so sad. I don't think about them every day anymore. But no, it's always going to be here."

We went to Ellie's grave later that same weekend, to see the plaque for the first time and place a vase of flowers in the knob that had cost us that extra thirty-five dollars. It was hard enough to know what to say during these visits—"Don't step in the standing water," Josie reminded me, pointing down at the ever-present puddle at the curb where we parked. "Look out for the standing water!" she always said, since she was allowed to be silly and uncensored during these visits by virtue of her age—but on this day I was anxious. All the mistakes I'd made in Shirley's office haunted me. Not knowing what to spell out and what to abbreviate. Having so little room, not even an extra inch in which to add *Forever in Our Hearts*. Not wanting to use up all the lines but not believing for a moment either that Cliff or Evan or I would ever share the niche or need our names on the plaque. Faxing over my corrections taking out the nagging *th* and *rd* and not hearing back. It was all such a mistake.

I stepped over the standing water, held back while Cliff got Evan from the car. Josie ran ahead, yelling for us to follow. It was as if this were the funeral, not the mechanical operation we'd performed in September. I wished for graves like those in Hawaii, glass-fronted niches where you could see inside and the urns themselves announced the relevant information. If that were the case we could see the pictures we'd put there, the note from Josie, the candle.

I avoided and stalled and kept my eyes averted for as long as possible. And there it was, finally: KAMIDA. ELEANOR ANNE. JULY 30–AUGUST 3, 2000. The plaque was tiny, a dull olive green, and, worst of all, placed on the niche at just the slightest angle.

"It's crooked," I said.

Cliff was silent. He placed the vase of flowers and assumed a graveside pose—hands in front of him with his head inclined in the direction of Ellie's niche. Josie grabbed on to him and chattered while in my mind I compared Ellie's marker to those around it and, finding it lacking, imagined all the ways I could fix this thing I'd known in advance would be wrong. I could climb up to the eighth row and chisel off the plaque myself. I'd re-order, get a bigger one, no matter what Shirley had told me was possible. We would engrave a message. I scanned the other markers and got mad at Shirley all over again. Surrounding me were phrases, and different fonts, and upper- and lowercase lettering, and all sorts of personalized combinations of names and dates and loving messages. All those Shirley had said were impossible. These other families with their superior plaques clearly had had a better shot at success than I'd had with Shirley Darling and all her fumbling. I'd wanted to get out of her office; I hadn't wanted to do the form again. The lousiness of the plaque was punishment for my impatience.

"It's crooked," I said again. "It's so small."

"Stop," Cliff said. "I can't do this. Please just stop." He avoided my eye, let Josie hang on him, ignored us both. "I'm sorry," I said, but we both knew I'd gone too far. "I just can't do this anymore," he said and he walked away, taking Josie with him.

We traded places in front of the niche a few more times, then left. It was the only time since the twins were born I'd really seen him angry. This was how marriages fell apart in times like ours, when needs were potent and conflicting, when one partner could not offer comfort or sympathy because his or her own pain was too great. I'd stepped over the line and asked him to need me in a way that was absolutely opposed to how he was feeling. The difference was profound, and I turned queasy with regret.

"I'm sorry," I said again.

"It's okay." He took my hand and held it. We were alone, each of us, in our sadness. We loved each other but were alone nonetheless.

A month after my trip to New Mexico, I arrived for a touch-therapy session with Evan at Ginger's office out by the airport. When I came into the office, Ginger told me she had received a package addressed to me. "I think it's from someone you met in Albuquerque," she said.

I was expecting something from Ally perhaps. I had given her my address and asked her to write. I quickly saw from the return label that whoever had sent the box Ginger now handed over to me had tracked me down through the offices at Desert Health. I opened the box and saw a card addressed to me.

Dear Vicki,

We met at Desert Health—I was the woman from Boulder. You may not have known it but you taught me a great character lesson and gave me a great gift. The lesson was your grace and generosity in adversity. The great gift was my understanding that a mom may love all her children equally but must attend to whichever child had the greatest need at the moment.

My younger brother was born with health problems that continued through childhood. I was a sturdy, independent little girl and so was left on my own. That may not have been great for any little girl but it was necessary. Because of you I now understand a small bit of what my mom had to juggle and how much she loved us all.

Enclosed you will find a token of esteem. It is something you said you liked but chose not to spend your resources on currently. It was my pleasure to find it for you. Best wishes to you, Evan, and all your family.

Inside the box: a lovely, expensive purse not unlike the one I'd seen this same woman carrying and had admired. My own, to keep.

Part Four

WHEN JOSIE WAS four years old, we were in the car coming home from preschool one afternoon, engaged in a typical end-of-the-day parent-child argument, one full of hairsplitting and salvos. I looked into the rearview mirror and asked, "Would it be possible, for once, for you not to use the word *but?*" A hard question to put to a child, certainly, let alone a four-year-old. A rhetorical, prickly question, given what awaited us at home: Evan; the round of therapies, medications, and doctors' appointments; her own life turned inside out; the conversations out her window to Ellie, the sister she never knew. Surely this girl at age four was entitled to an unlimited share of *buts*.

There came a long pause, and then: "Can there be a *well?*"

This was my other child, then, my smart and beautiful daughter, who once said, "If you don't like something your whole life you're not meant to be here on Earth." Of course there could be a *well*. We all needed one.

In telling the story of Evan and Ellie, I often found myself using the word *but*. So much of what I wanted to say involved argument: But why? But how? I tested myself daily in an effort to count the *buts*. Yes, Evan was beautiful, but no, he could not see. No, he was not unhappy, but what about his future?

I had lived my life before Evan and Ellie attached not only to a life without the shadow of disability but also to a life where words counted, where explanations could be given, where if I said the word *but* often enough, I would transcend argument and arrive at the truth, and with that truth, understanding. Most of my friends and I believed that, like the tough words surrounding Evan's life (*blindness, mental retardation, seizure disorder*), the truth of life and existence could reveal itself in language. What happened when Evan and Ellie were born was the absolute erasure of this reality for me. So what if I begged for the twins not to be resuscitated? My words were not heard. So what if I understood the medical reasons and terminology for why Evan went blind? That understanding didn't affect the hard reality of skipping straight ahead to the end of the chapter: *if your child becomes blind.* Those words on Ellie's crooked plaque? None of that changed what had happened. I fantasized one morning that I would make an appointment with Dr. Lamb and present to him all the arguments I had stored up, all the attempts to use words to make meaning. *What did you think you were doing?* I would ask. *What was on your mind when you said, "No DNR"? Did you not know how this might turn out? Could you not envision it? What are the words you would use to explain this to me, to my son, my husband, my daughter, our family?*

What words would he use? What would be his *but*, his *well*?

It was years before I finally opened up and read the medical records of the day I gave birth, to find my own truth beyond the arguments, my own understanding beyond the *but*s and the *well*s. I have read that grief brings with it the company of guilt and recrimination, our minds deceiving us into believing that we can change the outcome of a tragedy by changing the events leading up to it. I'd done this, rewritten the events, the night after the twins were born, and many nights afterward, just as I'd accepted more than my share of blame about my role in the twins' premature birth. And yet, until the morning I saw the record of my delivery, I'd never investigated the facts surrounding that birth, so convinced I was of the narrative I had constructed for myself, the only one that made sense to me as the years went on, the one that read like this: I was born to have these twins, to know what it was like to lose Ellie and love Evan, to live with the outcome and the sacrifice.

One night at dinner, Cliff, Josie, and I were discussing the facial expression she'd made when she was born. "It's the same droopy mouth Evan has when he's sad," Cliff said.

"Did Evan make a face when he was born?" she asked.

"I don't know," I said. "I wasn't looking."

"Why not?"

"Because I didn't want to know."

Because I was sure he would die. Because I didn't want him to live.

That kiss at Ellie's birth: "Your daughter. Give her a kiss." The next time I touched her, held her, she died in my arms.

I don't remember why I finally opened up the four-inch box of medical records I'd had on a shelf in my office since Evan came home. My dad wanted me to have the records; there was some talk of a lawsuit at one point. The service coordinator wanted me to have them; it would be important to have Evan's medical history on hand for the doctors. I suppose part of me wanted to have them too, as they were the only document I might possess of that time. What if, despite all my deep, specific recollections, my memory one day grew hazy and I wanted to know about a telltale moment? *Remember the time you talked to the social worker at Central about not wanting to answer questions about Evan's twin since it wasn't relevant to his case and she wrote in his chart, "Don't discuss twin with mom. Too painful." Or, What was it exactly that Dr. S. wrote after he told you those were slam-dunk seizures? Oh, right: "Recommend psychological counseling for mother."*

Holly once said to me that she often came up against the thing she least wanted to see or know by accident, that in looking for something else she would arrive at the thing itself, the thing she had been avoiding. She once found a photograph of Alexandra from those first days at Central in one of her own previously unopened boxes. *Did I really think she looked good when I took this?* she remembers asking herself, taking in Alexandra's vacant, drugged stare, the drool at her mouth. *What was wrong with me?* Maybe I myself opened the box of medical records that fall morning, four years after the twins were born, to find out something about Evan and his treatment in those early days. Maybe I wanted to read the few pages devoted to Ellie, to remind myself of the facts of her short life.

I don't remember what I was looking for when I took the top off that box, but what I found startled me. There, ten pages into the thick stack, I came across the record of the twins' delivery. My delivery, part of their medical records, inextricably bound from the start. I had had no idea this record was here, at my fingertips, all this time. I scanned the pages and read the words—simple, succinct—as if they had happened to someone else.

SUMMARY OF PARTURITION

HISTORY: The patient was admitted to Hampton Labor and Delivery as an outpatient for evaluation of vague lower abdominal cramping. She had a known twin intrauterine pregnancy, estimated to be at 24 weeks estimated gestational age.

On admission to Labor and Delivery, exam showed her to be 6–7 cm dilated. The typical workup for preterm labor was instantly initiated. These measures failed to resolve her contractions. It was elected to discontinue

magnesium sulfate and allow delivery to ensue. Detailed
discussion had been conducted with the patient and the
neonatologist in regard to the patient's desires for no heroic measures.

PROCEDURE IN DETAIL: The patient reached complete
dilation at 19:40 on July 30, 2000. Membranes were
ruptured artificially and subsequently a 1-pound 3-ounce
Baby A was delivered. The baby was instantly weighed
and handed to the attending neonatologist, who proceeded with a resuscitative attempt.

Baby B appeared to be in a transverse lie. Continued
vigorous attempts to rotate the fetus to a vertex presen-
tation were eventually successful and Baby B was then
delivered weighing 1 pound, 7 ounces. A second resuscitative effort was initiated.

Estimated blood loss for the procedures was 300 cc
and the mother was taken to the recovery room in satisfactory condition.

How different those words from mine, how profound the
gulf between what Dr. March had dictated and what I had experienced. Three hours, no more than a few hundred words,
so many lives changed forever. *The mother was taken to the recovery room in satisfactory condition.* No words could describe
this void that lay between the truth of the medical records and
the truth of my life, Evan's and Ellie's. I read the page again and
again, searching for some kind of release or understanding in
this story. Was there anything else I might have done, some
other outcome possible? In rereading the words of my delivery,
I saw there was not.

Following the record of the birth itself came a report from
the lab about what is commonly referred to as the afterbirth.
I have come to learn that in complicated births such as mine
the afterbirth is routinely sent off to a lab for inspection and

testing, since it can contain clues as to the source of the prematurity. I didn't know, nor had anyone told me at the time, that this had been the case with me—until I saw this report behind the record of my delivery, and read its dense language, the mention of twin placentas, *red/brown, spongy cotyledons, focally disrupted flattened cotyledons, a 3.5 cm aggregate of loosely adherent blood clot.*

It took several long minutes for me to parse this language and find a truth amid the description. I saw them then, two words buried in the diagnosis. *Acute chorioamnionitis.* Long and unpronounceable, in layman's terms those ten syllables described an infection that began in the placenta, inside me. That led to the delivery, Ellie's death, and Evan's disabilities. An invisible infection of which I had no awareness, signs, or symptoms until there was no means to change the outcome. One that could be traced only arbitrarily to Twin B. I had heard the word *infection* muttered only once around the time of the twins' birth, and that was in our first meeting with Dr. Lamb. No one had ever discussed it again as a source of my labor, or as an explanation of the birth. But here it was, finally, an answer, one I had ignored and had not sought. For years I had not known, nor had I asked. I had not even seen this report, ever, until that day.

Because I did not want to.

An infamous cliché in writing circles makes a simple, fundamental distinction between plot and story. "The king died, and the queen died" constitutes plot. "The king died, and the queen died of grief" is story. Cause and effect, in other words, constitutes the difference. In my case, if the twins' premature birth, Ellie's death, and Evan's survival gave me the plot, it was the record of my afterbirth that gave me the story.

Maternal infection, I learned, is sometimes the result of un-

derlying problems in the pregnancy rather than the cause of
them. Even if the doctors had discovered the infection prior to
my premature labor, there would have been no means to treat
it. Women with acute uterine infections must give birth or risk
the lives of their unborn children.

As for which twin had been the source of this infection inside me, there were no answers here either. Because of some
early bleeding associated with Evan, I had always thought of his
gestation as the problematic one, the potential source of trouble. But the report of the afterbirth offered nothing conclusive,
no way to trace the infection to my son.

Seeing nothing, no concrete source for this infection, no
ability to treat the infection other than exactly what happened
—that premature birth—and, consequently, finding no other
exit, no one to blame, not even a specific one of the twins, I
also knew I had elected to blame myself for the prematurity
rather than search for the answers or accept that there were no
answers. In blaming myself, I ensured my suffering, one that
included the ultimate sacrifice: giving my life over to my son's.
Beyond the love, there it was—the sacrifice.

As I turned over these mysteries, the shady truths and half
facts, the dead ends I kept coming up against in those pages,
I was overwhelmed by the spirit of Ellie. She was there, more
present than I have ever felt her, more present even than when
she was alive, or when I was at her gravesite, and I could feel
her pushing me, urging me to a conclusion I'd never allowed
myself. What if *she* had caused the prematurity, and the labor?
What if she was the agent of these profound changes? What if
she died so that Evan could live, as imperfectly as he did?

Why? I asked myself. *Why do I need to see it this way? Why
can't I blame him? Or myself? Why do I have to blame her?*

Because if she died so that Evan could live, I realized, *however imperfectly, then and only then could we learn what it meant to love him.*

These thoughts came to me so simply and powerfully I knew they were true, or as true as anything else I had theorized or told myself. And I knew too, in that moment, that if the words were true I must also see the ways in which Evan had suffered from these events. I could no longer continue to blame him, even in the subtle ways I had done. It also meant that I had not forgiven him—or her, or myself—at all.

Blame, I found, was a powerful force, an animistic human desire, one that continued to haunt me even amid these realizations about the truth behind my labor and delivery. The eventual release from my crucible of blame arrived in the most unexpected place: the same hospital where Evan and Ellie had been born. I had taken Evan to Hampton on a Monday morning early in December, the year he turned five, to have his G-tube replaced. He still had this tube even though when Dr. Lamb had sent us home all those years ago he had told us Evan would have it for all of eighteen months. Eighteen months! This had felt like a sentence at the time, and yet five years later, I still could only dream of Evan eating hamburgers and French fries, Cheetos, and frozen yogurt. I did not blame Dr. Lamb for being inaccurate; I knew my son was a hard case, a tough one he would not have wished on any parent. That Evan was the kind of ex–super-preemie for whom even the biggest crystal ball would not reveal the future. Five years later, Evan drank all his nutrition through a cup, which I knew to be quite a victory over the days and weeks we had struggled with rice cereal, slicing bottles' nipples with X-Acto knives so the cereal could flow through. He no longer had a feeding pump; there were no puddles of formula in his bed at night. The oxygen was long gone;

so too the apnea monitor and the med sheet on the kitchen cabinet. My boy had morning breath, a beautiful smile—finally —and even a laugh. He giggled when I tickled him, a galloping belly laugh that made everyone around him dissolve into laughter as well. His seizures, miraculously, with drugs and touch therapy and vigilance, had stopped. He'd even learned, in this last year, how to take steps. I now knew he would, eventually, walk. In many ways we were so very lucky.

That Monday morning, a brisk December wind greeted me as I took Evan from the car and put him into his stroller. I had parked in the underground structure, the same place I'd wrecked a rental car in those early, grief-stricken days. I carried my expensive purse, the one the woman from Boulder had sent me after Albuquerque, and I wore the denim coat I'd splurged on when Evan was in Nursery C, all those years ago. As I often tended to do whenever I found myself in a place from Evan's past (and my own), I let my mind wander among the details: the first days Cliff and I parked here after the twins were born. Running into Dr. Tam on my twins' second day of life to have her tell us they were being tested for meningitis. Finding out later how serious this was, having no sense of it at the time, nor the answers for my father when he asked them of me. "What does that mean, testing them for meningitis? What makes her think they might have meningitis?" How did I know? Had I asked, or had I been too dumbfounded to pursue the answers? I tried to remember but couldn't. Amid my grief and trauma, some moments, finally, had come to recede.

I got in the elevator then and pushed the wrong button for the ground level, the one marked 1 rather than G. How many times had I done that? Dozens, probably. I was always confused by the elevators in this hospital. Upstairs the doors opened onto the plaza and I saw, as if for the first time, that same cobbled brick path Cliff and I had taken the afternoon Ellie died. I remember being focused that afternoon on the arrangement of the bricks, their complicated crisscrossed pattern, something to take my mind off the thing that had just occurred, Ellie's slow death. We were in that stasis of grief, Cliff and I, one where I believed that if I stared at the bricks long enough I would not have to move either forward toward my future life as Evan's mother, or backward to the place where I was still only expecting. I walked up that same path this December morning and headed to the hospital's entrance. The one-story wing to my left held the suite of maternity rooms. I often tried to peer through the closed blinds as I went past, hoping to see . . . What? Someone like me? Being told by a helpful nurse, the way I was on the morning after the twins were born, not to pump my milk but to bind my breasts instead? Because why? Because my babies would no doubt die.

And then the garden area, set off from the main path, the same corner where I sat the afternoon of Evan's G-tube surgery. Remembering how the nurse had turned to me and said, "This can't be easy for you, seeing your baby into surgery," and how I'd answered, "I've done this four times before," and "I'm a pro," and how I'd then come down to this same spot and cried once I was alone.

I had lived a lifetime at this hospital.

If I turned around and looked north toward the mountains, I might remember sitting in the supermarket lot across the way, waiting in the car for Cliff to pick up the sleeping pills the doctor had so generously offered the morning I checked out of the maternity ward, a day after the twins were born. Ten juicy tablets to help me sleep without nightmares or dreams. It was hot that day and the smog covered the mountains in a yellow haze. It was hot the day we walked on those same bricks back to the elevator, back to our car, after Ellie had died in our arms.

That day with Evan, in the cool December air five years later, I felt myself travel to a place I'd never envisioned: a delivery room without nurses and arguments, no *buts* only a *well*, where instead of frantic medical interventions in the form of phone calls and resuscitation there was, instead, two very small babies handed to a stunned mother, the culmination of a very short pregnancy, a startling early labor. That mother held each child and touched their small limbs, let herself know her children in the quiet of a dark room. She was able to let them go, to say goodbye. They had come too soon. She was there with her partner, her lover, her friend. There was no one else but this mother, this father, and these two babies. There was compassion and kindness and a shared grief among them all. There was no fear or agonized pronouncements or turning away. In this space, there were only tears and sadness and grief.

I had never let myself imagine this scene. So much had happened, I could not take myself to this place, ever, the place where instead of insisting the twins survive, the doctors agreed that we should let them die. When I did take myself there, that morning, I understood immediately what I would have lost: a belief in love and loss and the sense that fear could be something I could face. The hot Sunday afternoon in July I walked into labor and delivery, I had no conception of true limits—the limits of love or medicine or compassion or language. I knew them now. I had learned all this in my time as Evan's and Ellie's mother.

That December morning, I stopped on the cobbled bricks outside the maternity ward, placed myself inside, in a dark room with my babies and my husband, and felt myself let them go. No Evan. No Ellie. No vigorous attempts to keep them alive, to make them stay. In that imagined moment of compassion and letting go, in a peaceful end to Evan's and Ellie's lives that had never happened, I finally found my forgiveness.

• • •

On the fifth anniversary of Ellie's death, I made my way to visit my daughter's grave by myself for the first time. In the same way that I had never allowed myself to look at the record of my delivery or to accept the underlying mystery of how and why I had come to be Evan and Ellie's mother, I had also never brought myself to this spot alone.

I parked by the curb, crossed over the puddle there, hearing Josie's voice in my head: "Don't step in the standing water." The day was hot, though not as hot as it was in my memory of the Sunday the twins were born. It was a Tuesday afternoon and the cemetery was empty. I walked up the path, past a familiar grave, also of a baby, one where the brass was always glossy and polished, the grave itself decorated with flowers and toys. At the outdoor sink I filled a vase with water and flowers. Inside the columbarium I looked up to the sky the way I always did, always grateful for the opening that gave light and sound. Then I looked up at Ellie's plaque and read the dates: July 30–August 3, 2000. Between July 30, when they were born, and August 3, when Ellie died, we had lived a lifetime. Evan had continued to live a lifetime. Ellie, we hoped, was at peace.

Over the years, from the time of Ellie's death until the day I went to her grave alone, I had allowed myself only fleeting moments of what it meant to be Ellie's mother. Certainly I had had my share of moments in which I imagined what it would be like to be her mother had she lived: another dark-haired daughter, more laughter in the dark at bedtime. Images have come to me many times of pushing her on a swing or listening to her talk to Josie in the back seat. The day I went to her grave by myself I realized that was the year she would have been starting kindergarten, and of course I imagined that too: first days, tears, the power of writing her name the kindergarten way. With Evan, my days were so caught up with the specifics of his needs, the frustration of never really understanding him, how tiring all the chores and therapies and all else could be. With Ellie, there was very little. Only an imagined daughter, and a deeply provisional future.

Looking back, I wondered if this was why it took us so long to bury her, not because of a deep connection to her or our inability to move on, but because of the fragile reality of her spirit in our lives. With a child who lives a life, even a short one, there are details and memories, photographs. In Ellie's case we had nothing except her ashes and this gravesite to remind us that she had even lived. Not even a photo, since the social worker culled her files years later and we had not had the presence of mind before then to ask her for that last picture. As a mother, what was I to make of that? I had learned how to be Evan's mother, to sacrifice myself and push and pull him along toward language, health, mobility. But how was I to be the mother of a child who'd lived for four days and whom I'd held only once?

That day at Ellie's grave, as I placed the lilies I'd brought in a vase on her niche, I knew with absolute certainty that I had never known Ellie except as spirit. To this day I find many photographs of Evan's ultrasounds and only one of Ellie's. In it she is a skeleton, a ghost. Even in the short time I was expecting the twins, it took much effort to tune in to Ellie, so much that on the day I went into labor I had to lie still for several long moments to be sure that she was still moving, and that both babies were still alive. "I felt them both this morning," I remember telling the doctor. Unlike Evan, who cried long and as soon as he appeared, Ellie wasn't moving when she was born. I thought about this again at the grave that day, how Ellie had always been, in so many ways, a ghost to me.

Without the connection to a physical body, without a being I could see or hold, all I had was the possibility of listening to Ellie's spirit and what it might tell me. Time and again, this was all I had. When she was inside me with her fluttery movements. The day she was born. The day she died. The day I read the medical records and she came to me to tell me I was not to blame Evan anymore, or myself. That day, at Ellie's grave, I sat myself down against the cool wall of the columbarium and closed my eyes. Immediately, I found myself underwater, in the dark. There was Evan, a baby, someone, in my arms. And there was Ellie, gone. Close enough to hear, too far to save. If I were to let go of Evan I would lose him too. If I held on to Evan, I would lose Ellie. In this moment, the sacrifice was so clear to me it was palpable, and I remembered again all the other moments in Evan's progress where I had had to make a choice: the drug at birth that would save his life and give him permanent neurological damage; the surgery that would save his sight but put him desperately far behind in everything else (breathing, eating); the next drug that would stop his seizures but take away any remaining eyesight he might have. The mysterious infection that had caused the birth in the first place, and how this meant the twins had to be born whether or not they were ready. And it was this complete and utter sense of sacrifice that grabbed me again. That Ellie had to die for Evan to live; that I had, somehow, done this before. That I was right to think she had brought him here so that we could know what it was like to love him, and, perhaps, to know what it meant to forgive ourselves for that original sacrifice.

When I left Ellie's grave that afternoon, an older woman came walking purposefully down the path toward me. Not Shirley Darling, but another Forest Lawn employee. She was there to tell visitors about the cemetery's one hundredth anniversary celebration, taking place that weekend. "We are inviting all our guests," she said. "Who are you here to visit?" I'd never been asked that question before, and was never asked it again, but in that moment I replied, simply and for the first time, "My daughter."

On the other side of blame, I have learned, lies forgiveness and redemption. That day by Ellie's graveside I understood how necessary it was to pass over to that other side, to reclaim my life, assume my place as Evan's mother, and let go of my need to be the only one responsible. To move on, if that was possible. I remembered back to the day Curt and I looked at cemeteries, how I couldn't find a way to bury Ellie in that beautiful ancient graveyard east of town, the one that looked down upon a basketball court, community pool, and preschool below. The sounds of childhood rang loud and I wanted so much to believe that Ellie belonged there but the pangs of grief outweighed my motherly sentiment and I could not bear to hear the loud sounds she would never know. I wasn't convinced that the dead could hear, or that they would care in the same way as the living. This graveyard where I now stood, the one where we finally found a way to bury our daughter, also lay atop a hill, and for the first time I looked out, after saying the words *my daughter* to this stranger, to see and hear that there were all kinds of sounds amid the stillness of that hot August day: the hum of the freeway traffic nearby; the drone of people and machines that kept the cemetery green and groomed; and, just across the hill to the south, a house that fronted the cemetery where I heard the voices and laughter of small children playing in the yard. When I listened this time, I heard in those sounds not loss but life.

EPILOGUE

OUR SON, EVAN, died of an acute intestinal blockage in the early-morning hours of July 24, 2008, just six days shy of his eighth birthday. Earlier in the day he'd been playing, happy. By two in the afternoon, I knew something was wrong. Three o'clock had us in an ambulance on the way to the emergency room, and by two the next morning he was gone.

Even the most anticipated ending can leave us lost, confused. Imagine an ending that comes without warning or preparation, one that is shocking, sudden, and unexpected. "I saved his life over and over," I told a friend, "and in the end, at the very end, I couldn't save him again." In eight years, I had indeed seen moments where I thought my son might die, and I often worried he would, but I never once considered his end might come in this way, so abruptly, without notice. When my husband and I left the hospital the night Evan died—the same hospital where Evan and his twin sister had been born—I said, "I am so done with this place," as if by putting my own words of finality on the subject, I might also bring the matter to a close.

We want, in an ending, a sense of justice and purpose, a feeling that the inexorable is also comprehensible. In truth, no ending is ever complete, no goodbye sufficient. I was not done with my son, and yet he died. Did that mean he was done with me?

Evan's death ultimately had its source in his extreme prematurity. The same obstruction that brought us to the emergency room came about due to internal scarring that dated back to his G-tube placement as a baby. For seven years, then, this potential had existed inside our boy, unknown to us. And within twelve hours from its ultimate onset, he was gone.

Evan's—and Ellie's—lives began too soon, and ended too quickly. But even a short life is a whole life; this I have learned. I dedicate this book to my son, who taught me how to recognize that life, and tell his story.

ACKNOWLEDGMENTS

Many people helped make this book happen over the years, including writer friends Michelle Latiolais, Susan Segal, Greg Bills, Jeff Solomon, Ben Huang, and Andrea Malin; the inner circle of critics and kindred souls: Rachel Simon, Kristen Spina, Jennifer Graf Groneberg, Jinin Kiem, Kyra Anderson, Lisa Alvarez, Tupelo Hassman, Suzanne Kamata, Karen De-Groot Carter, Susan Etlinger, Jordan Sadler, and Beth Andersen; all the terrific women at Literary Mama who first gave a home to this material: Marjorie Osterhout, Caroline Grant, Susan Ito, Ericka Lutz, Alissa McElreath, Shari McDonald Strong, Andi Buchanan, Rebecca Kaminsky, Rachel Sarah, and Heidi Raykell. Portions of this work found early supporters in Angela Rinaldi, Deborah Tall at the *Seneca Review,* Andrew Tonkovich at the *Santa Monica Review,* and Elizabeth Finn-Arnold at *Philosophical Mother.* I thank you.

My great friends have seen our family through unspeakable trials and have stood by us with love, support, and kindness: Sarah Picchi and Kalea Chapman; Robert Scott and Kim Nakakura; Susan and Paul Simon; Sheryl Madonna; Sarah Seager; Lee Goldstein; Ed Wacek; Rachel Roellke; James Kolker; Nancy Duncan; Holly and Brad Boyer; Bill Sorensen; Rachel Toles; fellow preemie moms Carrie Heckman, Traci Foyster, and Kelly Sanchez; Bruce Schwartz; Lisa LaValley; Sarah Todd;

Roberto Espinoza; Michael Pacyna; and Tim Nolan. Thank you all for not turning away from the hard stuff, every day.

Our extended family includes Curt and Susan Kamida, Michael, Bo, and Katie; Clayton and Betty Kamida; my brother and sister-in-law, Bill Forman and Lisa Forman Cody, and their three sons, Thomas, Nicholas, and Alexander; my sister, Alyssa Stamatakos, her husband, Ted, and their daughters, Sophia and Alexandra; and my brother Bob Forman. All of you have had to mend and readjust in the midst of our journey and have done so with grace and compassion.

My parents, Marc and Phyllis Forman, have been beside me from the start, and have proven every day their strength, courage, and love.

Therapists, doctors, and teachers made my son's life meaningful and proved their expertise and devotion really could make a difference: Elyse Holloway, Zena Begin, Judy Packard, Donald Shields, Gregory Lizer, Myrna McCune, Tejal Shah, Holly Wills, Joy Huguet, Sheryl Smith, Lesley Mayne, Diane Yuen, Tracy Prehn, and Wendy Watts all had a say in who Evan was and what he became. Thank you too to Osong Kim, Sora Choi, Kamuel Wo, and Steven Schayer.

Caregivers Gloria Ubieta, Elizabeth Boehm, and Monika McClellan made my writing life possible by being so present and constant with my children. Gloria especially loved Evan with the entirety of her enormous heart.

In a league all her own, for decades of support and friendship: Maria Theresa Maggi.

Nicole Angeloro at Houghton Mifflin Harcourt has been a gracious shepherdess from manuscript to print. Lisa Glover and Tracy Roe made the production process seamless. The generous folks from the Bread Loaf Writers' Conference at Middlebury College who sponsor the Bakeless Prize have earned my undying gratitude, including Michael Collier and Ian Pounds. And thank you most of all to Tom Bissell, who had the supreme munificence of spirit to choose this book and say such lovely things about it, thereby giving it not only a home, but a voice.

Finally, to my daughter Josie and my husband, Cliff. Always.

Bread Loaf and the Bakeless Prizes

The Katharine Bakeless Nason Literary Publication Prizes were established in 1995 to expand the Bread Loaf Writers' Conference's commitment to the support of emerging writers. Endowed by the LZ Francis Foundation, the prizes commemorate Middlebury College patron Katharine Bakeless Nason and launch the publication careers of a poet, a fiction writer, and a creative nonfiction writer annually. Winning manuscripts are chosen in an open national competition by a distinguished judge in each genre. Winners are published by Houghton Mifflin Harcourt Publishing Company in Mariner paperback original.

2008 JUDGES

Antonya Nelson, *fiction*

Tom Bissell, *nonfiction*

Eavan Boland, *poetry*